DOWN FROM EQUALITY

BLACKS IN THE NEW WORLD
August Meier, Series Editor
A list of books in the series appears at the end of this book.

DOWN FROM EQUALITY

BLACK CHICAGOANS
AND THE
PUBLIC SCHOOLS
1920-41

MICHAEL W. HOMEL

UNIVERSITY OF ILLINOIS PRESS

Urbana and Chicago

Publication of this work was supported in part
by a grant from the Andrew W. Mellon Foundation.

Acknowledgment is given to the Association
for the Study of Afro-American Life and
History for permission to use portions
of chapter 5 that first appeared in
the *Journal of Negro History* (July, 1974).

Library of Congress Cataloging in Publication Data

Homel, Michael W. (Michael Wallace), 1944-
Down from equality.

(Blacks in the New World)
Bibliography: p.
Includes index.
1. Afro-American children—Education—Illinois—
Chicago—History. 2. School integration—Illinois—
Chicago—History. I. Title. II. Series.
LC2803.C5H65   1983   370'.9773'11   83-6893
ISBN 0-252-00981-9

For Nina and for my Mother and Father

CONTENTS

Illustrations

Maps

Tables

PREFACE

Only one or two of my teachers seemed to take any interest in us black students. The classes were overcrowded and frequently kids would be passed along, grade to grade, simply because they had good attendance records . . . Even though I was unprepared, I found I could get along in class. It didn't take very much thinking to realize that these conditions were tolerated because of prejudice which kept white students apart from blacks. It's true I didn't know what kind of education whites were getting, but I reasoned it couldn't possibly be worse than mine.

Ralph Metcalfe

. . . from its inception Betsy Ross had been earmarked as a ghetto school, a school for black children and, therefore, one in which as many things as possible might be safely thought of as "expendable." That, after all, was why it existed: *not* to give education but to withhold as much as possible, just as the ghetto itself exists not to give people homes but to cheat them out of as much decent housing as possible.

Lorraine Hansberry

THE HISTORY of public education for blacks in Chicago, like the development of the public schools in general, rests on a tragic paradox. On the one hand, many Americans have given education the responsibility for personal liberation and social change by viewing the classroom as a staging ground for upward mobilty of blacks, immigrants, and other working-class children. Indeed, some did climb the ladder of success: Ralph Metcalfe became an Olympic athlete and United States congressman, and Lorraine Hansberry became a playwright—although the testimony of these black Chicagoans suggests that local classrooms contributed only marginally to their future achievements.[1] For the most part, however, the schools have not been catalysts for social change. Public education is necessarily society's creation and

---

[1] The passage from Metcalfe is found in Earl and Miriam Selby, *Odyssey: Journey through Black America* (New York, 1971), pp. 314-15; Hansberry is quoted in Robert Nemiroff, ed., *To Be Young, Gifted and Black: Lorraine Hansberry in Her Own Words* (Englewood Cliffs, N.J., 1969), p. 35.

is therefore a conserving institution rather than one which reorders social attitudes and relationships. Thus, black education in Chicago between the world wars reflected the influences that limited black life in general—confinement to a ghetto, employment discrimination, and crime, disease, and family disorganization. But the public schools did not merely mirror the external forces restricting black lives; they also reinforced blacks' subordinate status. While restrictive covenants kept blacks in the ghetto, school officials were intensifying segregation with techniques of their own. Similarly, the racism of teachers and textbooks nourished and strengthened the prejudice that flourished outside schoolhouse doors. In sum, because the schools were products of white middle-class society, they reduced rather than expanded opportunities for groups like Chicago's blacks.

This book describes the creation of a separate and unequal system of public education in one northern city and analyzes black responses to the growth of segregation and inequality in the 1920s and 1930s. These decades were especially important for black Chicagoans and the public schools. In 1920, there was substantial integration of black students and teachers, and schools that enrolled blacks were basically equal to the ones whites attended. By the eve of World War II, however, black pupils and instructors were rigidly segregated, and their schools received less money and were more overcrowded than those in white neighborhoods of varying economic and social status. While I have written a case study of a single city, the significance of black education in Chicago extends well beyond that city's borders. Chicago's black population was second only to New York among United States cities in 1930 and 1940. Moreover, while northern school systems between the world wars adopted varied policies toward black children, the patterns of segregation and inequality that Chicago's black public school pupils experienced became typical for the majority of northern blacks by the 1940s and 1950s.

On the other hand, readers should be aware of the boundaries I have imposed upon this book. First, it addresses the relationship between Chicago blacks and the public schools and is not a history of black education in Chicago. Accordingly, I have not dealt with many institutions that helped educate black people—non-public schools, fraternities and sororities, benevolent associations, churches, social clubs, civic organizations, the press, commercial amusements, and popular culture. Furthermore, although this study does address the educational process in public schools, discussion of the classroom experience is secondary to the focus on the emergence of segregation and inequality and black reactions to these two developments.

Readers will also notice that I devote relatively little attention to the residential, occupational, social, and political patterns of black life between the wars. These conditions, important to consider if one is to understand the story of public education, are treated at length in rich contemporary works like St. Clair Drake and Horace Cayton's *Black Metropolis,* Harold Gosnell's *Negro Politicians,* and E. Franklin Frazier's *The Negro Family in Chicago.* In addition, the fine historical scholarship of Allan Spear's *Black Chicago,* Thomas Lee Philpott's *The Slum and the Ghetto,* and William M. Tuttle's *Race Riot* enables me to concentrate on public school issues and to refer those desiring additional background information to my able predecessors.

Finally, some words about the sources for this study are in order. In reconstructing and analyzing the past, historians typically rely both upon published materials and other data available to the public and upon private letters, reports, and information collected by individuals and organizations. The student of black education in cities like Chicago faces serious problems with both types of sources. Employees at the Chicago Board of Education responded to my inquiries about unpublished records and correspondence by asserting that they no longer existed. If such materials have been destroyed, the history of public education in Chicago will never be more than partially told. The lack of official archival materials on black education is all the more unfortunate in view of the scarcity of such information in manuscript collections of private individuals and groups. Still other difficulties occur with public sources. While black children in northern schools may have been a "separate problem," as the title of a recently published study suggests, in the Chicago school system's published records, blacks were not separate but invisible. If our knowledge of black education were derived solely from the thousands of pages of Board of Education *Proceedings, Directories,* and *Annual Reports,* we could only conclude that Chicago was a city without black pupils or teachers. Supply purchases and personnel changes appear in minute detail, but the official policy of color blindness (often contradicted by administrators' actions) precluded any mention of race or race relations.

Therefore, I have relied heavily on non-official sources, such as newspapers (particularly the black press) and other periodicals, studies by scholars and civic agencies, interviews, and census data. While these yield substantial information, they also leave frustrating gaps and do not tell us all that we want to know about blacks and schooling. Perhaps more troubling than the incompleteness of the data is the fact that what is available represents critics of the school system far more thoroughly than it does those who ran public education in Chicago. Despite these problems, a significant story can be told. In addition to the light this book sheds on Chicago's ever-volatile school politics and race relations, the study explores an important but often-neglected aspect of the black urban experience. The public schools not only communicated information and values to thousands of black children but helped shape blacks' perceptions about the urban North. If public education did not help liberate blacks in the way that the myths of equal opportunity and social mobility promised, the schools were nonetheless a catalyst for social change. In Chicago, as elsewhere, blacks' experiences with the public schools heightened their sensitivity to racial injustice and stimulated civic action that promoted group solidarity and tried to improve black lives.

Even though much historical research and writing is solitary, I have been fortunate to receive valuable assistance from individuals and institutions. My greatest debt is to August Meier, whose skillful editing lengthened this book's gestation period but greatly improved the final product. Carole S. Appel of the University of Illinois Press ably supervised the transition from manuscript to finished book. Richard C. Wade first directed my attention to the subject of black education, and David B. Tyack expanded my knowledge about urban education in general. Christopher R. Reed generously shared his insights on black civic organization in Chicago. My colleagues Richard D. Goff and Lester B. Scherer not only commented on an earlier draft of the manuscript but also demonstrated by example how one can combine good teaching and historical scholarship. I thank Eastern Michigan University for a sabbatical leave and Ira M. Wheatley, head of the Department of History and Philosophy, for his unfailing support and encouragement. Gary R. Court served ably as my research assistant. Jane Spires typed two drafts of this study accurately and with an even temper, my provocations notwithstanding. John Hope Franklin and David Street read the first version of this work and offered useful criticism. A number of Chicagoans active in educational and civic affairs during the interwar years generously shared their time and their memories; although their names appear in the bibliographical essay, I thank them here for their contributions. Neither they nor the others I have named are responsible for errors this book may contain.

As every student knows, libraries are treasured resources. My biggest thanks here goes to the Chicago Historical Society library staff and its outstanding manuscripts librarian, Archie Motley, for providing a congenial working atmosphere during my long-term residence there. I also benefited from the collections and staffs at the libraries of the University of Chicago, Eastern Michigan University, the University of Michigan, and the Chicago Board of Education, as well as the Manuscripts Division of the Library of Congress, the National Archives, the Center for Research Libraries, the Chicago Public Library, the Municipal Reference Library of the City of Chicago, the Illinois State Library, and the Newberry Library.

My wife, Nina, not only assisted directly at every stage of this project from research to proofreading but also gave other support for which I am deeply grateful. The dedication only suggests my gratitude to her and to two other important people in my life.

M.W.H.

DOWN FROM EQUALITY

CHAPTER ONE

Black Chicagoans and the Public Schools before 1920

UNTIL THE 1920s, black Chicagoans could give their city relatively high grades for educational opportunity. Schooling for blacks in Chicago was far superior to that in the South, where scarce funds, short terms, inadequate facilities, and a severely limited curriculum hampered education. Moreover, Chicago's racially mixed classrooms and willingness to hire black teachers made its schools more attractive than those of many other northern communities. After 1900, however, a rising tide of white prejudice and discrimination increasingly endangered the educational advantages black Chicagoans enjoyed. Heightened racial tensions threatened to replace a fluid pattern with a rigid, restrictive one.

In early Chicago, public school policy toward black children swung from exclusion to integration to segregation, finally settling on mixed schools after 1865. Before the Civil War, Illinois was one of several midwestern states that allocated no public funds to educate blacks. Both an Illinois law of 1835 and Chicago's city charter of 1837 followed previous state statutes that restricted public school enrollment to whites. While such exclusion was obviously discriminatory, it had little actual impact. The majority of eligible children did not attend the public schools during the 1830s and 1840s, and few school-age blacks then lived in Chicago. By the late 1840s, as abolition sentiment and sympathy for fugitive slaves grew, Chicago broke with Illinois's policy of exclusion. Local ordinances of 1849 and 1851 removed the racial bar and granted all children access to the public schools. For more than a decade, blacks attended classes with whites, even though state education funds for Chicago were still based solely on the city's white enrollment.[1]

Although little is known about the first black pupils in the Chicago schools, evidence does suggest some intriguing patterns. Unlike their counterparts in the 1920s and 1930s, black children attended overwhelmingly white schools. Jones and Dearborn had black enrollments of 5.2 and 3.8 percent, respectively, in 1861, and the percentage was even lower at the rest of the school buildings. On the other hand, black students clustered in a few districts and were not distributed evenly throughout the city. In 1861, of 172 blacks enrolled, 138 attended the two South Side schools mentioned. This figure paralleled the residential concentration of Chicago's blacks in the Dearborn and Jones districts. Thus, despite the integrated classrooms and the lack of a largely black ghetto, the link between residential and educational segregation that would characterize twentieth-century Chicago had already emerged.[2]

In 1856, the city opened a high school to prepare students for college and to train teachers for local classrooms. Admission was by competitive examination; in 1860, the high school enrolled about 3 percent of the 14- to 18-year-old population. All the high school students were white. In July, 1861, Mary E. Mann, "a highly intelligent mulatto girl," applied for the high school's teacher-training program. While Chicago had expanded educational opportunities for black children, its residents were sharply divided over the desirability of black teachers. "A Citizen" asked readers of the *Chicago Evening Journal,* "Is it our determination that the African shall, in all respects, be placed in the same social position as the whites? Are they to be the husbands of our daughters, the companions of our sons, the models of our children?" But Mary Mann did not stand alone. "Another Citizen" retorted that southern whites let untutored slaves raise their children. "Cannot we trust the care of our children to the highly educated of that same race?" "Justice" contended that decisions based on color "insult the moral sense of our people." The majority of the school board evidently agreed. A motion excluding those "of African blood" from the normal department failed, and the board approved Mann's application, 6-3.[3]

The city schools' policy of integration, however, had not taken firm root. During the next few years, the Civil War intensified antiblack hostility in Chicago, as it did elsewhere in the North. Many whites blamed blacks for the long and costly war and worried that slave emancipation would promote miscegenation, social equality, and massive black migration to the North. Wartime elections reflected these fears. In June, 1862, Illinois voters reaffirmed the state's Black Laws and approved constitutional provisions barring Negro newcomers and denying black residents the ballot. Moreover, the Democrats won the state elections in 1862 and Chicago's municipal elections in 1862 and 1863 by assailing abolition and warning of the "Africanization" of Illinois.[4]

The newly elected lawmakers overturned the city's policy of racially integrated schools. In February, 1863, the Democratically controlled state legislature authorized a new city charter which required Chicago "to provide one or more schools for the instruction of negro and mulatto children, to be kept in a separate building" and which barred them from schools that enrolled whites. The *Chicago Times,* which a rival paper termed "the organ of Jeff. Davis in this city," rejoiced that soon "the white children attending our public schools shall not be subjected to the degrading necessity of associating with the negro." The Board of Education complied with the new charter by establishing the Colored School in a rented building in June, 1863.[5]

As elsewhere, separate education meant both inadequate accommodations for black children and jobs for black professionals. "The house is the best that could be procured at that time," Superintendent of Schools William H. Wells reported, "but it is not well suited to the wants of the school. It is entirely destitute of yard room and is in other respects quite inconvenient." At first, two white women, Roxanna Beecher and Emily Stevens, taught the black students, with Beecher acting as principal. In July, 1863, Mary Mann completed her two-year normal course at the high school. At graduation ceremonies, officials seated her in the audience instead of on the stage with her classmates. After thus insulting her, authorities gave Mann a job at the Colored School, which she held until the school was discontinued.[6]

Chicago's experiment with segregation proved short-lived. An aroused black citizenry, a wavering Board of Education, and the shifting tides of party politics combined to doom the Colored School. Many blacks refused to send their children to the separate building. It enrolled only 57 pupils in its first year and 108 during 1864-65. Whether this gain derived from the sharp rise in black population or from growing acquiescence to segregation is impossible to determine. Nevertheless, even at its peak, the Colored School attracted only about 100 pupils, half the number of Negroes found in integrated classrooms in 1862. Furthermore, daily attendance was comparatively sporadic, for the separate facility ranked last in attendance among all schools in the city in 1863 and thirteenth of eighteen in 1864-65. Several years later, an administrator recalled, "The school was disorderly and much trouble existed in the vicinity of the school." Instead of attending the Colored School, many black children simply remained in regular classrooms. According to the story told in one black family, "The teachers declined to assign them to classes or studies. The children, however, attended daily, taking their seats in an orderly fashion throughout the controversy that ensued."[7]

The Board of Education compounded confusion by ruling that students with one-eighth or less Negro ancestry could legally avoid the Colored School. This pronouncement stimulated a series of such requests. Officials rejected some, but others passed the color test. In October, 1864, school superintendent Josiah L. Pickard disclosed that thirty-six Negroes were attending predominantly white schools, "since according to statements of parents and guardians, all have less than one-fourth negro blood."[8]

Such compromises satisfied neither the dominant Democrats nor the black community. The same school trustee who three years before had attempted to bar Mary Mann from the teacher-training program called for an investigation of blacks attending white schools. Meanwhile, black activists stepped up their protest, perhaps worried that rising enrollment at the Colored School signified black acceptance of segregation. In an indignation meeting, Negro residents attacked separate education as "gross in its tendency, and uncharitable in its purpose, calculated to retard the moral and intellectual progress of the colored youth, and brand them with degradation." Charging that segregation "fosters a prejudice in the mind of the child which is difficult to eradicate," blacks called for an end to the Colored School and a return to integrated classrooms. When resolutions brought no results, blacks "invaded the offices of the Board of Education and the Mayor," according to one contemporary. No evidence exists as to whether this was a direct action protest or a more conventional lobbying effort.[9]

Although black protests and noncooperation made the life of the Colored School stormy, political change was decisive in halting segregation. By autumn, 1864, Union victories on the battlefield brought a reversal of Democratic electoral gains of the past two years. After Republicans won congressional and state campaigns in November, 1864, and captured three-fourths of the Chicago City Council the following April, they improved the legal status of Illinois blacks. In February, 1865, the legislature ratified the Thirteenth Amendment to the federal Constitution, repealed the Black Laws, and approved a new charter for Chicago which eliminated the separate schools requirement. In the same month that Abraham Lincoln was assassinated, the Colored School closed its doors.[10]

While the state did not pass its widely evaded law forbidding segregated education until 1874, the demise of the Colored School ended formal racial barriers in the Chicago public schools. During the last three decades of the nineteenth century, black pupils not only attended classes with whites but did so on relatively amicable terms. About 1871, Superintendent Pickard reported, "All difficulty with the children of color has disappeared, except such as may be common to all children who have had no better advantages than themselves; we certainly have less frequent complaints than in the separate system." A black who attended the city schools during the 1880s concurred with Pickard's judgment. "I was never treated any different from any of the other people in the class," he recalled in 1939. "Things were a little different then from what they seem to be now.'' Although some incidents of racial conflict occurred, whites seemed to treat the small black student minority with relative tolerance during the late nineteenth century.[11]

From around the turn of the century, a more turbulent racial atmosphere replaced the peaceful climate that had prevailed since the Civil War. There were several reasons for the changed conditions. A younger generation of whites, largely indifferent to blacks' concerns, had replaced older Chicagoans whose ties with the antislavery movement and the young Republican party had fostered sympathy for blacks. Second, blacks stirred popular hostility by serving as strikebreakers in several bitter labor disputes. The most important cause of the deteriorating racial situation, however, was the substantial rise in Chicago's black population. Owing mainly to migration, especially from the Upper South, the number of blacks in the city grew from 30,150 to 44,103 between 1900 and 1910. During World War I, when the mass migration from the Deep South began, Chicago's black community increased even faster. Between 1910 and 1920, the Negro population rose 148 percent, to 109,458. During this decade, the percentage increase in black population was seven times that of the white gain, and by 1920, blacks accounted for 4.1 percent of the city's residents. Steadily growing concentrations of blacks in certain South Side neighborhoods accompanied their overall population gains, and this fact helped shape race relations in the schools during these years.[12]

The rapid growth in the number of blacks enhanced tensions by intensifying rivalries for housing, jobs, and recreational facilities. As the black clubwoman and civic leader Fannie Barrier Williams observed in 1905, ''The increase of the Negro population . . . has not tended to liberalize public sentiment.'' Whites who had looked kindly upon blacks in distant Dixie and who had tolerated the small minority settlement of the nineteenth century felt threatened as the number of black migrants swelled. In 1919, one letter to a local newspaper claimed that the white Chicagoan had been ''suddenly shoved out of his environment by an influx of a race alien to him.'' The writer added that northern whites had been willing to abolish slavery but ''still do not want them to come up here and 'sit right in our laps.''' At the factory, on the picket line, at parks, playgrounds, and beaches, on streetcars, and in the neighborhoods, whites resisted the black ''invasion.'' Tensions broke into open warfare with fifty-eight bombings of homes and offices between 1917 and 1921 and the terrible riot in July, 1919, which killed thirty-eight people and injured more than five hundred.[13]

While the growing social turbulence left its mark on the public schools, some of the openness and tranquillity of the late nineteenth century lingered after 1900. As Chicago's black population grew, the number of black children in local classrooms also increased. Negro school attendance rose from 2,694 in 1900 (ages 5-20) to 4,160 (ages 6-18) in 1910. Thereafter, the number of black pupils increased more rapidly, reaching 11,866, 2.7 percent of the citywide total, by 1920. While total school attendance in Chicago advanced 26.4 percent between 1910 and 1920, the figure for blacks jumped 185.2 percent. Despite the gains in black enrollment, however, classrooms remained racially mixed. In 1905, Keith Elementary was about two-thirds black, but no other school in the city had a black enrollment exceeding 30 percent. A decade later, Keith had become over 90 percent black; no other school followed suit, however, and Keith accounted for only one-twelfth of the 4,500 blacks in the Chicago public schools.[14]

Black teachers also enjoyed relatively unrestricted opportunities within the school system. The Board of Education hired black instructors on an integrated basis at least as early as the 1880s. From thirteen in 1901, they increased to sixteen in 1908 and to forty-one in 1917. During these years, black teachers, while not scattered evenly throughout the city, were by no means confined to schools with sizeable black enrollments. In 1901, one observer of the black community reported, "The practice of the teachers is chiefly among whites in the public schools." Eight of the fifteen black instructors in 1905 worked at schools with few or no black children. Four taught where black pupil enrollments reached as high as 30 percent, while three others were at Keith Elementary. Despite an increasing tendency for black faculty members to cluster at schools with many black pupils, the group as a whole remained reasonably well dispersed in 1917. Of the twenty-eight instructors whose assignments are known, seventeen taught in predominantly or exclusively white institutions.[15]

When white students or parents objected to the presence of black faculty members, school officials came to the aid of the teachers. After the principal of Moseley Elementary shifted a black instructor from one room to another in 1909, white pupils threatened to "strike." The principal, however, defended the teacher and refused to rescind his decision. Admitting that black teachers often faced opposition, an assistant superintendent saw no way to satisfy protesting whites: "But what can we do? We can't bar them from taking the examinations." In 1916, *Crisis* reported that in the face of public agitation against black faculty members, "the Board of Education stood firm." About a year later, some white pupils at Phillips High objected to the hiring of Oscar Jordan, the school's first black teacher. The principal brushed aside the complaints. "I told them that this man was a graduate of the University of Illinois, a high school graduate in the city, and a cultured man. Go in there and forget the color, and see if you can get the subject matter," he told the dissidents.[16]

While such student unrest was becoming more common, a substantial degree of interracial harmony persisted in the Chicago schools at this time. The principal of Raymond Elementary School, located near the west edge of the black district, stated in 1910, "When one treats these dear little children, both black and white, with tenderness and makes no difference between them . . . they both lose their prejudice." A few months later, a visiting educator claimed that he found no trace of color consciousness among the pupils of Farren Elementary, which was 30 percent black. He marveled that white majorities occasionally elected black children class officers. In 1916, an unnamed principal asserted, "Among the children in school there is no trouble. When trouble does come it usually starts in the homes." Even in the wake of the wartime migration and postwar riot, tranquillity remained the norm in many districts. At most South Side schools that investigators for the Chicago Commission on Race Relations visited, youngsters of both races mingled freely in classrooms and on playgrounds. Often children chose classmates of the opposite color to share a desk or to cooperate on a project. Raymond's principal reaffirmed, "In their meetings the question of color never arises at all." Added the principal of Colman School, "The color makes no difference." As black Chicagoans evaluated their local schools in the early twentieth century, there were indeed some grounds for satisfaction. In a 1906 article entitled "Chicago's Impartial Schools," Fannie Barrier Williams reached a positive verdict about public education in her city. "Do they offer equal opportunities to all classes of children? Is there a democratic spirit that, for the time being at least, makes the child of the alley equal to the child of the avenue?" she asked. "I think these questions can be answered with a more or less emphatic yes."[17]

Even as Williams wrote, however, the same forces that were worsening race relations in general were making their mark upon the public schools. One measure of the rising color tension was the increased frequency of interracial clashes. Interracial pupil combat took place not only in schools which blacks were entering for the first time or in districts with large and growing black enrollments, but also in stable integrated areas as well. In November, 1909, when the two children of a Pullman porter enrolled at the all-white Harvard School on the Far South Side, classmates greeted them with "sneering glances and covert insults." That afternoon, a group of white pupils pushed one of the youngsters down and beat him. A year later, white students battled black newcomers at Doolittle Elementary, which was located east of the black district, in an area that was undergoing racial change.[18]

Meanwhile, in several neighborhoods where Negroes were rapidly attaining a majority, black children were typically the aggressors in interracial conflicts. "Feeling their strength, they have undertaken to 'clean out' the pale faces," a black observer reported in 1907. "In various ways, more or less emphatic, they have served notice on their white schoolmates that they are not wanted and that the sooner they get out the better." A teenaged student at Moseley Elementary, which was about one-half black by 1908, sighed, "They're always having fights at school." At Keith Elementary, whites complained of periodic "race wars" and begged authorities for transfers. In September, 1908, after the ten-year-old daughter of a white grocery store owner identified several blacks who had searched a teacher's desk, she became the target for retaliation. A "horde of blacks" chased the girl and allegedly beat her and threatened to kill her.[19]

School districts with a stable racial balance also experienced pupil discord. After a black youth slugged a white girl at Tilden School in 1905, "a pitched battle" between the races ensued. Declared a shopkeeper, "It was as near a riot as any fight I ever saw." Color strife was common along the western edge of the South Side black district. Fights between blacks and working-class whites of Irish and eastern European origins erupted intermittently along the Wentworth Avenue "dead line" for many years. One such feud in 1914 ended when a train hit a white combatant and severed one of his arms.[20]

Whereas white segregationists argued that such clashes justified separate schools, blacks tended to minimize the significance of these episodes or to attribute the problems to nonracial causes. Fannie Barrier Williams asserted in 1905, "It is true that now and then colored and white children have their little race quarrels, but not more than do the children of other races." During the wartime migration, Robert S. Abbott, the Georgia-born printer who made the *Chicago Defender* the nation's leading black newspaper, struck a similar note. "Perhaps a few school children, white and Black, have some petty differences which they are attempting to adjust in the usual schoolboy way . . . ," he declared. "Every girl or boy who has attended public school even where there was no mixture of races has seen differences adjusted this way." The *Defender* accused the white press of exaggerating these incidents and wrongly portraying them in racial terms. For example, in 1915, a battle that a white newspaper reported as "Children in Race Riot" appeared in the *Defender* as a good-natured fray in which both sides were racially mixed. In another case, blacks proved that a *Chicago Tribune* account of "a miniature race war" at Phillips High School was false, and the paper admitted its error. While racial peace may have been typical and some reports of strife were clearly overdrawn, no one could deny that color tensions within the public schools were rising.[21]

Interaction among pupils, of course, largely mirrored attitudes among adults. After 1900, periodic school segregation movements arose among white Chicagoans, some limited to a single district or neighborhood, others aimed at establishing separate education throughout the city. In 1903, Chicago's leading black integrationists detected "a seeming desire on the part of a certain class of citizens to separate the Afro-American pupils in the public schools from the whites." The blacks, who included the dentist Charles Bentley and the attorneys Ferdinand L. Barnett and Edward H. Morris, organized the Equal Opportunity League, which briefly functioned as a protest group friendly to W. E. B. Du Bois and critical of Booker T. Washington. After the League spoke out against separate schools, the ill-defined segregation threat failed to materialize.[22]

Local race relations, however, worsened substantially in the wake of a stockyards strike in 1904 and a teamsters' strike in 1905. When employers imported black strikebreakers from the South, whites retaliated against Chicago blacks; a series of minor attacks culminated in a deadly riot in May, 1905. The labor clashes spilled into the schools as well. During the teamsters' strike, several hundred white students, encouraged by adults, left classes to protest coal deliveries to school buildings by black scabs. One principal announced, "I will invite the pupils to strike if the dirty niggers deliver coal at this school." Although the strikes were settled, race relations in Chicago had been damaged permanently.[23]

When fall classes resumed four months after the teamsters' strike, white parents began to switch their children from integrated districts to schools with few or no black students. Though the neighborhood school system was the norm in Chicago, authorities often permitted parents to transfer their children to other districts upon request. Racial, ethnic, and social class differences lay behind many transfer applications. As one journalist reported: "The applicants all have what appears to them good reasons why 'Freddie' and 'Clara' should not be compelled to attend a certain school. The environments, it will be stated, are not ideal or the finer sensibilities of the pupils from the boulevard are harried by daily contact with the children from the humble back street." Superintendent of Schools Ella Flagg Young confirmed that the same factors motivated the transfer requests reaching her administration. "It is purely a social matter," she stated. "The parents wish to get away from a certain element, a certain nationality which may dominate their neighborhood and the transfer is decided upon." While school officials sometimes criticized this trend, they did not stop it by enforcing the neighborhood system for all.[24]

In the fall of 1905, authorities at first routinely approved the wave of transfer requests. By December, however, the exodus had cut attendance sharply at five racially mixed schools, while nearby white schools had become overcrowded. When authorities refused new transfer applications, some white students turned truant. The school superintendent and Board of Education were baffled by the dilemma. Only a plan to separate the races would satisfy white parents, but approving transfers in a racially selective manner might violate the state's ban on segregated schools. On the other hand, denying transfer applications would provoke popular pressure against the school system, increase color conflict in the classroom, and encourage whites to move away from integrated areas. Either way, school integration would be the casualty. Late in 1905, several school trustees did suggest transferring whites out of mixed schools but withholding that privilege from blacks. One Board of Education member explained, "Other schools would have to be built just outside the 'black belt' to accommodate the white children transferred, but I believe this to be the only possible solution of the problem." Although the *Tribune* reported that the board intended to implement this plan, it reached no such agreement, and the situation dragged on inconclusively.[25]

Blacks regarded the *Tribune's* treatment of the transfer issue as a campaign for segregated education. "The *Tribune* is laboring to abolish the mixed school system of Chicago," said Ferdinand Barnett pessimistically, "and I would be willing to wager that within the next five years it will achieve its object." Barnett's wife, Ida B. Wells-Barnett, persuaded Jane Addams to call a meeting at Hull-House to discuss the *Tribune's* campaign. Prominent white clergymen, lawyers, editors, and social workers joined black leaders. One enthusiastic black exclaimed, "In this assembly of earnest men and women who have a right to be heard and are respectfully heard on every public question, one could easily fancy himself in New England in the stirring days of the Abolitionist movement." Wells-Barnett stated that segregated black schools were inferior to accommodations for whites, and she begged the prestigious group to defend blacks and the principle of equality. "Would they use that power," she asked, "to help us, the weaker brothers, secure here in Chicago an equal chance with the children of white races?" Her plea succeeded, for Addams headed a committee of seven which quickly convinced the *Tribune* to end its speculations about separate schools.[26]

In 1906, Chicagoans began to consider a new city charter, and blacks again grew apprehensive about school segregation. The local branch of the Niagara Movement, the civil rights protest group founded the previous year by Du Bois, convinced Mayor Edward F. Dunne to name a black to the charter commission. Charles Bentley, the prominent black dentist who had helped establish the Niagara Movement both nationally and in Illinois, testified on behalf of a ban on separate schools in the proposed charter, and such a clause was included. Chicago voters, however, rejected the document by a wide margin.[27]

Within a few years, agitation by whites in Hyde Park once again thrust the school segregation question to the forefront. Hyde Park, bounded by Fifty-first and Fifty-ninth Streets, Washington Park, and Lake Michigan, had been part of Chicago since its annexation in 1889. In the 1890s, the Columbian Exposition and the establishment of the University of Chicago helped develop the area and determine its character. Hyde Park had several black enclaves, whose 2,500 residents supported themselves mainly through domestic and personal service jobs in local homes and hotels.[28]

In September, 1908, whites who opposed the movement of blacks into white-occupied blocks created the Hyde Park Improvement Protective Club. The association restricted newly arriving blacks to the existing enclaves and forced blacks out of areas the HPIPC designated for whites. The group coerced local landlords, realtors, and merchants into supporting the cause and through threats, financial incentives, and vandalism reduced the area's black population by two-thirds by 1920.[29]

Hyde Park whites not only wanted segregated housing but sought separate schools as well. HPIPC president Henry T. Davis claimed that few whites believed that "constant association between negro and white children helps the education of either." HPIPC leaders warned that interracial dancing might occur, maintained that black teachers should not instruct white children, and claimed that segregation would foster racial peace. Davis asserted, "Where there are but a few negro boys at a school they are often abused by the white boys and it would be a protection for them if they were kept by themselves." Finally, the group believed separate schools would assure a segregated neighborhood. A local physician explained, "I think that if the negro children are separated from the white children in Hyde Park schools the result will be that their parents will leave this neighborhood, and that our property will soon return to its normal value." Whereas HPIPC initially proposed that the Board of Education separate the races only in Hyde Park classrooms, by 1912, leaders urged that the whole school system be segregated. One member predicted, "It is only a question of time when there will be separate schools for Negroes throughout Illinois."[30]

Blacks were outraged at "this small coterie of no-account caucasians," as the *Defender* called the HPIPC activists. At an indignation meeting, five hundred blacks heard the attorney John G. Jones, a former state legislator and outspoken adversary of Booker T. Washington, declare, "Separate schools create and perpetuate race prejudice. The man who advocates such a thing is a menace to society." A black journalist agreed. "Let Negroes and white boys study and play together as children," he announced, "and they will grow to a better understanding and live more peaceably . . . when they grow to be citizens." As during the *Tribune's* segregation series several years earlier, blacks had the support of highly placed white Chicagoans. The *Chicago Evening Post* scoffed, "Those property owners in Hyde Park . . . should save their breath." The newspaper's editors predicted, "There are too many citizens of Chicago—both men and women—who went to school with colored children and are unconscious of any contamination thereby to make it possible, we believe, for such a proposal to gain any headway." Democratic mayor Carter Harrison II, who had appointed several prominent blacks to high-ranking patronage jobs and successfully courted many black voters, dismissed the segregation plan as unlawful and indicated that authorities would ignore it. School officials agreed with Harrison. The *Defender* purred confidently, "There are too many 'real white folks' in this city to allow Southern or ancient Roman ideas to prevail in modern Chicago."[31]

In spite of the strong sentiment among blacks during the pre-war period for mixed schools, agitation for separate education came not only from whites but from some Negroes as well. In November, 1910, a number of blacks reportedly circulated petitions for segregated education, and similar efforts continued intermittently for the next several years. In April, 1912, the *Crisis* attacked white "reactionaries and their colored tools" who were calling for dual school systems in Chicago, and a year later the *Defender* bemoaned the fact that "people of supposed intelligence amongst us constantly appeal to the Board of Education for separate schools here." The prospect of more jobs for black instructors was the main appeal black separatists used in Chicago as elsewhere. Although an officially segregated school system would have enhanced job opportunities and provided a refuge from racial tensions, it won no public support from black Chicago's civic leadership and provoked vigorous attack from many activists. The *Defender* spoke for most local blacks when it blasted black separatists as "tools of unscrupulous, prejudiced whites or unprincipled, self-aggrandizement seeking parasites" and told one to "beat it back to her dear old southern home, where all the Uncle Toms and Topsys should be."[32]

White protests against administrative policies that increased school integration were another problem prior to the mass migration of World War I. In the pre-war years, school officials placed greater value on using classroom accommodations efficiently than on catering to the racial prejudices of white parents. When officials ordered pupil transfers or redrew school attendance boundaries so that white children came in contact with black youngsters, white parents resisted bitterly. A reporter summarized the situation in 1908: "When one school becomes overcrowded the only remedy is to change the boundary lines between that district and an adjoining district, where there are vacant rooms, but the protests which follow every change only emphasize the impossibility of making divisions which will serve to accommodate the greatest number of pupils and satisfy parents who demand discrimination." Six years later, Superintendent Young confirmed, "Every attempt to force parents to send their children to those schools which were once crowded, but today have accommodations to spare, is met with protests from parents and their representatives in the city government."[33]

In September, 1908, a month after several attacks upon black adults by white mobs, school officials transferred 350 white elementary pupils out of a high school building to make room for additional high school students. Administrators sent 150 of the children to nearby Hancock Elementary School, which was about one-tenth black. Fights broke out among students at Hancock, which was near the stockyards, scene of clashes between union men and black strikebreakers four years before. Thirtieth Ward alderman Michael McInerney spoke for the aggrieved whites: "It's a hardship that seems unjust to these pupils. They come from good families and they have been at a good building. Now they are told to go to an old building and to sit side by side with—well, with children they don't wish to sit beside. There's going to be trouble out there and something ought to be done."[34]

Encouraged by parents, nearly all the newly assigned pupils boycotted Hancock. A committee of parents reported that nearby white schools had room for the 150 children. Authorities seemed divided. Board of Education president Otto C. Schneider announced, "No favoritism will be shown any one" and blamed white parents for the trouble. "A clean negro boy is better than a dirty white boy," Schneider declared. "The parents of some of the negro children who attend the Keith and Hancock schools are a far better class than the parents of some of the white pupils there." Superintendent of Schools Edwin G. Cooley, however, bowed to the whites and rescinded the mass transfer.

Some children returned to their former rooms, and others went to a nearby white elementary school.[35]

Officials did not always give in to public opposition. In December, 1906, overcrowding in a school district in Englewood on the Southwest Side resulted in a boundary change that sent some additional white students to Copernicus Elementary, which was about 30 percent black. Almost immediately, trouble began. After whites and blacks traded threats for several days, several hundred pupils fought with stones, clubs, and hatpins. Though the principal and the parents' club denied reports of violence, parents of recently arrived whites were unconvinced. One anguished mother cried, "I am afraid my children will not reach home alive after attending school." Parents of forty new pupils asked the Board of Education to return their offspring to the overcrowded school they had previously attended. Authorities spurned the request, and clashes at Copernicus continued. A year and a half later, a reporter noted, "The two races have an attitude of armed neutrality which gives way every few days to an open fight."[36]

A similar episode took place on the city's West Side, where the school board changed boundaries in an effort to curtail overcrowding in 1910. Pupils formerly attending all-white institutions found themselves in integrated classes at Hayes and Mitchell schools. Disgruntled parents enlisted two aldermen on their behalf, but their complaints were unheeded. Once again, officials were more concerned with reducing the number of children on half-day schedules and in makeshift facilities than in catering to racial bias.[37]

Besides boundary and transfer disputes, a second source of racial controversy before 1920 was Wendell Phillips High School, named after the eloquent abolitionist. Although Phillips had a largely white student enrollment when it opened in 1904 on the South Side, black population growth in the Phillips district soon made it Chicago's first predominantly black high school. Whereas about 290 Negroes, one-sixth of the total, attended Phillips in 1915, by early 1921 blacks accounted for three-fourths of the school's student population. With its socially diverse enrollment and extensive extracurricular program, a high school like Phillips was more susceptible to ethnic and class conflicts than the smaller elementary institutions.[38]

In 1908, the Board of Education attempted to undermine secret high school fraternities and sororities by suggesting that each high school establish a social room open to all students. Both blacks and whites used the Phillips social room, and sometimes interracial dancing occurred. This distressed white parents, many of whom lived in neighborhoods that blacks were beginning to enter. One white asserted that black immorality justified segregation and warned, "Unless this separation is made you will ruin the future generation and debauch your home."[39]

These cues were sufficient for the Phillips dean of girls, Fanny R. Smith. Smith was not well liked in the black community. In November, 1913, some blacks accused her of advocating separate schools and urging Negro pupils to do the same. In January, 1915, Chicagoans discovered that for three years Smith had scheduled social hours for blacks and whites on separate days. She explained that white protests necessitated the arrangement but claimed that the situation also offered an educational lesson. "The colored pupils are learning," she wrote, "just as the white ones have to learn, that people have political rights, but social privileges; that kindly interest in others cannot be forced." Assistant Principal Charles Perrine defended the policy by distinguishing between the school's educational and social functions. Ignoring the question of public responsibility, Perrine contended that "no one could complain because another would not associate with them in a social dance or otherwise."[40]

Black parents persuaded their children to avoid the segregated social room, but black leaders did not publicly protest the situation. As Ida B. Wells-Barnett remarked, "It was not the colored people who rushed into print with this." Interracial dancing was a relatively unimportant, yet potentially inflammatory, issue. Blacks realized that race relations were deteriorating, and that protracted conflict over the social room would place their rights in greater danger. As one black put it, "Let the least trouble arise in one of these social gatherings whether thru accident or intention and popular feeling would flame out and the schools be closed against us entirely." An emotional issue and the worsening climate of opinion had compromised the militant integrationism of nineteenth-century blacks.[41]

Ironically, it was a pair of well-known whites who openly challenged segregation at Phillips. In January, 1915, the University of Chicago dean of women, Marion Talbot, and Celia Parker Woolley, a social worker, sent protests to Superintendent Young. Talbot declared, "A good many people believe that if ever there was a time when discrimination between races should be made, socially or otherwise, this surely is not the time." Citing a traditional argument for universal education, Talbot concluded, "Our public school certainly is an agency for fostering sympathy and democracy which must not be allowed to fail the community." Woolley, who operated Frederick Douglass Center, a settlement house offering cultural activities for educated blacks, seconded Talbot's views. Rebutting Smith and Perrine, Woolley proclaimed, "The color line has no more place in the social gatherings of the school than in the classroom or laboratory." Segregation was unacceptable, she said, for it "sets at naught the fundamental principles on which our public school was based."[42]

With the affair made public, blacks began openly criticizing the Phillips arrangement. The Progressive Negro League, a South Side civic organization, reminded authorities that Phillips was "a public institution conducted in all branches for all the people." Wells-Barnett blasted "the class spirit" inherent in segregation and added, "Miss Smith speaks of social privileges. There should be no privilege connected with our public schools." The black weeklies also joined the attack. Julius F. Taylor, the anticlerical Bryan Democrat who edited the *Broad Ax,* warned of "the germ of southern racial prejudice." The previously silent *Defender,* now crusading against "the Monster Prejudice," advised educators to encourage fairness and cooperation. If white children "wanted to crush and humiliate pupils," the *Defender* suggested, "let them go to a private school, where they can have all the caste and 'society' they desire." An editorial writer guessed that if Wendell Phillips knew what happened at the school named for him, "He must turn over in his grave and sigh."[43]

For blacks floridly to denounce separation in the social room was almost obligatory in view of Talbot's and Woolley's dissent. Significantly, however, black and white antisegregationists, sensitive to the perils of "social equality," did not insist upon integrated social hours and the explosive confrontation they would have produced. Beauregard F. Moseley, a Georgia-born attorney, businessman, and Republican politician, suggested that officials make no policy and permit students to decide the question informally. The most popular choice, though, was to abolish the program. The *Defender* counseled, "If socials bring on such race contempt, let there be no dances." Forcing unwilling students to mingle socially would benefit no one, Woolley declared. Since race mixing in the social room invited contention over a minor issue, avoiding the problem was the wisest course. "Let us abandon the dancing class in the public school and every other purely social function," she pleaded.[44]

School authorities eventually took this advice. Superintendent Ella Flagg Young, who headed the Chicago schools from 1909 to 1915, won black admiration by praising black pupils and defending integration. In 1913, a black journalist wrote of Young, "She has nipped in the bud many designs to separate the races . . . and has righted many individual cases of mistreatment on account of color." Although Young at first refused to intervene in the Phillips dispute, she finally imposed the option suggested by Woolley and the *Defender.* Young explained that whereas race bias was absent when pupils did academic work, "it was only when they were together on a purely social basis that difficulty came." Therefore, in April, 1915, she eliminated the Phillips social hours and substituted programs of "intellectual uplift." "Instead of the tango and the fox trot," remarked one spectator, "the students now listen to a lecture on Mexico, look at stereopticon views of the Yosemite valley, or debate the question of woman suffrage." Black spokesmen lauded Young's decision, but racial equality had been defended at the cost of the program involved. Such a solution was hardly a useful blueprint for racial peace in the public schools.[45]

As black enrollment at Phillips rose even more sharply after 1915, relations between blacks and whites deteriorated still further. Phillips whites, who became a minority during World War I, still sought to isolate themselves through segregation. When the U.S. Army introduced an officer-training program at Phillips in 1917, the sergeant in charge tried to restrict blacks to a separate company. Opposition from students and principal Spencer Smith derailed the plan. The following year, two black aldermen claimed credit for thwarting a move by a Phillips evening school instructor to place black and white students in separate rooms. As Phillips's principal from 1917 to 1921, Charles Perrine tried to limit blacks' presence at the high school. Perrine, who had favored Fannie Smith's segregated social rooms, advocated separate schools, denounced social equality of the races, and segregated students at graduation ceremonies. Under Perrine, school clubs and social affairs were closed to black students. Perrine believed that black pupils lowered his school's academic standards and vowed to keep Phillips a "white" institution. He told a reporter, "I don't think the time has come when the whites should be crowded out of the Wendell Phillips by the Negro." Perrine, however, was the champion of a lost cause. His plan to reduce black enrollment at Phillips by opening a junior high for blacks aroused little response from authorities, and Perrine left Phillips after blacks called for his removal.[46]

Since black population growth and the expansion of black residential areas were making Phillips predominantly black, some of the remaining whites sought an escape route. In April, 1917, a group of parents from Willard Elementary, a largely white school which sent its graduates to Phillips, complained about conditions at the high school. Although parents first denounced the taverns and pool halls near Phillips, one woman admitted, "The real reason is that the Phillips school has a large number of Negroes. So why mince matters and refer to conditions as immoral when we mean there are colored students there?" A physician who led the Willard group added, "There is no denying the fact that the Phillips school is two-thirds colored and that white children should not

be compelled to sit with colored children." School administrators, who
a decade earlier might well have rejected segregation pressure, satisfied
the parents by shifting Willard from the Phillips district to the territory
of largely white Hyde Park High School.[47]

Meanwhile, the causes which made race relations tense at Phillips
High produced renewed talk of separate schools on a citywide basis. In
August, 1918, Max Loeb, a thirty-four-year-old Jewish businessman
and Board of Education member, sent a letter to fifty black Chicagoans
which asked some explosive questions. Loeb wrote:

> How best can the Race antagonisms be avoided which often spring
> up when the two races are brought into close juxtaposition—espe-
> cially when white and Colored children are in attendance under the
> same [teachers] and in the same classes? Do you think it wiser,
> when there is a large Colored population, to have separate schools
> for white and Colored children? If the separation came at the de-
> sire and upon the initiative of the Colored people, would the sym-
> pathetic understanding of Colored by whites, and vice versa, be
> heightened, or would such a separation increase prejudice and an-
> tagonism? Do you think it wiser to have separate classes for Col-
> ored and whites, with Colored and white teachers, in the same
> school rather than to have separate schools? It seems much wiser to
> have separation (if any at all is necessary) by voluntary action
> rather than through the operation of law. How, in your opinion,
> should a separation movement, if under any circumstances it is
> wise, be begun?[48]

Blacks reacted indignantly. Beauregard Moseley told Loeb, "I must
confess your letter astonished me, and almost made me feel that I had
been insulted." The black press pointed out that it was ironic for a
member of a group victimized by bigotry to consider similar bias
against Negroes. Black journalists also declared that Loeb violated the
ideals for which the nation had gone to war. As the *New York Age*
remarked, "The inconsistency of such a movement should be patent to
the blindest color-phobist at this time, when America is engaged in the
struggle to bring about a world-wide democracy." "Mr. Loeb's new
propaganda is as dangerous within as the kaiser's kultur is without,"
the *Defender* editorialized. "He could do no more to help the kaiser
among our people than be raising the issue of separate schools while we
are engaged in a war to convince the Hun that class and race distinctions
must forever be banished."[49]

Max Loeb had more than an abstract interest in race relations. His
home, at 4854 Grand Boulevard (South Parkway), lay in the path of
black residential expansion and within the Willard Elementary district,

which blacks were beginning to enter. Loeb himself had been on the Board of Education when Willard residents filed their grievances about Phillips High in 1917. But Republican politics might well have motivated Loeb's inflammatory letter as much as racism. Loeb came to the school board as an appointee of Mayor William Hale Thompson (1915-23, 1927-31). When the state legislature approved a law reorganizing Chicago's school administration in April, 1917, Thompson selected a new Board of Education. The former board members, including Loeb, refused to step aside, and for more than a year the city had two competing school boards.[50]

Loeb, ousted by his former patron, was angry at Thompson, and his schools letter was aimed at "Big Bill" at least as much as against black Chicagoans. From his earliest days in politics, Thompson had assiduously courted black voters. As mayor, he gave blacks jobs in city government, protected illicit South Side businesses, and publicly identified himself as a friend of the race. In return, blacks gave Thompson overwhelming and crucial support. For example, "Big Bill" won the 1915 Republican mayoral primary by 2,500 votes but would have lost had he not carried the largely black second ward by 6,763.[51]

Loeb's segregation inquiry, therefore, ensured political fireworks. As Moseley observed, for a Thompson appointee to promote separate schools "is, to say the least, surprising." The letter attempted to alienate or confuse Thompson's most steadfast followers less than a month before he faced Medill McCormick, a former *Tribune* publisher and an incumbent congressman-at-large, in the Illinois Republican senatorial primary. Thompson's opponents exploited the Loeb episode, hoping to deny the mayor some of the black vote. For example, the *Tribune* was the only major Chicago daily newspaper to report the Loeb letter and blacks' reaction, and its stories carefully drew the Loeb-Thompson connection. Furthermore, most of the black response also came from outside Thompson's camp. *Broad Ax* editor Julius Taylor, a Democrat, wrote, "If Mayor Thompson and his loud-mouthed Colored supporters, those who are getting rich at the public crib, expect the decent and self-respecting colored people to vote and shout for him he must lay away from Max Loeb." Oscar De Priest had risen through the Thompson faction of the Republican party to become Chicago's first black alderman (1915) but was temporarily estranged from the Republican regulars after acquittal on bribery charges in 1917. De Priest created his own political group, the People's Movement, to support his candidacies for City Council in 1918 and 1919. The People's Movement also criticized Loeb's segregation bid and warned Thompson, "We shall oppose unalterably for public office any men or group, who, for any purpose whatever, sanction or give support, openly or covertly, to the suggestion of segregation in the public schools."[52]

Thompson skillfully hastened to repair the damage. He assured a delegation of prominent blacks that Loeb was a liar, a crook, and a tool of the *Tribune.* With characteristic flourish, "Big Bill" told South Siders, "There is no more danger of segregation in the schools in the city of Chicago than the kaiser to be President of the United States." Black Thompsonites asserted that the mayor deserved their race's continued support and charged the *Tribune* with using the affair to advance McCormick's election hopes. Meanwhile, having made his point, Loeb publicly retreated: "My letter was one of inquiry only, designed to get the point of view of the Colored parent who has children in the public school. I DID NOT, DO NOT, and SHALL NOT advocate segregation. Nothing could be further from my mind than to advocate anything undemocratic or subversive. . . . My position has been altogether misunderstood." Loeb's political purposes fared as poorly as his racial ones. Although McCormick did win the statewide primary, Thompson scored his usual landslide among black voters, winning the second ward by better than six to one.[53]

Within a year, the tragic race riot of July, 1919, increased white interest in formally segregating the public schools. As one woman stated, "It is all wrong for colored children and white children to be in school together. There should be separate schools, because the two races of children are as different in everything as in their color." For the most part, whites opposing racially mixed classrooms also hoped to separate blacks and whites in every other way as well. Cries arose for "complete segregation of the two races . . . two entirely distinct and separate castes." *The Economist,* voice of the city's white commercial and real estate leaders, urged segregated housing and transportation as in the South. On behalf of citizens favoring "an intelligent and equitable separation of the races," Southwest Side alderman Terence F. Moran proposed a biracial commission to probe the riot's causes and "equitably fix a zone or zones which shall be created for the purpose of limiting within its borders the residence of only colored or white persons." Before the City Council could consider the plan, Louis B. Anderson, Mayor Thompson's floor leader and one of two black aldermen, obtained a ruling that the resolution was out of order.[54]

The biracial riot-study commission envisioned by Alderman Moran was soon appointed by Illinois governor Frank O. Lowden. Black suspicion of the twelve-member Chicago Commission on Race Relations was widespread. The *Chicago Whip* declared itself "opposed to the commission because it means segregation, and we are uncompromisingly against segregation of any sort." The *Broad Ax* detected "a silent and well laid plan . . . to separate the White and the Colored race every way that it will be possible to do so." Julius Taylor gloomily predicted that "a long chain of other evils and almost insurmountable obstacles are more than likely to follow in the deadly wake of the Illinois Race Commission." Only the *Defender,* whose editor was a commission member, refrained from the pessimistic chorus.[55]

The fear that the race relations commission would promote segregation was well founded. Moran's resolution had made many blacks apprehensive about a riot study agency, especially one named by Governor Lowden, a rival of Thompson. The *Whip* warned, "Segregation measures are in the air. Lowden's forces are at work. BEWARE, BEWARE, BEWARE!" The commission's membership also caused concern. The *Broad Ax* accused one black member of favoring separate schools and identified one of the whites as an officer of the Kenwood and Hyde Park Property Owners Association. Both Lowden and Francis Shepardson, Lowden's race relations adviser and vice-chairman of the commission, favored segregation. Lowden urged an agreement on separate neighborhoods for each race, and Shepardson declared, "The negro does not desire to scatter himself over the entire city" and endorsed "intelligent segregation that will permit the negro to live among those of his own kind whom he prefers."[56]

At first glance, the race relations commission's school recommendations, which appeared in 1922, seemed to prove the *Whip* and *Broad Ax* unduly alarmist. Instead of calling for formally separate schools, the commission urged that extracurricular activities be open to black pupils and that the schools hire "principals and teachers who have a sympathetic and intelligent interest in promoting good race relations in the schools." However, the commission did not advocate or defend school integration. Its top priority educational recommendation, headed "More Schools in Negro Areas," stressed improved facilities and less overcrowding in the black belt, even though black schools already compared favorably with immigrant schools in these respects. As the historian Thomas Philpott has shown, the Chicago Commission on Race Relations sought a "dual solution," in which blacks' housing and public services would be improved in exchange for a tacit acceptance of segregation. Unfortunately, separation appeared but the quality of facilities continued to deteriorate.[57]

In 1920, prosegregation forces had an additional opportunity when Illinois residents considered a new state constitution. The *Broad Ax* anticipated proposals "that the Colored race should be stripped of its manhood rights in this state, that segregation or 'Jim Crowism' in some form or other must prevail." Some white Chicagoans did demand formally separate schools. One suggested permitting segregation statutes, explaining, "Definite blocks in Chicago could be set apart for the homes of the negroes. They could be given separate residence sections, separate schools and separate bathing beaches." But the U.S. Supreme Court had struck down such laws three years earlier, and convention delegates did not wish to challenge the decision. Even if segregationists had prevailed at the convention, their success would have been hollow, since Illinois voters rejected the proposed constitution for reasons unrelated to race.[58]

Although legally authorized segregation did not appear in the Chicago schools between 1900 and 1920, blacks had little cause for complacency. The rapid increase in black population and the expansion of black residential districts had changed the public school system just as they had affected Chicago's neighborhoods, workplaces, and parks. Racial tensions among pupils had grown, and white parents were increasingly insistent upon segregation. Furthermore, during and after the mass migration of World War I, school officials and white civic leaders were less inclined to defend blacks against popular pressure than they had been before 1915. Finally, the mass migration, combined with black confinement to specific blocks and neighborhoods, was concentrating black pupil enrollment in certain school districts. The separate school system which blacks so feared seemed to be emerging even without formal action by state or local authorities.

NOTES

1. Mary J. Herrick, *The Chicago Schools: A Social and Political History* (Beverly Hills, Calif., 1971), pp. 24, 400; Bessie Louise Pierce, *A History of Chicago* (New York, 1937-57), I, 270-71, II, 390; Chicago Board of Education, *Annual Report of the Board of Education,* VI (1859-60), 18; *Chicago Evening Journal,* July 30, 1861, p. 3

2. Board of Education, *Annual Report,* VII (1860-61), 81, VIII (1861), 34, 59; U.S. Census Office, *Population of the United States in 1860* (Washington, 1864), p. 90.

3. Herrick, *The Chicago Schools,* pp. 38, 41-42, 403; U.S. Census Office, *Population of the United States in 1860,* pp. 78-79, 90; *Evening Journal,* July 30, 1861, pp. 2-3, July 31, 1861, p. 3; *Chicago Times,* July 29, 1861, p. 1; *Chicago Tribune,* July 29, 1861, p. 1, July 30 and 31, 1861, p. 4, July 11, 1863, p. 4.

4. V. Jacque Voegeli, *Free but Not Equal: The Midwest and the Negro during the Civil War* (Chicago, 1967); Forrest G. Wood, *Black Scare* (Berkeley, Calif., 1968); Arthur Charles Cole, *The Era of the Civil War,*

1848-1870 (Springfield, Ill., 1919), pp. 266-71, 296-97, 333-37; Pierce, *History of Chicago,* II, 265-69.

5. Board of Education, *Annual Report,* XXV (1878-79), 38; Pierce *History of Chicago,* II, 12, 339; *Times,* Feb. 17, 1863, p. 3; *Tribune,* Feb. 18, 1863, p. 2; City of Chicago, *Journal of the Proceedings of the City Council,* Mar. 23, 1863, p. 3.

6. Board of Education, *Annual Report,* X (1863), 24, 62; *Evening Journal,* July 11, 1863, p. 4; *Tribune,* July 11, 1863, p. 4; Chicago Board of Education Library, Notebooks on School Histories.

7. Board of Education, *Annual Report,* X (1863), 24, 52, XI (1864-65), 17, 78; U.S. Commissioner of Education, *History of Schools for the Colored Population* (New York, 1969), p. 343; St. Clair Drake and Horace R. Cayton, *Black Metropolis: A Study of Negro Life in a Northern City* (New York, 1945), p. 44.

8. *Tribune,* Sept. 18, 1864, p. 4; *Evening Journal,* Oct. 5, 1864, p. 4.

9. *Tribune,* Sept. 18 and Oct. 6, 1864, p. 4; *Evening Journal,* Oct. 5, 1864, p. 4; Drake and Cayton, *Black Metropolis,* p. 44.

10. Cole, *Era of the Civil War,* pp. 327-28, 387-88; Pierce, *History of Chicago,* II, 281, 284, 339; Board of Education, *Annual Report,* XXV (1878-79), 38.

11. U.S. Commissioner of Education, *Schools for the Colored Population,* p. 343; Charles S. Johnson, "Source Material for Patterns of Negro Segregation: Chicago, Illinois" (working memorandum for Gunnar Myrdal, *An American Dilemma*); Illinois Writers Project of the Works Progress Administration, "The Negro in Illinois" (George Cleveland Hall Branch, Chicago Public Library).

12. Allan H. Spear, *Black Chicago: The Making of a Negro Ghetto, 1890-1920* (Chicago, 1967), pp. 12-19.

13. Fannie Barrier Williams, "Social Bonds in the 'Black Belt' of Chicago," *Charities,* 15 (Oct. 7, 1905), 43; *Chicago Daily News,* Aug. 1, 1919, p. 9; William M. Tuttle, Jr., *Race Riot: Chicago in the Red Summer of 1919* (New York, 1970); Chicago Commission on Race Relations, *The Negro in Chicago: A Study of Race Relations and a Race Riot* (Chicago, 1922); Spear, *Black Chicago,* pp. 11-23, 29-42, 201-22.

14. Department of Commerce and Labor, Bureau of the Census, *Negroes in the United States* (Washington, 1904), p. 237; Ernest W. Burgess and Charles Newcomb, eds., *Census Data of the City of Chicago, 1920* (Chicago, 1931), pp. 34-35; *Tribune,* Dec. 5, 1905, p. 9, *Daily News,* Dec. 20, 1916, p. 11.

15. Richard R. Wright, Jr., "The Industrial Condition of Negroes in Chicago" (B.D. thesis, University of Chicago, 1901), pp. 13, 16; U.S. Immigration Commission, *The Children of Immigrants in Schools* (Washington, 1911), II, 558-59, 678; *Daily News,* Dec. 15, 1916, p. 7; Ford S. Black, *Black's Blue Book* (Chicago, 1917), pp. 57-58, 67; D. A. Bethea, *Colored People's Blue Book and Business Directory of Chicago, Illinois* (Chicago, 1905), p. 126; Chicago Board of Education, *Annual Directory,* 1905-6, pp. 111-223, 1917-18, pp. 208-375; *Tribune,* Dec. 5, 1905, p. 9.

16. *Chicago Record-Herald,* May 1, 1909, p. 4; *Crisis,* 13 (Nov., 1916), 35; Chicago Commission on Race Relations, *Negro in Chicago,* pp. 252-53.

17. *Chicago Defender,* Nov. 12, 1910, p. 1; "John Farren School, Chicago," *Journal of Education,* 73 (Feb. 2, 1911), 119; *Daily News,* Dec. 20,

1916, p. 11; Chicago Commission on Race Relations, *Negro in Chicago,* pp. 246-47, 249-50; *New York Age,* Apr. 5, 1906, p. 7.

18. *Record-Herald,* Nov. 11, 1909, p. 3; Spear, *Black Chicago,* pp. 20-21; *Crisis,* 1 (Nov., 1910), 4.

19. *New York Age,* Oct. 10, 1907, p. 1; *Broad Ax* (Chicago), Oct. 3, 1908, p. 3; *Tribune,* Mar. 18, 1908, p. 7; *Chicago Evening Post,* Sept. 24, 1908, p. 3; *Inter-Ocean* (Chicago), Sept. 25, 1908, p. 12.

20. *New York Age,* Dec. 7, 1905, p. 1; *Tribune,* Nov. 29, 1905, p. 7, Jan. 30, 1914, p. 3; *Defender,* Oct. 6, 1917, p. 6, Jan. 19, 1918, p. 6, June 21, 1919, p. 1.

21. *New York Age,* Dec. 14, 1905, p. 7; Spear, *Black Chicago,* pp. 81-82, 114-115; *Chicago Herald,* Mar. 9, 1915, p. 3; *Tribune,* Nov. 1, 1912, p. 3; *Defender,* Nov. 9, 1912, pp. 1, 3, Mar. 13, 1915, p. 1, May 3, 1919, p. 20; *Crisis,* 5 (Feb., 1911), 195-96.

22. *Appeal* (St. Paul), Oct. 24, 1903, p. 4; *Tribune,* Oct. 19, 1903, p. 2; Spear, *Black Chicago,* p. 85.

23. William M. Tuttle, Jr., "Labor Conflict and Racial Violence: The Black Worker in Chicago, 1894-1919," *Labor History,* 10 (Summer, 1969), 408-32; Spear, *Black Chicago,* pp. 36-40.

24. *Record-Herald,* Oct. 14, 1908, p. 7; *Daily News,* Jan. 29, 1915, p. 5; Board of Education, *Annual Report,* LX (1914), 123.

25. *Daily News,* Dec. 5, 1905, p. 14; *Evening Post,* Dec. 5, 1905, p. 7; *Tribune,* Dec. 5 and 6, 1905, p. 9.

26. Alfreda M. Duster, ed., *Crusade for Justice: The Autobiography of Ida B. Wells* (Chicago, 1970), pp. 274-78; *New York Age,* Apr. 5, 1906, p. 7.

27. *New York Age,* Apr. 5, 1906, p. 7; J. Max Barber, "The Niagara Movement at Harpers Ferry," *Voice of the Negro,* 3 (Oct., 1906), 406; Spear, *Black Chicago,* pp. 57-58, 85-86; *Appeal,* June 30, 1906, p. 2. For the Niagara Movement, see Elliott Rudwick, "The Niagara Movement," *Journal of Negro History,* 42 (July, 1957), 177-200.

28. Harold M. Mayer and Richard C. Wade, *Chicago: Growth of a Metropolis* (Chicago, 1969), pp. 90, 172, 177; Chicago Commission on Race Relations, *Negro in Chicago,* p. 107; Spear, *Black Chicago,* pp. 21-22.

29. Thomas Lee Philpott, *The Slum and the Ghetto: Neighborhood Deterioration and Middle-Class Reform, Chicago, 1880-1930* (New York, 1978), pp. 154-55; Spear, *Black Chicago,* pp. 22-23; Chicago Commission on Race Relations, *Negro in Chicago,* pp. 107, 114.

30. *Tribune,* Feb. 17, 1912, p. 1; *Record-Herald,* Feb. 17, 1912, p. 3, May 19, 1912, p. 12; *Broad Ax,* Sept. 18, 1909, p. 1.

31. *Defender,* Feb. 24, 1912, p. 6, June 22, 1912, p. 1; *Record-Herald,* Feb. 18 and 26, 1912, p. 3; Spear, *Black Chicago,* pp. 62-64, 125; *Evening Post,* Feb. 17, 1912, p. 6; *Chicago Daily Journal,* Feb. 17, 1912, p. 2; Drake and Cayton, *Black Metropolis,* pp. 344-45.

32. *Defender,* Nov. 12, 1910, p. 1, Sept. 9, 1911, p. 3, Apr. 5, 1913, p. 4, Jan. 24, 1920, p. 16; *Broad Ax,* Dec. 31, 1910, pp. 1, 4; *Crisis,* 3 (Apr., 1912), 228.

33. *Record-Herald,* Oct. 14, 1908, p. 7; Board of Education, *Annual Report,* LX (1914), 122-23.

34. Spear, *Black Chicago,* pp. 47-48; *Tribune,* Sept. 25, 1908, p. 1, Sept. 29, 1908, p. 5.

35. *Tribune,* Sept. 28, 1908, p. 9, Sept. 29, 1908, p. 5; *Daily News,* Sept. 25, 1908, p. 20; *Evening Post,* Sept. 25, 1908, p. 3; *Inter-Ocean,* Sept. 25, 1908, p.

12, Sept. 26, 1908, p. 4; *Record-Herald,* Sept. 26, 1908, p. 9.

36. Chicago Commission on Race Relations, *Negro in Chicago,* p. 107; Board of Education, *Proceedings,* Dec. 19, 1906, p. 658; *Tribune,* Jan. 11, 1907, p. 3, Sept. 29, 1908, p. 5; *Daily News,* Jan. 11, 1907, p. 2; *Record-Herald,* Jan. 12, 1907, p. 1.

37. *Tribune,* Sept. 14, 1910, p. 5; *Inter-Ocean,* Sept. 14, 1910, p. 10.

38. *Broad Ax,* Jan. 23, 1915, p. 4; Board of Education, *Annual Directory,* 1914-15, p. 69; *Daily News,* Dec. 20, 1916, p. 11; *Crisis,* 21 (Mar., 1921), 224.

39. Board of Education, *Annual Report,* LIV (1908), 230-31; *Tribune,* Jan. 6, 1915, p. 1, Jan. 19, 1915, p. 6.

40. *Defender,* Nov. 1, 1913, p. 4; *Daily Journal,* Jan. 6, 1915, p. 3; *Tribune,* Jan. 6, 1915, p. 1; *Broad Ax,* Jan. 23, 1915, p. 4.

41. *Defender,* Mar. 14, 1914, pp. 1, 7; *Daily Journal,* Jan. 6, 1915, p. 3; *Evening Post,* Jan. 27, 1915, p. 6.

42. *Chicago Herald,* Jan. 6, 1915, p. 11; *Evening Post,* Jan. 27, 1915, p. 6.

43. *Herald,* Jan. 8, 1915, p. 16; *Daily Journal,* Jan. 6, 1915, p. 3; *Broad Ax,* Jan. 23, 1915, p. 4; Spear, *Black Chicago,* pp. 82-83, 114; *Defender,* Jan. 16, 1915, p. 2, Jan. 9, 1915, pp. 6, 8.

44. Spear, *Black Chicago,* p. 79; *Broad Ax,* Jan. 23, 1915, p. 4; *Defender,* Jan. 16, 1915, p. 2; *Evening Post,* Jan. 27, 1915, p. 6.

45. *Herald,* Jan. 6, 1915, p. 11, Apr. 13, 1915, p. 5; *Tribune,* Apr. 13, 1915, p. 13; *Defender,* Aug. 2, 1913, p. 4, Apr. 24, 1915, p. 8.

46. "Military Drill in High Schools," *School Review,* 24 (Feb., 1916), 156-58; *Defender,* Mar. 17, 1917, p. 1; clipping from *Chicago Plain Dealer,* Oct. 5, 1918, NAACP Papers, Box C402, Library of Congress; Chicago Commission on Race Relations, *Negro in Chicago,* p. 255; *Defender,* Oct. 6, 1917, p. 1, July 3, 1920, p. 1; Board of Education, *Annual Directory,* 1921-22, pp. 18-27.

47. *Tribune,* Apr. 6, 1917, p. 15; Board of Education, *Proceedings,* Aug. 7, 1917, p. 238.

48. Albert Nelson Marquis, ed., *The Book of Chicagoans* (Chicago, 1917), p. 421; *Defender,* Aug. 17, 1918, p. 16.

49. Spear, *Black Chicago,* p. 106; *Tribune,* Aug. 14, 1918, p. 7, Aug. 20, 1918, p. 8; *Broad Ax,* Aug. 17, 1918, pp. 2-3; *New York Age,* Aug. 24, 1918, p. 4; *Defender,* Aug. 17 and 24, 1918, p. 16.

50. *Tribune,* Apr. 6, 1917, p. 15; "The Chicago School Board," *School and Society,* 5 (Apr. 28, 1917), 492; Glen Edwards, "Schools and Politics in Chicago," *Survey,* 42 (Aug. 16, 1919), 724-25, and "School Board Situation in Chicago," *National Municipal Review,* 8 (Mar., 1919), 196-97; "Chicago's Public School Tangle," *Survey,* 38 (June 16, 1917), 259-60; "The Chicago School Situation," *School and Society,* 6 (July 7, 1917), 19. The courts finally ruled in favor of the old board, which resumed office in October, 1918.

51. Harold F. Gosnell, *Negro Politicians: The Rise of Negro Politics in Chicago* (Chicago, 1935), pp. 37-62; Tuttle, *Race Riot,* pp. 184-203; Spear, *Black Chicago,* pp. 187-189; Victor S. Yarros, "Presenting Big Bill Thompson of Chicago," *Independent,* 119 (Nov. 5, 1927), 446-48; Harold F. Gosnell, "How Negroes Vote in Chicago," *National Municipal Review,* 22 (May, 1933), 238.

52. William T. Hutchinson, *Lowden of Illinois* (Chicago, 1957), II, 383-84; *Tribune,* Aug. 14, 1918, p. 7, Aug. 15, 1918, p. 13, Aug. 19, 1918, p. 5; *Broad Ax,* Aug. 17, 1918, p. 2, Aug. 24, 1918, pp. 2, 4; Gosnell, *Negro Politicians,*

26   *Down from Equality*

pp. 163-76; Spear, *Black Chicago,* pp. 78-79, 122-24, 189-90.
53. *Defender,* Aug. 17, 1918, p. 11, Sept. 7, 1918, p. 10; *Broad Ax,* Aug. 24, 1918, p. 2, Aug. 31, 1918, p. 4; Charles Edward Merriam, *Chicago: A More Intimate View of Urban Politics* (New York, 1929), p. 145; *New York Times,* Sept. 12, 1918, p. 1; Tuttle, *Race Riot,* pp. 204-6.
54. Tuttle, *Race Riot,* pp. 3-10, 32-66; Charles W. Holman, "Race Riots in Chicago," *Outlook,* 122 (Aug. 13, 1919), 567; Philpott, *The Slum and the Ghetto,* pp. 209-210; *Tribune,* Aug. 6, 1919, p. 3; *Daily News,* Aug. 5, 1919, p. 1, Aug. 6 and 8, 1919, p. 9; Chicago Commission on Race Relations, *Negro in Chicago,* p. 458; *Proceedings of the City Council,* Aug. 5, 1919, p. 1115.
55. Arthur I. Waskow, *From Race Riot to Sit-In, 1919 and the 1960's* (Garden City, N.Y., 1967), pp. 60-104; *Chicago Whip,* Aug. 9, 1919, p. 10; *Broad Ax,* Aug. 30, 1919, p. 1; *Crisis,* 21 (Jan., 1921), 102.
56. *Whip,* Nov. 15, 1919, p. 8; *Broad Ax,* Aug. 30, 1919, p. 1; Waskow, *From Race Riot to Sit-In,* pp. 61-63, 65-66, 75, 101-2.
57. Chicago Commission on Race Relations, *Negro in Chicago,* p. 643; Waskow, *From Race Riot to Sit-In,* pp. 97-104; Philpott, *The Slum and the Ghetto,* pp. 209-27.
58. *Broad Ax,* Nov. 24, 1917, p. 3, Aug. 30, 1919, p. 1; *Defender,* Jan. 10, 1920, p. 16; *Daily News,* Aug. 4, 1919, p. 9.

CHAPTER TWO

Creating a Segregated School System

BETWEEN 1915 AND 1940, the Chicago public schools underwent a significant transformation. As I have indicated in the first chapter, before the onset of the mass migration of southern blacks to the city, black students had attended racially mixed schools, and most Negro instructors taught in classrooms with few or no black students. By the beginning of the Great Depression, however, the distribution of blacks within the system had changed dramatically. The great majority of black pupils and teachers learned and worked in predominantly Negro schools. During the 1930s, this pattern grew even more rigid. By 1945, the president of the local branch of the NAACP declared without much exaggeration, "We have segregated schools outright. . . . They are as much segregated as the schools in Savannah, Georgia, or Vicksburg, Mississippi."[1]

Despite the absence of racial data in Board of Education statistics and records, it is still possible to trace the growth of segregation in the local schools. If we define a segregated school as one with 90-100 percent black pupil enrollment, for 1916 only Keith Elementary fits the description. Of the 4,500 blacks in the public school system, 91.3 percent went to integrated schools. Four years later, the balance had shifted considerably. The number of segregated black schools had jumped from one to six, and these schools contained 40 percent of the black students who attended school in Chicago. Another four elementary schools and Phillips High had black enrollments of 50-89 percent. Between 1920 and 1930, segregated education became the norm. The list of segregated black schools expanded from six to twenty-six (twenty-three grade schools, two junior highs, and Phillips High), and the proportion of black pupils in segregated buildings more than doubled to 82.4 percent. Although the lack of figures for 1940 precludes an exact measure of segregation, racial isolation in the schools apparently increased still further during the Depression.[2]

Just as black students became more numerous and more segregated, so did Chicago's black public school teachers. In 1917, 41 of the city's 8,316 instructors were black. By 1930, the number of black faculty members increased more than sevenfold to 308, while the total teaching force had risen to 13,268. Like blacks in other occupations, Negro instructors clustered in less prestigious and remunerative job categories. Whereas blacks constituted 2.3 percent of the regularly assigned faculty in 1930, they made up 6 percent of the substitutes. In 1934, although blacks accounted for 3.4 percent of the elementary staff, only thirty-six Negroes, .9 percent of the city's total, filled the higher paying and academically advanced high school positions. For example, two-thirds of the Phillips High faculty was white in the late 1920s, even though the student body was almost entirely black. Furthermore, just two blacks became principals before 1940.[3]

As we have seen, black teachers were reasonably well distributed within the public school system before World War I. But between the war and the start of the Depression, black instructors became as segregated as black students. Of the seventeen instructors in predominantly white schools in 1917, just four retained similar posts in 1930. Nine could not be traced, and four others moved from white to black schools. More important, the large numbers of new black faculty members in the 1920s were concentrated in black schools. By 1930, 85.4 percent of the city's black instructors served at schools with 90-100 percent black pupil enrollments. Whereas in 1917 three-fifths of the black teachers had worked at buildings at least 90 percent white, by 1930, only 9 percent taught at such schools. No detailed studies of black faculty placement exist for the thirties or early forties, but racial isolation of teachers and pupils continued in tandem. In 1945, the Mayor's Committee on Race Relations reported, "Approximately 90 percent of non-white teachers in Chicago are in schools with 95 percent or more Negro pupils."[4]

Why did Chicago's public schools become almost completely segregated within so short a time? From the periodic discussions about separate schools before 1920, one might suppose that whites enacted laws or other regulations formally segregating public education. But this never occurred, and after 1920, talk of officially separate schools subsided. Rather, racial isolation came about as a result of the striking demographic changes in the city's black community, new informal racial policies by school authorities, and the color bias of Chicago's white residents. As this chapter will demonstrate, although racism among the white public was widespread, it was not constant throughout the city and therefore did not underlie school segregation in a uniform way. Instead, white racism varied in intensity and forms of expression from one neighborhood to another, and these differences resulted in distinctive patterns of segregation for black students and especially for black teachers.

The sharp increase in the black population after 1915 and accompanying rigid housing segregation produced most of the racial isolation in the schools. The black population of Chicago jumped from 109,458 (4.1 percent of the total) in 1920 to 233,903 (6.9 percent) ten years later. During the Depression, even though the city's overall growth halted, the number of blacks continued to climb. By 1940, 277,731 blacks made their homes in the city, and they accounted for 8.2 percent of the population. Blacks' numerical gains came mainly through migration, especially from the Deep South; between 1915 and 1940, about 190,000 black newcomers arrived.[5]

As black Chicago's population rose, its school attendance figures did likewise. Whereas in 1910 only 4,160 blacks ages six through eighteen (1.2 percent of the city total) had attended classes in public and private schools, by 1920, this figure nearly tripled to 12,299, or 2.8 percent of the whole (ages 5-18). During the 1920s, while white school attendance rose by more than one-third, the number of blacks going to school in Chicago swelled 175 percent and reached 33,856 (5.4 percent of the total) by 1930. During the Depression, white school attendance plunged nearly 80,000, but blacks continued their substantial gains. From 1930 to 1940, black school attendance rose nearly 50 percent to 50,670, 8.9 percent of the citywide total. Black school attendance increased at a more rapid rate than did the Negro population as a whole in the 1920s and 1930s because many of the earlier migrants were in their late teens and early twenties and did not have school-age children. But as the newcomers established themselves and had families, school enrollments advanced steadily, even when migration slowed, as in the 1930s. Thus, the proportion of the total black population that was attending school doubled between 1910 and 1940 (from 9.4 to 18.2 percent), while the comparable figure for whites showed no clear direction. Overcrowded school facilities in black neighborhoods would be one consequence of this trend.[6]

Thus far, we have examined census data on classroom attendance that includes both public and private schools. Since the public schools did not compile statistics by race, precise figures on black enrollment in the public system are unavailable. Nevertheless, because more than one-fourth of Chicago's white children enrolled in private schools whereas few blacks did so, blacks made up a larger share of public school enrollment than census reports would suggest. In 1964, Robert J. Havighurst of the University of Chicago estimated that black public school enrollment climbed from 30,000 in 1930 (6.4 percent of the total) to 46,000 in 1940, which was 11.0 percent of the public school total and 2 percentage points above census statistics encompassing both public and private school attendance.[7]

As more blacks came to Chicago, small black districts steadily expanded into a vast ghetto. Prior to World War I, about three-fourths of the city's black residents lived in a narrow strip of land stretching from Roosevelt Road (1200 South) to Fifty-ninth Street between the Rock Island Railroad and State Street (and Michigan Avenue north of Thirty-ninth Street)—see map 1. Although blacks were highly segregated, they were too few to produce separate schools. During the war, the black section spread east to Cottage Grove above Thirty-ninth Street and broadened two blocks (from State to Michigan) south of Thirty-ninth. In the 1920s, as southern migrants replaced whites leaving for newer outlying neighborhoods, blacks filled in most of the remaining territory from Michigan east to Cottage Grove and pushed southward to Sixty-third Street and west to Wentworth Avenue. Segregation, meanwhile, became even more intense than it had been before World War I. An index of segregation compiled by the sociologist David Wallace shows 91.8 for as early as 1898, rising to 98.4 by 1930.[8]

Others have described the process of ghetto formation and expansion, so the story deserves only brief mention here.[9] The same tactics whites used before World War I in Hyde Park and elsewhere persisted in later years. If blacks attempted to settle outside the ghetto, whites threatened them, tried to buy their property, and vandalized or bombed their homes. Realtors either refused to deal with blacks or steered them to areas which were already predominantly black or designated for black occupancy. Banks and savings associations financed homes in a racially discriminatory fashion. Property owners' associations, which numbered about 175 in Chicago by World War II, used a variety of methods to keep neighborhoods free of black people. One of the best-known techniques was the restrictive covenant, a deed provision prohibiting rental or sale of property to blacks and other named minorities for a fixed period of time, such as twenty to twenty-five years. Covenants took effect only when a specified portion of local property (often three-fourths) carried the restriction. By the 1940s, however, covenants had closed an estimated 25 to 50 percent of Chicago's South Side to blacks.[10]

To what extent does the ghetto account for segregation of black students in the public schools? One might expect to answer this question by comparing racial isolation in housing with that in classrooms. Similar figures would suggest that school segregation resulted from residential segregation, whereas if the former exceeded the latter, one could suppose that actions by school authorities accounted for the discrepancy. Unfortunately, several difficulties cast doubt on the value of such statistics. First, the lack of official data on enrollment by race in the public schools means that we must rely on contemporary independent surveys of racial patterns in Chicago classrooms. Such studies exist for 1920 and 1930 but not for 1940. Second, data on housing segregation, derived from the federal census, are inadequate in important respects. Census statistics may minimize the degree of residential segregation, since in racially mixed census tracts, blacks and whites may have been segregated instead of evenly distributed within the tract. Moreover, a simple comparison of housing and school segregation ignores age differences between the races, the greater white enrollment in nonpublic classrooms, and the fact that census tracts are smaller than school districts. Keeping these cautions in mind, one may nevertheless advance some tentative conclusions. On the one hand, housing patterns seem to explain the proportion of black children attending schools 50-100 percent black. In 1920, when 60.2 percent of Chicago's blacks lived in census tracts with black majorities, 67.2 percent of black school enrollment was in schools at least one-half black. In 1930, the respective figures were 89.6 and 88.3 percent. On the other hand, it appears that actions of school officials did significantly increase the number of black students in 90-100 percent black schools. In 1930, 63.2 percent of the city's blacks lived in census tracts at least nine-tenths black, but 82.4 percent of black enrollment was at 90-100 percent black schools.[11]

School authorities not only helped isolate black pupils but also played a decisive role in segregating black teachers after World War I. While some teachers wanted to work near their homes and others may have preferred to teach children of their own race, the existence of the black ghetto per se was a minimal factor in the segregation of black faculty members. Since Board of Education employees assigned instructors, the school system was responsible for whatever teacher distribution patterns resulted. As mentioned earlier, before World War I, officials placed the majority of black instructors in mostly white schools and denounced racial bias when white parents or children objected to black faculty members. During the interwar decades, on the other hand, school authorities readily capitulated to whites who did not want black teachers. In 1920, when a black substitute took an eighth-grade classroom at all-white Altgeld Elementary, several children behaved rowdily. Daily newspapers declared, "Students Defy Negro Teacher," spoke of "revolt," and predicted "a general strike" against the black instructor. Students at other schools with black faculty members began to discuss boycotts of their own. Although officials claimed publicly that the incident was not racial, they sent the substitute to another school even though the regular teacher had not yet returned to work. Before 1920, school board headquarters had apparently utilized substitutes without regard to race. But in the wake of the Altgeld incident, Superintendent of Schools Peter Mortenson announced, "It is not the intention of the officials to assign colored teachers to white schools where it is liable to create a disturbance."[12]

After 1920, school authorities were not only more responsive to white protests against black instructors but also took the initiative by assigning them in a discriminatory manner. About 1930, an assistant superintendent who supervised the assignment of teachers told a researcher that white districts often did not accept blacks. Since applications did not distinguish job candidates by race, office employees skipped persons whose addresses identified them as Negroes when vacancies arose at white schools.[13]

The substitute bureau conducted its business in a similar fashion. In 1930, the 2,500-member substitute list included 150 Negroes. The bureau director declared that she identified individuals on her list by race and channeled blacks exclusively to black schools. A graduate of Howard University testified, "The assignment clerks just refused to send a Negro girl to an all-white neighborhood, or to any white principal, of whom there were many, who did not want a Negro teacher." She once called school headquarters to complain about her lack of substituting assignments. She said, "The clerk asked over the phone whether I was white or Negro." An assistant examiner added that black applicants did not receive substitute certificates unless a principal requested a black substitute or a specific black individual.[14]

School principals also played an important role in segregating black faculty members. Officials at the Board of Education assigned instructors to schools, but principals could both request specific teachers and reject instructors of whom they disapproved. As one observer put it in 1924, "As every teacher already in the 'system' is aware, the formality of employment is executed by the Board of Education, but the real choice is made by the school principal." During a teacher's first three years of service, a principal's unsatisfactory rating would result in a transfer to another school. Principals could also drive out tenured faculty members by giving them problem students, unpleasant working conditions, and low evaluations. "All he's got to do is say, 'I don't think you'll be very happy at our school,'" one black educator explained. "You take the hint. Because if the principal decides you're going to be unhappy, you will be, don't worry."[15]

Principals often used their prerogatives to either exclude black teachers or keep them to a minimum. "I was sent to a South Side school where there was a prejudiced principal," a black instructor declared in

1931. "About two o'clock of my first day's work, the assistant principal came to me and said that I had better waive my appointment, as my work was unsatisfactory." Don Rogers, who served in a variety of administrative posts in the 1920s and 1930s, told a state investigatory commission in 1941, "Certain principals, yes—they are individualistic, some not wanting, for instance, colored teachers and things like that. That is the individualism of the principal." The motives behind such practices were mixed. Some principals simply disliked blacks or believed that they made inferior teachers. Others lacked strong racial animosity themselves but feared that black instructors would anger parents or provoke conflict among the faculty. Finally, since only low-status schools had black teachers, principals reasoned that black staff members would erode their school's prestige and injure the principal's reputation.[16]

The decisions made by employees at Board of Education headquarters and by principals of individual schools distributed black instructors in a curious way. As stated earlier, during the Depression, sixth-sevenths of the city's black public school teachers were in 90-100 percent Negro institutions. But black faculty members did not enjoy unrestricted job opportunities within the ghetto. In 1930, in the twenty-six segregated black schools, only slightly over one-third of the instructional staff was black (264 of 764, 34.6 percent). Moreover, within the ghetto, black representation on faculties varied widely. At nine grade schools, blacks constituted a majority of the teaching force; more than half of all the black elementary instructors in the system worked at these few schools. On the other hand, eight other segregated black schools with 251 instructors had only 21 blacks on their staffs (8.4 percent of the total). Contemporaries agreed that the racial attitude of the principal was decisive in accounting for these differences among black institutions.[17]

The few black teachers in predominantly or exclusively white schools were also clustered in a peculiar fashion. In 1930, the thirty black instructors in white schools were found in the neighborhoods of West Town (Near Northwest Side), Near West Side, South Lawndale, Burnside, Pullman, Archer Heights, and the Lower West Side (see map 4 in chapter 3). These areas ranked among the lowest in the city in housing cost and in educational achievement of their adult populations and among the highest in the city in percentage of foreign-born residents. In other words, the blacks who taught in white schools were in areas that other faculty members and administrators regarded as relatively undesirable.[18]

Spokesmen for the black community objected that segregating their race's teachers necessarily reduced their opportunities for employment within the public school system. Since most schools were closed to black instructors, they had to wait longer than whites for permanent assignments. A former white teacher claimed that on one occasion, a black ranked first on an examination for high school art instructors. Since the first ten openings were in white schools, administrators filled the jobs with temporary appointees. Finally, a position at all-black Du Sable High became available, and the front-runner received the job. As the *Defender* stated in reviewing the plight of black teachers in 1930, "Many who graduated three years ago have never been placed as regulars, all vacancies in these schools in which they might have been placed being given to young girls of other races."[19]

Segregation in the schools also limited blacks' chances at Chicago Normal College, the teacher-training institution operated by the Board of Education. During the 1920s, when black representation on school faculties was increasing, blacks expressed no major complaints about CNC policies. In the Depression, however, black enrollment at the normal school fell from 72 of 1,090 students (6.6 percent) in 1930 to 24 of 625 in 1934 (3.8 percent). Of 400 pupils CNC admitted in 1940, only 11 were black. With so many ghetto residents unable to find work, blacks were bitter about the declining opportunities at CNC. In 1941, the *Defender* noted the "suspicion that politics and prejudice keep many qualified Negro applicants from being admitted to the Chicago Teachers college." A group of blacks from West Woodlawn, which contained more black teachers than any area in the city, protested the scarcity of Negro pupils at CNC. The civic leader Irene McCoy Gaines reported, "They were told that the proportion of Negro students had to be kept down because after graduation there would be no place for them, as they would not be accepted by the principals in white districts." Job bias and discrimination in training had become as interdependent in the school system as they were in the economy as a whole.[20]

School officials, as we have seen, were less responsible for the segregation of black students than of black teachers. Nevertheless, pupil segregation was not solely a result of living patterns. On the contrary, school administrators' actions produced more racial separation than occurred merely from the combination of the housing ghetto and the neighborhood attendance structure. Segregation policies of school authorities did not stem from a single decision by the Board of Education or from explicit direction by personnel at school headquarters. Rather, measures to isolate the races sometimes arose at the request of white residents and in other cases grew out of antiblack attitudes of individual officials. Between the world wars, authorities increased segregation by skewing three procedures of school administration: drawing district boundaries, approving pupil transfers, and establishing branch schools.

Board of Education personnel drew school district boundaries based on pupils' travel distance to class, capacity of school buildings, and location of barriers and safety hazards like parks, railroads, and busy streets. Often, however, these criteria were in conflict. For instance, administrators might have to choose between forcing children to walk several more blocks or requiring them to cross a dangerous thoroughfare. Often a neighborhood's changing population rendered previous boundaries obsolete by channeling students into half-filled classrooms or makeshift accommodations. Since changes in attendance districts might evoke protests from affected parents, authorities generally preferred to retain existing boundaries as long as possible. Mapping attendance districts was not a simple task.[21]

To determine the extent to which school boundaries increased segregation, we can compare district lines with the racial composition of census tracts. As usual, a series of complicating factors make our results more approximate than precise. First, as noted earlier, in racially mixed census tracts, blacks and whites may have been either evenly scattered throughout or segregated within the tract. Where a school boundary split such a tract, we do not always know whether officials were color-blind or simply observing intratract differences. Second, railroad tracks or busy streets, landmarks used in drawing boundaries, often also separated black and white neighborhoods. Where "natural" and racial borders coincided, were school officials responsible for classroom segregation when they followed normally acceptable districting practices? In addition to this dilemma, the lack of racial censuses of the public schools, the incompleteness of districting information, and attendance of some children at private institutions all make it impossible to determine how much segregation originated in boundary decisions.

Nonetheless, some conclusions are possible. For one thing, white and black responses to districting controversies changed sharply between the pre-migration period and the interwar era. Before 1915, fully segregated neighborhoods did not exist, so racial gerrymandering was unlikely. Race-related boundary disputes during these years consisted of whites' objections to redistricting that moved their children into classes with blacks. Between the wars, the tables turned, and blacks were on the defensive. In the 1920s and 1930s, ghetto residents complained that authorities drew attendance lines to separate the races. In 1937, the Chicago Council of Negro Organizations called for "a change of boundaries which will remove segregation in the schools." Two years later, the Chicago and Northern District Federation of Colored Women's Clubs demanded that the Board of Education remap attendance areas "so that children will be permitted to attend the school nearest their home instead of making boundaries which will make certain schools 'all colored,' as is now the practice.''[22]

Map 1, which depicts South Side elementary school boundaries during the interwar decades, yields some answers to blacks' charges of racial gerrymandering. First, school districts faithfully observed Cottage Grove Avenue, the ghetto's eastern edge. Oakland Elementary was an exception at first, but in 1926, the school board assigned the white portion of Oakland's district to Shakespeare School, an all-white institution. Oakland's enrollment shifted from 26 percent black in 1920 to 98 percent black ten years later. Blacks believed that the Cottage Grove line proved that school authorities followed separatist policies. To the explanation that Cottage Grove was a principal thoroughfare and therefore a rational boundary marker, blacks retorted that neither South Parkway nor State Street, main north-south arteries within the ghetto, were as consistently employed to form district lines.[23]

Along Wentworth Avenue, the ghetto's western edge, a different situation prevailed. Though Wentworth separated the races from Twenty-sixth to Fifty-fifth, it served as a boundary marker only until Thirty-third Street. South of this point, districts overlapped the Wentworth line, often following the Rock Island Railroad tracks two blocks east. As a result, most of the schools just west of Wentworth were racially integrated. Sherwood, Mann Branch of Raymond at Thirty-seventh and Wells, and Webster each were between 25 and 30 percent black in 1920 and between 30 and 50 percent black in 1930. Other schools in the vicinity also had black children.[24]

As map 2 reveals, South Side high school districts duplicated the elementary pattern. Again, Cottage Grove Avenue was a nearly impenetrable wall. White students living less than a mile from Phillips but east of Cottage Grove traveled nearly four miles to attend classes at Hyde Park High School. Along the western edge of the ghetto, high school boundaries ignored racial divisions in housing. At no point did district lines coincide with Wentworth Avenue. The territory of Phillips High included some white neighborhoods, and Englewood High, which was 30 percent black in 1930, drew graduates from three ghetto elementary schools.

What accounts for the variations in districting practices between one side of the ghetto and the other? The most likely explanation lies in the differences among the white neighborhoods adjacent to the black belt. Kenwood and Hyde Park, east of Cottage Grove, ranked near the top of Chicago neighborhoods in the educational achievements and affluence of their populations. Many residents of these areas were influential in the city's political and social affairs. During the 1930s, Mayor Ed-

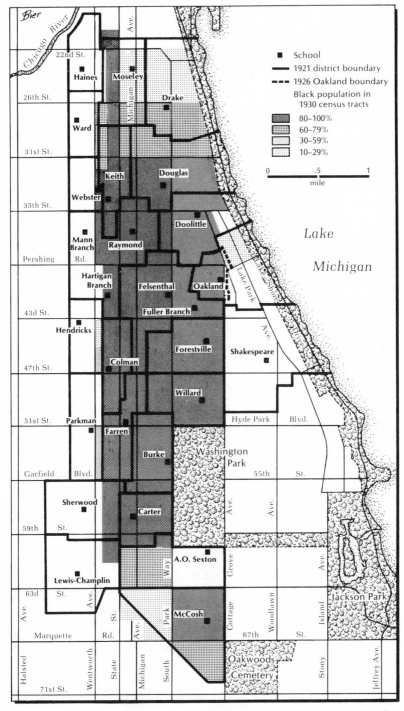

1. Chicago Public Elementary School Districts in the South Side Ghetto, 1921-40

Based on Ernest W. Burgess and Charles Newcomb, eds., *Census Data of the City of Chicago, 1930* (Chicago, 1933), and Chicago Board of Education, *Proceedings,* Feb. 23, 1921, July 28 and Aug. 25, 1926.

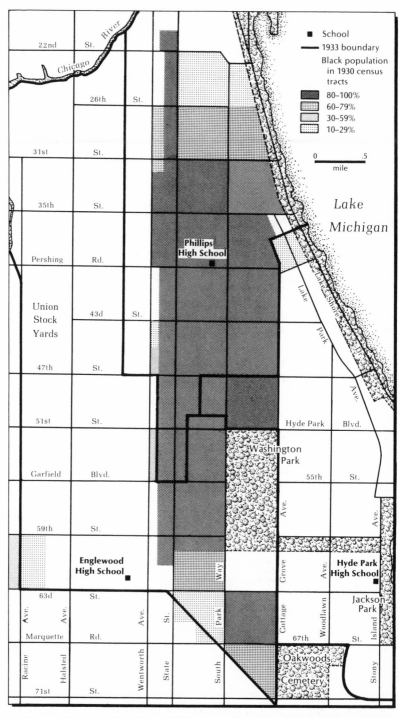

2. Chicago Public High School Districts in the South Side Ghetto, 1933

Based on Ernest W. Burgess and Charles Newcomb, eds., *Census Data of the City of Chicago, 1930* (Chicago, 1933), and Chicago Board of Education, *Proceedings,* Sept. 13, 1933.

ward Kelly and Board of Education president James B. McCahey lived in this section. Neighborhood improvement associations flourished there and helped blanket property with race-restrictive covenants. School officials knew that additional school integration would elicit a vocal and potent response. On the other hand, the four communities immediately west of the ghetto (Armour Square, Fuller Park, Bridgeport, and New City, map 4) were among the city's lowest in housing rentals and educational levels. Though residents there often dealt forcefully with blacks, they did not organize property owners' groups or wield as much political influence as did inhabitants of Kenwood, Hyde Park, and Woodlawn. Hence, authorities mapping boundaries on the Wentworth side were less constrained by the possibility of local resistance.[25]

Districting policies on the east and west sides of the black ghetto did have one thing in common: in both places in the 1920s and 1930s, the few changes officials made intensified racial segregation. For most of the interwar period, all-black Willard Elementary was the only school to breach the Cottage Grove barrier. During World War I, when Willard was largely white, parents complained about having to send their children to Phillips High. The Board of Education therefore placed Willard in the Hyde Park district. During the 1920s, the Willard neighborhood became part of the ghetto and contained the homes of prominent black journalists, physicians, and clergymen. For a time, Willard continued to send its graduates to Hyde Park, but in 1935, a new black high school (at first called New Wendell Phillips but later named Du Sable) opened. Though school board proceedings did not specify the new school's attendance area, the *Defender* reported that the school board had switched Willard into the New Phillips district. "When Wendell Phillips was opened last year," the paper said in 1936, "the Hyde Park high school began transferring pupils to Wendell Phillips and now very few Race students remain in Hyde Park." The Cottage Grove wall now kept out black secondary and elementary pupils alike.[26]

The same trend occurred on the Wentworth side. In 1921, ten predominantly white grade schools west of the black section lay in the Phillips district. Five years later, the Board of Education removed six of these schools from Phillips's territory. Superintendent of Schools William McAndrew reported, "For some time past, very few of the graduates of these schools have attended the Phillips school. This rearrangement of school districts will permit [the students] . . . to attend high schools they can reach conveniently." Since these whites already were avoiding all-black Phillips by transferring to other schools or giving false addresses, authorities ratified student preferences rather than attempting to enforce integration.[27]

Where district lines did not produce racial separation, whites could desert neighborhood schools by obtaining transfer permits. Parents asked authorities to enroll their children at a specified school outside their home district. If a middle-level administrator approved, the student received the necessary permit. Although many pupils transferred for nonracial reasons, blacks charged that administrators issued permits in a racially discriminatory manner. Blacks alleged that officials readily granted transfers to whites who lived in predominantly black areas. Similar requests by blacks, however, were usually rejected unless they carried the endorsement of an influential sponsor. Moreover, some principals and faculty members actively encouraged whites to emigrate from black schools. A black teacher testified, "I know also of several cases where white principals had told children that they ought to transfer to schools where there are not so many Colored pupils." One such principal noticed a light-skinned woman calling for her child at a mostly black institution. He explained that the youngster did not have to remain there, for he would recommend a transfer to a nearby white school. Such bias in the use of transfer permits was, according to one ghetto civic leader, "another sore spot" for South Side blacks.[28]

The number of whites escaping black schools on transfers is unknown, but the movement merited frequent comment in the black press. In 1933, the *Defender* estimated that five hundred high-school-age whites resided in the Phillips district but enrolled elsewhere. These transfers stemmed from two sources. First, along the ghetto's western edge, boundary lines put whites living between Wentworth and Stewart avenues in the Phillips district. These students used transfers to avoid the overwhelmingly black high school. The former principal of a white elementary school in this vicinity stated that authorities had ordered him to direct his graduates to Englewood High instead of to Phillips, as official districting policy prescribed. The second group of whites transferring from Phillips were the children of storeowners who lived in or adjacent to their ghetto businesses. High prices, credit disputes, and competition with black businesses had already made these merchants unpopular with their neighbors. When the sons and daughters of the shopkeepers obtained transfers, blacks complained that such merchants profited from their businesses but otherwise stood apart from ghetto life. The *Defender* announced, "Children of white merchants on the South side should go to school with the children of their patrons, thus encouraging a spirit of friendliness and good will on the part of both parent and child." Robert Abbott's journal recommended, "A rule should be laid down that all children attend the schools in the districts in which they live."[29]

School officials occasionally tried to eliminate transfers because they threw enrollments out of balance with building capacities and produced jealousy and complaints. After administrators revised high school boundaries in 1933, Superintendent of Schools William Bogan canceled all transfer permits for secondary pupils, but many students ignored Bogan's order. During World War II, William Johnson, Bogan's successor, also revoked transfer permits of between 10,000 and 15,000 children. But citywide protests by white parents forced Johnson to reverse the order. Efforts to close the transfer loophole failed because parents throughout the city demanded the special privilege. Politicians also liked the permit system, since it provided an opportunity to perform favors for constituents. Even blacks did not consistently oppose the transfer permits, for while they denounced whites who left ghetto schools, some blacks sought the same exemption for their own children.[30]

A few blacks living in the Phillips High district secured transfers to other South Side high schools. The two most popular destinations of black permit-holders, Hyde Park and Englewood, had middle-class students and offered a more competitive academic climate than did Phillips. But black students who entered these schools on transfers occupied a precarious position. As outsiders they were vulnerable targets for white segregationists. When about sixty Phillips youths transferred to Tilden High about 1920, Tilden students harassed the newcomers until they withdrew. At Parker High in 1923, administrators told the faculty to "check on any colored people in the division room to see if they live in this district. Please report any who do not." When the local NAACP objected that such action should apply to whites and blacks alike, Mayor William E. Dever agreed and quashed the proposed census. A decade later, Negroes charged that Board of Education personnel were forcing black secondary pupils with permits to return to Phillips. The *Defender* complained, "As a result of the hounding down of Race children by these paid sleuths, the Race attendance at Englewood and Hyde Park high schools has been cut in half."[31]

The branch school was a third device officials might use for racial purposes. Authorities created branches where they did not want facilities operating as regular schools. For instance, enrollments at neighboring schools could decline below the point where two principals and clerical staffs could be justified, so one school would become a branch of the other. Branches were also common in sparsely settled outlying parts of the city. Here some students attended class in portable units, one-room wooden structures with metal roofs. Such portables were branches of parent schools until the board constructed permanent buildings. In other cases, officials established high school branches in elementary buildings or even designated the vocational program at a regular building as a branch of a vocational school. Branch arrangements usually did not involve racial bias, but sometimes they did.

Fuller and Felsenthal were nearby elementary schools located in a South Side neighborhood that was about two-fifths black in 1920. In 1917, declining enrollment at Fuller caused authorities to make it a branch of Felsenthal. Soon blacks objected that Felsenthal's principal assigned students to the schools in such a manner that Felsenthal was four-fifths white, while the Fuller branch became 90 percent black. Blacks also contended that inferior education accompanied segregation at Fuller. They alleged it was a dumping ground for problem pupils, had a poorly maintained building and inferior teachers, and lacked a playground of its own.[32]

A second case in which a branch school served as a vehicle for segregation occurred in Morgan Park on the Far South Side. An upper-status white majority dominated Morgan Park and kept housing for the large black minority (35 percent of the population in 1930) strictly segregated. Morgan Park High School was a hostile environment for black students, who in 1930 numbered about 100 (5 percent of the total). Blacks accused white teachers of excluding them from extracurricular activities, unjustly giving them lower grades, and practicing bias in graduation seating arrangements. In 1920, when a black women's club asked Principal William Schoch to ban a football cheer which began, "Nigger, nigger, pull the trigger," he refused; the offensive chant ceased only upon orders from Board of Education headquarters. A decade later, an irate mother alleged that Schoch "spoke of the Colored pupils as 'blackies' and 'black as the ace of spades' to my face and in the presence of my two children." She added: "The Colored pupils are reminded that they needn't expect the same treatment as the whites. . . . The use of the word 'nigger' is even heard in the classrooms. . . . Colored students are suspended for the most trivial offenses and everything is done to discourage them. . . . The teachers are openly hostile, refuse in many cases to help Colored pupils. The principal is very open in his contempt of our people and shows us very little courtesy." A black student described the impact of this harassment on his Negro classmates: "The boys and girls seem to be afraid of a frown on a white face—they are immediately cowered and thrown into abject terror." This anonymous pupil confirmed the mother's charges and concluded, "The Colored students are not getting a fair deal."[33]

In such an atmosphere, any change in the status of Morgan Park's black pupils would increase racial friction in the community. In September, 1934, the high school was severely overcrowded, with 2,100 students (about 120 of them black) occupying a building with a capacity of 1,500. To relieve the situation, the school board created branches of the high school at two nearby elementary buildings. Officials assigned some white freshmen to classes at Clissold Elementary and sent all thirty-two first-year blacks to all-black Shoop Elementary. Blacks, however, charged that overcrowding was not the real motive for the new arrangement. "This excuse is as vicious as it is false and deceptive," one asserted. Blacks pointed out that while authorities barred all minority freshmen, an estimated 75 to 200 whites who had transferred to Morgan Park from other Chicago and suburban districts remained at the high school. Blacks regarded the Shoop branch as "a definite movement to separate the public schools of Chicago" and feared that the assignment of freshmen to Shoop was a first step toward placing all black high school pupils there. Black spokesmen offered a different remedy for overcrowding. "Let those who do not belong in Morgan Park high school get out," advised the *Defender,* "and there will be room enough for those who do belong in it."[34]

Aggrieved blacks found an ally in Democratic mayor Edward J. Kelly. In office a little more than a year, Kelly had already begun to lure blacks from their traditional Republican home. Kelly cultivated ghetto politicians such as aldermen William L. Dawson and Robert R. Jackson, and the Democrats had nominated a black, Arthur W. Mitchell, for the United States House of Representatives. A month before the 1934 election, Kelly enhanced his party's reputation in the ghetto even more by overruling the school board and ordering the black freshmen returned to Morgan Park High's main building. The mayor declared, "I am definitely opposed to any movement that denies the free right of any citizen of Chicago the privilege of attending any public institution of learning regardless of race, color or creed." Alluding to suburban pupils attending Morgan Park, Kelly added, "The sons and daughters of citizens and taxpayers of the city MUST be given preference in attending the schools which they help support."[35]

Although the mayor's action delighted black Chicagoans, it enraged Morgan Park whites. They launched a week-long boycott of the high school. Though some claimed that they were protesting overcrowding, the actual cause of their distress was ill-concealed. One demonstrator complained, "We moved out in Morgan Park to get away from these niggers. And now we've got to contend with them again." The boycotters criticized Kelly for interfering with school affairs and demanded that the Board of Education send the black freshmen to Shoop. Protesters felt that the continued use of Clissold for some first-year whites

meant that blacks were receiving favored treatment. Whites also denounced the behavior of black Morgan Park students. One white man
reported, "The familiarities charged against some of the Negro boys
have consisted of such acts as 'chucking' white girls under the chin and
stepping on their toes in the corridors." A school adminstrator asked a
black delegation, "I am quoting others now, but isn't the real trouble
out there due to the Colored students being after the white girls?" An
Urban League committee regretted "the behavior of some of the students in the high school who admittedly are not conducting themselves
in the proper manner."[36]

Authorities dampened the dissent by a combination of evasion and
threat. When a hundred whites met with Superintendent of Schools
Bogan, he supported a branch of Shoop but explained that "he was
powerless in view of subsequent developments." Meanwhile, Kelly
confused matters further by denying that he had suppressed the
branch plan and declaring "that this was a matter for the board of
education and that it was not to be interfered with in the performance
of its duties." Bogan finally capped the protest by warning that students who stayed away from school might forfeit credits for their
courses. Although whites returned to classes and black freshmen remained at the main building, ill feeling persisted. School officials
assured whites that authorities would enforce discipline and penalize
violators "of rules or proprieties," and prejudice and discrimination
continued unabated. While Mayor Kelly's concern for ghetto votes
had sustained integration in Morgan Park, he did not have the power
to bring harmony to racially mixed classrooms. Accordingly, for
blacks the taste of victory was bittersweet.[37]

As an alternative to stratifying schools by race, some systems segregated children within the same school. In a number of northern cities,
authorities assigned blacks to separate rooms or seated them at the back
or side of racially mixed classes. While Chicago's teachers and administrators rarely formally separated pupils by race within classrooms,
segregation in or exclusion from extracurricular activities was common.
This was particularly true in high schools, where interracial contact between the sexes was a sensitive issue. Black students at schools with
white majorities generally ate lunch and socialized among themselves,
and blacks tended to stay away from school clubs. When they did try to
participate, whites often objected and threatened protests. At school-
sponsored parties and dances, black children clustered together on
those occasions that they did attend. A high school official commented
about 1920, "The colored never come to social affairs. They are so

much in the minority here that they leave all organizations to the whites."[38]

The senior prom was the most racially troublesome high school activity. Inconsistency characterized prom policy toward black pupils. "In one school graduates not only are invited, but urged to attend," the *Defender* attested; "in another school they are not only overlooked, but in some cases actually forbidden to attend these affairs." High schools that did discriminate attempted to transfer their responsibility to private hands. Tilden High authorized a private "Booster Club" to sponsor its proms. Lindblom and Bowen scheduled their dances at ballrooms that either barred blacks or humiliated them by requiring use of a separate entrance and elevator. One principal justified excluding Negroes by philosophizing, "If you satisfy one group, you make another group dissatisfied, so you haven't solved a problem." For many years, dark-skinned students accepted prom segregation, and at some schools they organized their own separate affairs. "Children are being turned out of our schools more snobbish, priggish and more arrogant than they were when they entered," a black editor complained in 1935. "At the same time, other students are being turned out with a feeling of inferiority more definitely stamped upon them than ever before."[39]

During the 1930s, blacks began to resist prom segregation and succeeded in toppling barriers at several high schools. At Tilden in 1935, a dozen black seniors obtained prom bids by mistake. School personnel tried to recover the tickets and, when this failed, warned the students that they would be arrested if they showed up at the dance. A biracial coalition of women's clubs protested to Superintendent Bogan, who commanded Tilden to admit black pupils to all future dances. Two years later, Bowen High School officials repeated Tilden's earlier tactics after a black girl acquired a prom bid. Mayor Kelly, alerted by the local NAACP, ordered all five black seniors admitted to the dance. Bowen then switched the prom site to one that did not practice racial bias, and high school officials welcomed the black students and their dates.[40]

While incidents such as the prom controversies reveal the large degree of hatred toward black pupils among white Chicagoans, these episodes also suggest that white hostility toward blacks in the public schools was not equally intense throughout the city. For example, immigrant neighborhoods on the West, Near Northwest, and Far South Sides were least likely to resist the presence of black pupils and teachers. These districts experienced some racial conflict, but as the sociologist Harvey Zorbaugh's account of the Near North Side in the 1920s demonstrated, recent immigrants rarely tried to segregate blacks or drive them away from their neighborhoods. Indeed, such districts apparently displayed considerable tolerance; a woman who attended a West Side high school in the 1920s recalled peaceful relations between black and white pupils.[41]

Immigrant areas were the only white sectors of the city that accepted black teachers. As a principal observed about 1920, "The European people do not seem to resent the presence of a colored teacher." The assistant principal of heavily Italian Skinner Elementary reported that former students who returned to the building rarely failed to visit "the most beloved teacher," a black first-grade instructor. Froebel's principal praised a Negro instructor for having but one discipline case in the past three years. Another school official labeled a black teaching at the Near West Side's Cregier Junior High "so refined and cultured a woman." A black who had served in largely immigrant schools for a decade beginning in the mid-twenties commented, "I have never had any trouble with the pupils or the parents. . . . I have had some very enjoyable contacts." Pressures for school segregation were relatively weak in immigrant districts for a combination of reasons. Greater respect for authority, less race consciousness, and lack of time for political activism may explain why "new ethnic" areas tolerated blacks in their schools.[42]

By contrast, whites in old-stock, middle-income neighborhoods of Chicago fiercely opposed blacks in their classrooms. Regularly assigned black faculty members were unknown in these districts, and even the appearance of a black substitute would provoke disruption, as the Altgeld case illustrated. Evidence from Morgan Park and Hyde Park given earlier indicates the icy reception whites in middle-class areas gave their small black minorities. Two other incidents show the ways in which whites resisted the arrival of new black students and tried to drive out those already there.

In September, 1928, twenty-five black girls transferred from Morgan Park to Fenger High to take household arts courses not offered at their former school. Fenger, on the Far South Side, previously had only twenty-five blacks among its 2,200 pupils, and the white majority greeted the newcomers with a boycott. On Friday, September 21, between 500 and 2,000 students walked out of the high school building and paraded outside, yelling and singing. Police nabbed many of the protestors, and the demonstration disintegrated. But on Monday, 150 to 200 students sustained the "strike" for a second day. Whites complained about eating and swimming with blacks and objected to black youths asking white girls to dance at school socials. Fenger whites also said that accepting more blacks would make their school less prestigious than nearby Morgan Park High, a rival of Fenger. One pupil reasoned,

"If they don't want colored pupils at their high-hat school, neither do we."[43]

The protest received mixed reactions from whites in the Fenger community. Student government officers denounced the walkout and asked absentees to return to classes. Principal Thomas C. Hill, who at first dismissed the boycott as a misguided scheme of a tiny minority, summoned police to crush the protest and warned that pupils who remained away would be punished. On the other hand, the local Chamber of Commerce helped persuade the boycotters to return to school but supported the goals of the walkout and urged school officials to remove blacks who lived outside the Fenger district.[44]

At first, Superintendent Bogan defended the blacks. He pronounced the transfer "perfectly regular" and threatened to expel white demonstrators. After the businessmen announced their agreement with the boycott's aims, Bogan promised to study the transfer question and to revoke dishonestly acquired permits. A week later, the school chief ordered the newly arrived blacks back to Morgan Park and promised to make household arts courses available there. Blacks objected that nonresident whites at Fenger were unmolested.[45]

When only eight of the twenty-five girls returned to Morgan Park, between 100 and 500 whites staged a second strike at Fenger on October 9 and 10. The school's beleaguered principal exclaimed, "We will not tolerate these absurd walkouts any longer." Hill repeated earlier disciplinary threats, and the protest finally subsided. Small numbers of Morgan Park blacks remained at Fenger, but whites there regarded them as intruders. In 1933, the Chamber of Commerce again tried to purge Fenger of its black transfer students. The merchants' association predicted racial conflict unless authorities created a segregated junior high school for Negro youngsters. The *Defender* exploded, "The evil bird, Jim Crow, flapped his wings loudly . . . and from every side rose the harsh cries of Race hating, un-American bigots." Officials turned their backs on the businessmen's plan, and racial troubles at Fenger were muted for the remainder of the Depression.[46]

At Fenger, school officials dampened white protest without completely satisfying it. Closer to the ghetto, where whites were ardently determined to keep blacks out of their neighborhoods, the Board of Education was more responsive to public opinion. A boundary dispute in the Washington Park subdivision in 1933 aptly illustrated the interplay between popular pressure and official action in segregating Chicago schools. The subdivision was a white enclave bordering the ghetto; black-occupied housing lay to the west and south, while Washington Park, which served ghetto inhabitants, was north of the area (map 3).

Limited to overcrowded, expensive quarters, blacks envied the "island of whites" nearby. The decline in the subdivision's population from 8,124 in 1930 to 7,138 in 1934 made it especially open to racial change.[47]

In 1928, whites in the subdivision implemented a restrictive covenant policy, sponsored by the Woodlawn Business Men's Association. For the next twelve years, the subdivision became the focus of racial housing rivalry in Chicago between whites east of Cottage Grove who regarded the subdivision as a buffer protecting their homes from black invasion and blacks challenging the legality of restrictive covenants. During the 1930s, the Woodlawn Property Owners' Association (WPOA) led the campaign to save the subdivision from "colored encroachment." Although some blacks moved into the western part of the section in 1932 and 1933, by the spring of 1934, the WPOA claimed, "Every negro family which has moved into the community since the new administration took office has been evicted, and suits are pending against families who were in the district before." For the next five years, the WPOA nearly halted the arrival of black residents in the subdivision and seemingly secured its goal of racial exclusivity.[48]

Although the WPOA emphasized housing, it also made school conditions a matter of concern. In 1931 and 1932, WPOA founder Fred L. Helman took credit for the removal of at least some of the few blacks attending elementary schools east of Cottage Grove Avenue. Helman also agitated against the presence of black pupils at Hyde Park High School, declaring, "They are all over and if we get them out of the Hyde Park school we can get this district back to what it once was." WPOA's main target, though, was A. O. Sexton Elementary School, located in the Washington Park subdivision. Sexton's boundaries encompassed both the subdivision and black-occupied territory between South Parkway and State Street. Sexton's large black enrollment (30 percent in 1930) violated the WPOA's ideal of an all-white enclave. As Helman said, "The property owners near the Sexton school have restricted their property to white people and they are now finding it hard to get tenants with children who have to be sent to school along with the negroes."[49]

The WPOA therefore launched a campaign to eject blacks from Sexton. In 1931, the whites persuaded the school board to place two portable units west of South Parkway to, in Helman's words, "take care of some of the Negroes attending our school." This change accommodated ninety students. When new officers assumed command of the WPOA in mid-1933, the group renewed its labors against Sexton's blacks. The new leaders pledged "immediate action to supply other

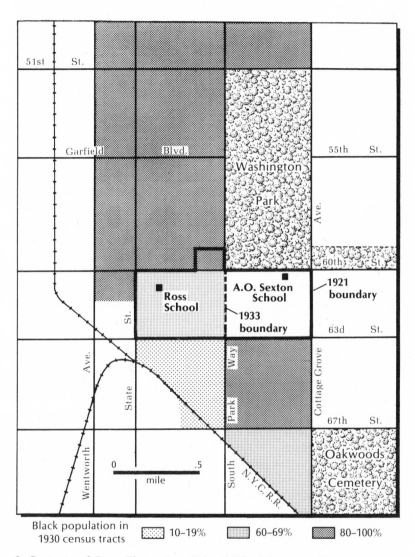

Black population in
1930 census tracts
☐ 10–19% ☐ 60–69% ■ 80–100%

3. Sexton and Ross Elementary School Districts, 1921-40

Based on Ernest W. Burgess and Charles Newcomb, eds., *Census Data of the City of Chicago, 1930* (Chicago, 1933), and Chicago Board of Education, *Proceedings,* Feb. 23, 1921, Sept. 13, 1933.

school accommodations for the colored children now attending the Sexton school, and open said school in the fall for the exclusive use of the white children in our restricted district.'' The newly elected president, James Joseph Burke, urged authorities to shift the Sexton boundary from State Street eastward to South Parkway, thereby severing the black portion of the district. This change, declared Burke, "will accomplish more than anything else to prevent the negro encroachment from traveling further eastward."[50]

Such a boundary revision would require some expansion of ghetto school facilities. At first, the WPOA suggested that the recently created federal Public Works Administration could finance a new school building in the black belt. The *Defender* fumed, "The insolence of the property owners in brazenly attempting . . . to use Race people's tax money to further malicious schemes of Jim Crowism and prejudice is declared without parallel in the history of Chicago." PWA director and U.S. interior secretary Harold L. Ickes, a former president of the local NAACP, reportedly spurned the proposal. According to a black journalist, Ickes declared that federal funds were "not a grab bag" for racial discrimination.[51]

Although the new school plan foundered, Woodlawn whites attained their goal by a different route. The Chicago schools had been in precarious financial condition for a number of years. Rising enrollment, numerous building projects, and new educational programs expanded the school budget fivefold between 1915 and 1929. The need for increased revenue, however, did not result in a comparable rise in the tax rate or property assessments. The schools sold tax anticipation warrants to meet expenses, but the Depression cut tax payments and made local banks less willing to purchase the warrants. The public schools therefore ran out of money: in the winter of 1929-30, teachers' paychecks arrived late; and by mid-1931, faculty members received scrip for their services. Under pressure from the city's business community, the Board of Education approved a retrenchment program in the summer of 1933. The board fired 1,400 teachers, increased the work loads of principals and high school instructors, shortened the school year, and closed the only municipal junior college. In addition, trustees abolished all junior high schools, elementary manual training, household arts, and physical education, and halved the number of kindergartens. Still other services were either cut or eliminated.[52]

One of the schools affected was the all-black Betsy Ross Junior High, five blocks west of South Parkway. The Board of Education made Ross an elementary school and, following the WPOA's advice, gave Ross the same boundaries as the black portion of the Sexton district. For the first time, Sexton's attendance area was limited to the Washington Park subdivision. Significantly, the WPOA publicized its triumph on August 1, though the school board did not formally approve the change until mid-September. When the new academic year began, blacks found the doors of Sexton closed to them. Parents were angry and confused, and many seemed unaware of the boundary change. One woman vowed, "Those children who live in the Sexton district must go to Sexton or we'll find the reason why." "It isn't our purpose to fight for our children to go to Sexton school merely to be associated with white children," another explained. "What we want is that our children shall attend school in the district in which they live and that the school they attend is up to the standard." Other parents had learned about the redistricting and obtained transfers permitting their youngsters to enroll at Sexton. When these pupils appeared there, however, Sexton personnel sent them to Ross.[53]

Conditions at Ross made the change especially galling to blacks. The Ross building was nearly thirty years older than Sexton and, according to black residents, "wholly unfit for occupancy, with positively none of the facilities that are found in the modern school." As a result of overcrowding at Ross, pupils there received less instruction than provided for in the standard school schedule. Black parents complained to school administrators that their offspring "were cut off from well-equipped Sexton school and jammed into the tumble-down, already overstuffed Betsy Ross building." Meanwhile, whites in the subdivision celebrated their victory and felt certain that the redistricting would guarantee the section's racial exclusivity. The sympathetic *Woodlawn Booster* observed, "With the assurance that the Sexton school district will be rezoned, the property owners are filling their apartments gradually with tenants who had moved elsewhere last year." WPOA's Burke, according to a press report, "took the stand that the board's action not merely 'saved that school' but that it saved their homes as well."[54]

Success, however, had its perils. The loss of perhaps five hundred black students left Sexton underpopulated. Indignant blacks charged that the subdivision's school had a pupil-teacher ratio of 24-1, more than 50 percent under the citywide norm. Fearing that black youngsters might refill the empty seats, the WPOA sought more white students for Sexton. The Board of Education quickly cooperated by giving Sexton a branch of Tilden Technical High School, which enrolled 190 white freshmen living east of Cottage Grove Avenue. An official explained that the branch reduced overcrowding at Tilden's main building, and that the Board of Education had chosen Sexton since it was a modern structure easily convertible to high school use. Blacks, however, regarded the maneuver as ill-disguised separatism. "The fact remains that the Ross school was a good enough building for a junior high school for our girls and is still good enough to be used as an elementary school for our children of elementary school age," one remarked, "but is not good enough to be made a branch of Tilden Technical high school." A black reporter grumbled, "It thus appears that Race children are to be kept out of Sexton school at any costs."[55]

Local blacks did not give up. Parents of Ross students established the Fifth Ward Civic and Protective Association, which showered officials with criticism for the poor facilities at Ross and the empty seats in Sexton's classrooms. The latter so embarrassed administrators that they soon permitted some blacks to return to Sexton. By the mid-thirties, the issue had reached an uneasy balance which paralleled the housing rivalry in Washington Park.[56]

White dominance in the neighborhood, however, was short-lived. Though the WPOA's court suits and informal pressure seemed to halt the black influx, they had, in fact, only delayed the final outcome. Whites continued to move elsewhere, leaving landlords with vacant units. In 1939, some owners placed profit before racial solidarity and began to defy the WPOA and the restrictive agreements. Blacks entered the western half of Washington Park, where they accounted for 15 percent of the population in the 1940 census. In October, 1940, the United States Supreme Court announced its decision in *Hansberry* v. *Lee,* a case in which the Chicago NAACP attempted to undermine restrictive covenants. The Court sidestepped a definitive position on racial covenants, but it did overturn the Washington Park agreement, since it had not carried the signatures of the owners of 95 percent of the subdivision's property frontage, as the covenant required. After the Hansberry decision, white resistance in Washington Park collapsed, and by the following summer, the subdivision was predominantly black. Although Sexton's boundary remained at South Parkway, the school, too, became overwhelmingly Negro. The expansion of the ghetto had settled the districting dispute.[57]

In this chapter, we have seen how a segregated system of public education emerged in Chicago between 1915 and 1940 without formal or legal sanction. The small pre-World War I black district quickly spread on the South Side after 1915, and the rise of the ghetto, combined with the practice of basing school assignment on home address, placed most of Chicago's black children in 90-100 percent black schools by the 1930s. Policies of public school officials also changed. Instead of defending black students and teachers, as they had done prior to the great migration, school administrators during the 1920s and 1930s assigned Negro instructors in a racially discriminatory manner and used transfers, boundaries, and branches to intensify separation of pupils. The impact of white racism on the placement of black teachers and students varied from neighborhood to neighborhood. With ghetto children isolated in mostly black classrooms, the school board could provide them with inferior buildings, smaller school budgets, fewer supplies, and different academic standards. But without the legally prescribed dual systems found throughout the South and in many parts of the North, black Chicagoans had little opportunity to obtain administrative positions and held only a minority of teaching jobs in ghetto schools. By the eve of World War II, Chicago blacks were enduring the evils of segregation without savoring its limited benefits.

NOTES

1. Chicago Conference on Home Front Unity, *Home Front Unity* (Chicago, 1945), p. 23.
2. *Chicago Daily News,* Dec. 20, 1916, p. 11; Chicago Board of Education, *Annual Directory,* 1916-17, pp. 59-205, 1920-21, pp. 50-184, 1930-31, pp. 38-230; Chicago Commission on Race Relations, *The Negro in Chicago: A Study of Race Relations and a Race Riot* (Chicago, 1922), p. 242; Mary Josephine Herrick, "Negro Employees of the Chicago Board of Education" (M.A. thesis, University of Chicago, 1931), pp. 92-108; Ernest W. Burgess and Charles Newcomb, eds., *Census Data of the City of Chicago, 1920* (Chicago, 1931), p. 34; U.S. Department of Commerce, Bureau of the Census, *Fifteenth Census, 1930: Population,* II (Washington, 1933), pp. 743, 1147.
3. Board of Education, *Annual Directory,* 1917-18, pp. 208-375; Chicago Board of Education, *School Facts,* 1 (June 18, 1930), 4; Ford S. Black, *Black's Blue Book* (Chicago, 1917), pp. 57-58, 67; Chicago Commission on Race Relations, *Negro in Chicago,* p. 242; Herrick, "Negro Employees," pp. 32, 92-108; Harold F. Gosnell, *Negro Politicians: The Rise of Negro Politics in Chicago* (Chicago, 1935), pp. 292, 300; Frederick H. Robb, ed., *1927 Intercollegian Wonder Book, or, The Negro in Chicago, 1779-1927* (Chicago, 1927), p. 45.
4. Black, *Black's Blue Book,* p. 67; Board of Education, *Annual Directory,* 1930-31, pp. 242-505; Herrick, "Negro Employees," pp. 92-108; Chicago Conference on Home Front Unity, *Human Relations in Chicago* (Chicago, 1945), p. 31.
5. Otis Dudley Duncan and Beverly Duncan, *The Negro Population of Chicago: A Study of Residential Succession* (Chicago, 1957), pp. 34, 40-41.
6. Burgess and Newcomb, *Census Data...1920,* p. 35; Duncan and Duncan, *Negro Population of Chicago,* pp. 35-38, 42-43; Alzada P. Comstock, "Chicago Housing Conditions, VI: The Problem of the Negro," *American Journal of Sociology,* 18 (Sept., 1912), 245; Louise Venable Kennedy, *The*

Negro Peasant Turns Cityward (New York, 1930), pp. 135-37.

7. Robert J. Havighurst, *The Public Schools of Chicago* (Chicago, 1964), p. 54.

8. Thomas Lee Philpott, *The Slum and the Ghetto: Neighborhood Deterioration and Middle-Class Reform, Chicago, 1880-1930* (New York, 1978), pp. 119-34. Philpott uses the segregation index devised by David Wallace in "Residential Concentration of Negroes in Chicago" (Ph.D. diss., Harvard University, 1953). A score of 100 on the Wallace Index signifies complete segregation, while 0 means perfectly even residential settlement by race.

9. Allan H. Spear, *Black Chicago: The Making of a Negro Ghetto, 1890-1920* (Chicago, 1967), pp. 11-27, 142-46, 209-14; Philpott, *The Slum and the Ghetto,* pp. 113-200; Kenneth L. Kusmer, *A Ghetto Takes Shape: Black Cleveland, 1870-1930* (Urbana, Ill., 1976); Gilbert Osofsky, *Harlem: The Making of a Ghetto* (New York, 1966). For a useful collection of articles, see John H. Bracey, Jr., August Meier, and Elliott Rudwick, eds., *The Rise of the Ghetto* (Belmont, Calif., 1971).

10. Chicago Commission on Race Relations, *Negro in Chicago,* pp. 115, 251-52; Herman H. Long and Charles S. Johnson, *People vs. Property: Race Restrictive Covenants in Housing* (Nashville, Tenn., 1947), pp. 10-33, 39-44, 56-58; Rose Helper, "The Racial Practices of Real Estate Institutions in Selected Areas of Chicago" (Ph.D. diss., University of Chicago, 1958), pp. 2, 586-88; Robert C. Weaver, *The Negro Ghetto* (New York, 1948), pp. 212-17, 231-51; "Saving a Neighborhood," *Business Week,* Apr. 27, 1940, pp. 22-23.

11. Duncan and Duncan, *Negro Population of Chicago,* p. 96; Chicago Commission on Race Relations, *Negro in Chicago,* p. 242; Herrick, "Negro Employees," pp. 92-108; Board of Education, *Annual Directory,* 1920-21, pp. 50-184, 1930-31, pp. 38-230.

12. Chicago Commission on Race Relations, *Negro in Chicago,* pp. 521-23; Graham Romeyn Taylor, "Race Relations and Public Opinion," *Opportunity,* 1 (July, 1923), 199; *Chicago Evening Post,* Jan. 23, 1920, p. 1; *Chicago Daily Journal,* Jan. 23, 1920, p. 4; *Chicago Defender,* Jan. 31, 1920, p. 1; *Daily News,* Jan. 23, 1920, p. 3; *Chicago Herald and Examiner,* Jan. 24, 1920, p. 5.

13. Herrick, "Negro Employees," p. 12.

14. *Ibid.,* pp. 33-35, 90-91; Gosnell, *Negro Politicians,* pp. 283, 285.

15. Reuben Freedman, "The Problem of the Unassigned Teacher," *Chicago Schools Journal,* 6 (Jan., 1924), 170-71; Gosnell, *Negro Politicians,* p. 286; Annabelle Carey Prescott, interview, Chicago, May, 1973; Howard S. Becker, "Role and Career Problems of the Chicago Public School Teacher" (Ph.D. diss., University of Chicago, 1951), pp. 193-94.

16. Prescott, interview; Ethel M. Hilliard, interview, Chicago, Nov., 1969; Gosnell, *Negro Politicians,* pp. 288-90; Illinois State Commission on the Condition of the Urban Colored Population, hearings transcript, Jan. 3-4, 1941, pp. 190-223, Fair Employment Practices Commission, RG 228, National Archives; "Report of the Illinois State Commission on the Condition of the Urban Colored Population," March, 1941, pp. 125-26, Illinois State Library.

17. Herrick, "Negro Employees," pp. 92-108; Hilliard, interview.

18. Herrick, "Negro Employees," pp. 20-21, 92-108; Louis Wirth and Margaret Furez, eds., *Local Community Fact Book 1938* (Chicago, 1938).

19. Mary J. Herrick, interview, Chicago, Nov., 1969; *Defender,* Feb. 22, 1930, p. 12.

20. *Defender,* Apr. 5, 1941, p. 16; Herrick, "Negro Employees," p. 35; Gosnell, *Negro Politicians,* pp. 282-83; "Report of the Illinois State Commission on the Condition of the Urban Colored Population," March, 1941, p. 125, Illinois State Library; Commission on the Condition of the Urban Colored Population, hearings transcript, Jan. 3-4, 1941, p. 191.

21. Don C. Rogers, "Planning School-Building Construction Programs," *American School Board Journal,* 96 (Jan., 1938), 52-53; Meyer Weinberg, *Race and Place: A Legal History of the Neighborhood School* (Washington, 1967).

22. W. Lloyd Warner, Buford H. Junker, and Walter A. Adams, *Color and Human Nature* (Washington, 1941), p. 24; *Defender,* Nov. 20, 1937, p. 1, Feb. 11, 1939, p. 16.

23. Chicago Board of Education, *Proceedings,* July 28, 1926, p. 15, Aug. 25, 1926, pp. 166-67; Chicago Commission on Race Relations, *Negro in Chicago,* p. 242; Herrick, "Negro Employees," pp. 92-108.

24. Chicago Commission on Race Relations, *Negro in Chicago,* p. 242; Herrick, "Negro Employees," pp. 92-108.

25. Wirth and Furez, *Local Community Fact Book 1938.*

26. *Chicago Tribune,* Apr. 6, 1917, p. 15; Board of Education, *Proceedings,* Aug. 7, 1917, p. 238; *Defender,* Jan. 12, 1929, sec. 1, p. 2, Jan. 19, 1929, sec. 1, p. 4, Feb. 8, 1936, p. 6.

27. Board of Education, *Proceedings,* Feb. 23, 1921, pp. 521-22, June 9, 1926, p. 1686, June 23, 1926, p. 1779.

28. *Defender,* Apr. 15, 1916, p. 4, Apr. 13, 1929, pp. 1, 3, Feb. 6, 1932, p. 4, Dec. 16, 1933, p. 16, Dec. 23, 1939, p. 8; Doxey A. Wilkerson, "The Negro in American Education" (working memorandum for Gunnar Myrdal, *An American Dilemma),* pp. 217-18.

29. *Defender,* Oct. 28, 1933, p. 2, Dec. 30, 1933, p. 22, Sept. 30, 1933, p. 24, Aug. 27, 1932, p. 13, Sept. 10, 1932, p. 3, Dec. 16, 1933, p. 16.

30. *Tribune,* Sept. 13, 1933, p. 5; *Defender,* Dec. 21, 1935, p. 18, Dec. 23, 1939, p. 8; Board of Education, *Proceedings,* Sept. 27, 1944, pp. 345-46; *Chicago Sun,* Sept. 8, 1944, pp. 1, 5, Sept. 9, 1944, p. 1, Sept. 10, 1944, p. 16; Martin Levit, "The Chicago Citizens Schools Committee: A Study of a Pressure Group" (M.A. thesis, University of Chicago, 1947), pp. 37-38; Earl B. Dickerson, interview, Chicago, Dec., 1969.

31. Chicago Commission on Race Relations, *Negro in Chicago,* pp. 253-54; Annual Report of the Executive Secretary, Chicago Branch NAACP, Feb. 1-Dec. 31, 1923, p. 9; Morris Lewis to Walter F. White, Oct. 3, 1923, NAACP Papers, Branch Files, Box G48, Library of Congress; *Defender,* Sept. 23, 1933, p. 3.

32. Board of Education, *Proceedings,* Oct. 3, 1917, p. 465, Nov. 7, 1917, pp. 633-34; Chicago Commission on Race Relations, *Negro in Chicago,* p. 242.

33. Ernest W. Burgess and Charles Newcomb, eds., *Census Data of the City of Chicago, 1930* (Chicago, 1933), p. 189; Herrick, "Negro Employees," pp. 92-108; *Defender,* Oct. 6, 1917, p. 6, July 3, 1926, sec. 1, p. 10, May 24, 1930, p. 16, Nov. 20, 1920, p. 2, July 12, 1930, p. 14.

34. *Pittsburgh Courier,* Oct. 20, 1934, sec. 2, p. 3; Board of Education,

Proceedings, Sept. 12, 1934, pp. 189, 191, Sept. 26, 1934, pp. 238, 241; *Defender,* Sept. 22, 1934, pp. 1-2, Oct. 13, 1934, p. 3; Wilkerson, "Negro in American Education," p. 220.

35. John M. Allswang, "The Chicago Negro Voter and the Democratic Consensus: A Case Study, 1918-1936," *Journal of the Illinois State Historical Society,* 60 (Summer, 1967), 145-75; *Pittsburgh Courier,* Oct. 6, 1934, sec. 1, p. 6; *Defender,* Oct. 6, 1934, p. 1.

36. *Daily News,* Oct. 8, 1934, p. 1, Oct. 9, 1934, p. 5, Oct. 15, 1934, p. 1; *Chicago Times,* Oct. 7, 1934, p. 8, Oct. 8, 1934, p. 5, Oct. 9, 1934, p. 4, Oct. 10 and 11, 1934, p. 2; *Defender,* Sept. 22, 1934, p. 1, Sept. 29, 1934, p. 2, Oct. 13, 1934, p. 1.

37. *Times,* Oct. 7, 1934, p. 8, Oct. 11, 1934, p. 2; *Daily News,* Oct, 8, 1934, p. 1, Oct. 11, 1934, p. 3, Oct. 15, 1934, p. 1; *Defender,* Oct. 13, 1934, p. 1, Apr. 10, 1937, p. 29, June 15, 1940, pp. 1-2, July 6, 1940, p. 22; *Tribune,* Oct. 9, 1934, p. 2, June 12, 1940, p. 16, June 22, 1940, p. 10.

38. Chicago Commission on Race Relations, *Negro in Chicago,* pp. 252-56; Herrick, interview.

39. *Defender,* Jan. 26, 1935, pp. 1-2, June 15, 1929, p. 1, Jan. 25, 1936, p. 1; undated press release, Chicago Branch NAACP, May-June, 1937, Branch Files, Box G53; Warner et al., *Color and Human Nature,* p. 200.

40. *Defender,* June 15, 1935, p. 7, June 12, 1937, pp. 1, 3; undated press release, Chicago Branch NAACP, May-June, 1937, Branch Files, Box G53.

41. Harvey Warren Zorbaugh, *The Gold Coast and the Slum* (Chicago, 1929), p. 148; Irene K. Berger, interview, Chicago, Aug., 1978.

42. Chicago Commission on Race Relations, *Negro in Chicago,* p. 248; John T. Rose, interview, Chicago, March, 1970; Herrick, "Negro Employees," pp. 21-22; Gosnell, *Negro Politicians,* pp. 291-92.

43. *Daily Journal,* Sept. 21, 1928, p. 1, Sept. 24, 1928, p. 2; *Daily News,* Sept. 21, 1928, p. 6; *Evening Post,* Sept. 21, 1928, p. 1, Sept. 24, 1928, p. 2; *Herald and Examiner,* Sept. 22, 1928, p. 3, Sept. 25, 1928, p. 5.

44. *Tribune,* Sept. 21, 1928, p. 3, Sept. 22, 1928, p. 6, Sept. 25, 1928, p. 16; *Herald and Examiner,* Sept. 22, 1928, p. 3, Sept. 25, 1928, p. 5; *Daily News,* Sept. 21, 1928, p. 6; *Evening Post,* Sept. 22 and 24, 1928, p. 2; *Defender,* Oct. 6, 1928, p. 1.

45. *Tribune,* Sept. 22, 1928, p. 6, Sept. 25, 1928, p. 16; *Herald and Examiner,* Sept. 26, 1928, p. 21; *Defender,* Oct. 6, 1928, p. 1.

46. *Tribune,* Oct. 11, 1928, p. 5, Oct. 12, 1928, p.7; *Daily News,* Oct. 11, 1928, p. 6; *Evening Post,* Oct. 11, 1928, p. 1; *Defender,* Oct. 13, 1928, sec. 1, p. 5, Feb. 25, 1933, pp. 1-2.

47. Frederick Burgess Lindstrom, "The Negro Invasion of the Washington Park Subdivision" (M.A. thesis, University of Chicago, 1941), pp. 5, 26-28; Robert E. Martin, "Racial Invasion," *Opportunity,* 19 (Nov., 1941), 324; Horace R. Cayton, "Negroes Live in Chicago," *Opportunity,* 15 (Dec., 1937), 369.

48. Lindstrom, "Negro Invasion," pp. 6-7, 9, 21-24; St. Clair Drake and Horace R. Cayton, *Black Metropolis: A Study of Negro Life in a Northern City* (New York, 1945), pp. 184-89; *Woodlawn Booster,* Mar. 8, 1934, p. 5.

49. *Defender,* Mar. 28, 1931, p. 13, Oct. 29, 1932, pp. 1-2; Board of Education, *Annual Directory,* 1930-31, p. 202; Board of Education, *Proceedings,* Feb. 23, 1921, p. 534; Herrick, "Negro Employees," pp. 92-108; Fred L. Helman,

"To Property Owners in Woodlawn," received by NAACP, May 22, 1930, NAACP Papers, Box C402.

50. *Defender,* Mar. 28, 1931, p. 13; Board of Education, *Annual Directory,* 1931-32, p. 200; *Woodlawn Booster,* July 13, 1933, p. 7.

51. *Woodlawn Booster,* July 13, 1933, pp. 1, 7; *Defender,* July 22, 1933, p. 4.

52. Mary J. Herrick, *The Chicago Schools: A Social and Political History* (Beverly Hills, Calif., 1971), pp. 177-215; "The Assault on the Schoolhouse," *Nation,* 137 (Aug. 16, 1933), 173; S. J. Duncan-Clark, "The Chicago School Situation," *School and Society,* 38 (July 29, 1933), 153-54; Levit, "Chicago Citizens Schools Committee," pp. 11-15.

53. *Woodlawn Booster,* Aug. 3 and Sept. 7, 1933, p. 1; Board of Education, *Proceedings,* Sept. 13, 1933, p. 165; *Defender,* Sept. 23, 1933, pp. 1, 3.

54. *Defender,* Sept. 23, 1933, p. 1, Sept. 30, 1933, p. 15; *Woodlawn Booster,* Aug. 31, 1933, p. 4, Jan. 11, 1934, p. 8.

55. *Woodlawn Booster,* Oct. 5 and 26, 1933, p. 1; Board of Education, *Proceedings,* Sept. 27, 1933, p. 187; *Defender,* Sept. 30, 1933, p. 15, Oct. 14, 1933, pp. 1-2, Nov. 4, 1933, p. 3.

56. *Defender,* Nov. 4, 1933, p. 3, Nov. 18, 1933, p. 16, May 23, 1936, p. 4.

57. *Ibid.,* Sept. 23, 1933, pp. 1, 3; Lindstrom, "Negro Invasion," pp. 9-16, 24-25, 34; U.S. Department of Commerce, Bureau of the Census, *Sixteenth Census of the United States: 1940, Population and Housing Statistics for Census Tracts and Community Areas, Chicago, Ill.* (Washington, 1943), p. 136; Martin, "Racial Invasion," pp. 324, 326-27; "Report of the Illinois State Commission on the Condition of the Urban Colored Population"; I. F. Stone, "The Rat and Res Judicata," *Nation,* 151 (Nov. 23, 1940), 495.

CHAPTER THREE

The Triumph of Inequality:
School Funding and Facilities in the Black Community

FROM THE TURN of the century into the mid-1920s, members of Chicago's black community had frequently praised the school facilities that served their children. The black press often termed classroom accommodations "splendid." In 1915, an editor remarked, "Magnificent buildings dot the entire city and are so situated that no child is compelled to walk more than four or five blocks from its home." During these years, southern education was the standard by which blacks judged local conditions. In 1924, the *Defender* published a sketch of a proposed addition to a South Side elementary school and advised its readers, "Compare this structure with the schoolhouses built for our boys and girls in the South. The equipment is first class and not of the 'secondhand' variety that is dumped on our people in Dixie." Four months later, a photograph of Phillips High School carried a similar caption. "This massive structure, which houses children of both races, is very much unlike the contemplated schoolhouses to be erected in the vicinity of Clarksdale, Miss., where Jim-Crowism is to be the first lesson taught."[1]

By the 1930s, however, celebration had given way to complaint. Ghetto residents charged that the Board of Education provided them with old and outmoded facilities, spent less money on their schools than on those in white districts, and tolerated severe overcrowding. In 1939, a black social worker observed, "It seems that the schools which have the oldest equipment and the lowest salaries are in the Negro district." The same year, George McCray of the National Negro Congress revised the once-popular contrast of North and South when he declared, ". . . the Chicago school system is one of the most expensive systems in the world, yet in it the treatment of Negro children is on a level with education of Negroes in Mississippi."[2]

During the Depression, allegations of inadequate school accommodations came from all parts of Chicago's black ghetto. On the West Side, citizens in the Hayes Elementary district branded their school building a fire trap with an "ancient fire escape, which in case of fire would be more dangerous than the fire itself." Residents also criticized the location of boys' toilets in a separate unit behind the schoolhouse. Most objectionable, however, were the unhealthful conditions inside Hayes, which had been constructed in 1867. The school's kitchen was near a cesspool, and doorways led from the kitchen to a coal bin and an alley. Unclean drinking fountains were also a potential source of disease. A black journalist remarked, "The horrifying conditions . . . would impress one as being more suitable and more fit to be classified as a horse stable than an advanced institution of learning." In 1936, Hayes made headlines when seventy of its pupils contracted trench mouth (Vincent's infection). Hayes was not unique, for dissatisfaction with school facilities was apparent in other sections of the ghetto as well. About the time children were becoming ill at Hayes, parents in the Far South Side community of Lilydale waged a militant protest against the dilapidated portables their youngsters attended. And in the heart of the South Side ghetto, complaints against substandard building conditions rocked the Ross Elementary district in 1933 and the Phillips High district in 1936. In the late 1930s, parents of Colman Elementary students complained that the nearly seventy-year-old structure was obsolete and susceptible to fire. A subsequent blaze at Colman proved their point.[3]

What was the meaning of these incidents? Was the change in black Chicagoans' opinions about local school facilities due to people's increased expectations or had the quality of ghetto school accommodations actually deteriorated? How typical were conditions at Hayes, Ross, and Colman? And how similar were black schools to those in the city's white neighborhoods? A study of building age and quality, pupil-teacher ratios, budgets, new construction, and overcrowding in Chicago between 1920 and 1940 can answer these questions.

Since elementary schools are numerous and have small, relatively homogenous attendance areas, they are best-suited for a comparative survey of school facilities. I have created four categories of schools for this purpose:

1. *Black:* This group includes every Chicago public elementary school whose estimated pupil enrollment was 90 to 100 percent black. Since the Board of Education did not classify pupils by race, to designate black schools in 1920 and 1925 I used principals' estimates of black enrollment found in the report of the Chicago Commission on Race

Relations. For later years, data collected in Mary Herrick's 1931 master's thesis, "Negro Employees of the Chicago Board of Education," identified black schools. Census and school board information permitted adjustments to Herrick's list for 1935 and 1940.

2. *High status:* To identify this group, I devised a social status ranking for all seventy-five community areas in Chicago as listed in the *Local Community Fact Book* edited by Louis Wirth and Margaret Furez (Chicago, 1938). To obtain the status ranking, I rated each community according to the median school grade its residents had completed in 1934 and "median equivalent rental" in 1930 (the years for which the respective data were given). Wirth and Furez defined the latter as the "median of the actual rental of homes rented . . . together with 1 per cent of the value of homes owned, which was considered the approximate monthly rental." I added each community's rank for education and rental together and divided by two to produce a social status ranking. The nine communities with the highest rankings were Beverly, South Shore, West Ridge, Rogers Park, Hyde Park, Edison Park, Avalon Park, Kenwood, and Uptown (map 4). In these areas, median school grade completed ranged from 9.7 to 11.7 years, compared to Chicago's median of 8.1 years, while median equivalent rentals were between $71.96 and $136.13 monthly, well above the city median of $58.00. The high status category for 1920 to 1940 consists of every elementary school located within these nine neighborhoods, which were almost exclusively white.

3. *Low status:* I used the same process to identify the nine communities with the lowest education-rental rankings. These areas were Armour Square, Lower West Side, Bridgeport, Hegewisch, West Town, Near West Side, Fuller Park, New City, and Garfield Ridge (map 4). Here median schooling was between 6.1 and 7.0 years, and median equivalent rental fell between $19.99 and $32.67 monthly, except for Garfield Ridge, where it was $43.95. The low status category for 1920 to 1940 includes all elementary schools within these communities whose estimated black enrollments were less than 10 percent.

4. *Immigrant:* The nine Chicago communities with the highest proportion of foreign-born persons in their populations in 1930 provide the basis for this category. Three areas — West Town, Hegewisch, and Lower West Side — are also part of the low status group. The remaining six were North Lawndale, Pullman, Burnside, Lincoln Park, Albany Park, and Archer Heights (map 4). The percentage of foreign-born residents in these districts ranged from 32 to 45, con-

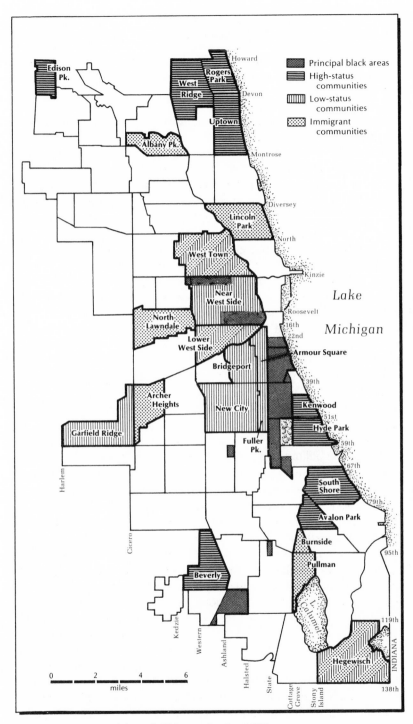

Principal black areas
High-status communities
Low-status communities
Immigrant communities

Howard
Rogers Park
Edison Pk.
West Ridge
Devon
Uptown
Albany Pk.
Montrose

Diversey

Lincoln Park

West Town
North
Kinzie

Near West Side
Lake Michigan
Roosevelt
North Lawndale
16th
22nd
Lower West Side
Armour Square
Bridgeport
39th

Archer Heights
New City
Kenwood
51st
Hyde Park
Garfield Ridge
Fuller Pk.
59th

67th

South Shore
79th

Avalon Park

Burnside
95th

Pullman

Beverly

L. Calumet

119th
INDIANA
Hegewisch
138th

Harlem
Cicero
Kedzie
Western
Ashland
Halsted
State
Cottage Grove
Stony Island

0   2   4   6
miles

4. Local Communities of Chicago in the 1930s

Based on Louis Wirth and Margaret Furez, eds., *Local Community Fact Book* (Chicago, 1938).

siderably higher than the 25 percent in the city as a whole. "Immigrant schools" for 1920 to 1940 are all grade schools located in these nine areas.

Building age is one measure of the quality of school facilities. Authorities believe that older structures are less likely to meet current health and safety standards or educational requirements. As George D. Strayer and his Columbia University associates maintained in their 1931 survey of public education in Chicago, "The age of a school building is an important factor in the determination of its present adequacy, potential adaptability, and future service." When we compare construction dates for the twenty-two black elementary schools in 1931 with Strayer's data for all 304 public elementary buildings in Chicago, we find black schools as a group to be much older. While 46 percent of all local grade schools were less than thirty years old at the time of Strayer's study, only 18 percent of the black schools were. By contrast, 55 percent of the black grade schools were constructed before 1892, while only three in ten throughout the city were that old. Do these figures suggest racial bias by school authorities or do they reflect the greater age of black neighborhoods? One analyst of black education in the North, Charles Predmore, commented in 1934, "It often happens that the colored child attends the older and less desirable schools, but this is the result of their residence in the older and more outmoded sections of the city." A comparison of elementary school age in differing types of Chicago neighborhoods in 1940 confirms his conclusion. Although black school buildings were much older than those in high status districts, they compared favorably with schools in white low status and immigrant areas. High status schools, often located in outlying parts of the city, were the youngest of the four categories with a median age of 26 in 1940. Only one of every eight high status schools was built before 1890, while nearly 70 percent had been finished since the start of the twentieth century. More than two-fifths, in fact, were erected between the world wars. While the remaining three groups (low status, immigrant, and black) each differed sharply from the high status set, they exhibited only minor variations among themselves. In these categories, between 45 and 53 percent of the buildings began service before 1890, and median school age in 1940 ranged from 48 to 54 years. By contrast, only one-fourth to one-third of the structures in these groups opened after 1900, and just 4 to 8 percent were products of the interwar decades. The main distinction among these three groups was that low status schools tended to be somewhat older than those in black and immigrant areas. Thus, despite the fact that black schools were significantly older than either the citywide average or those in high status districts, they were similar in age to facilities in immigrant sections and slightly younger than buildings in white neighborhoods of low social status.[4]

For their 1931 survey of the Chicago schools, Strayer's team also studied the quality of the city's public elementary school buildings. Researchers graded every public school in Chicago, rating classrooms, building structure and features, and school sites. Physical plants that received less than 400 points "drop below the dead-line of service, safety, or justified further investment," and Strayer urged authorities to close these buildings as soon as possible. Schools scoring 400-699 points did not meet acceptable standards but were worth renovating. Buildings earning 700 points or more ranged from "fairly satisfactory" to "thoroughly satisfactory" and required few or minor changes to meet the survey's measure of adequacy. Since structural quality was in large part a function of age, it is not surprising that results were similar for each. Although black schools received lower scores than high status schools or the citywide aggregate, they closely resembled schools in immigrant and low status districts and actually did better at the 600-799 level than the latter set. Whereas only one-fifth of the high status buildings were not worth saving, between 42 and 46 percent of the other three groups' structures were beyond repair. Nearly one-third of the high status schools were rated satisfactory, but only from 2 to 6 percent of the other groups' buildings were so designated. As with age, the quality of blacks' schoolhouses was about the same as that for immigrant and somewhat better than for low status whites.[5]

Building age and quality, however, reveal but one aspect of school resources. While officials in any period authorize some new buildings, they must rely primarily on the physical plant built by earlier generations. Therefore, to learn more about actions of school administrators, we must turn from buildings themselves to conditions inside them. One good measure of authorities' preferences in allocating resources is the number of pupils per teacher in a given school or group of schools. (Class-size data would also be helpful, but it is not available.) Table 1 illustrates pupil-teacher ratios in different types of schools during the interwar years. Although high status institutions performed worst (highest ratios) in absolute terms for most of the period, black schools had the poorest relative record. Ghetto institutions were best (lowest ratios) in 1920 and 1925, fell behind low status and immigrant schools in 1930 and 1935, and dropped to the bottom (albeit by a slim margin) by 1940. While pupil-teacher ratios in most schools declined substantially during the interwar era, this did not happen in black districts. Be-

Table 1

Number of Pupils per Teacher
at Selected Chicago Public Elementary Schools, 1920-40

Group	1920	1925	1930	1935	1940
High status	42.50	40.33	39.34	42.37	35.91
Low status	41.98	39.46	37.54	37.40	33.37
Immigrant	41.77	39.98	38.07	38.75	33.92
Black	36.63	37.91	38.84	40.48	35.95

Source: Chicago Board of Education, *Annual Directory*, 1920-21, pp. 51-184; 1925-26, pp. 59-195; 1930-31, pp. 65-230; 1935-36, pp. 64-218; 1940-41, pp. 52-203.

tween 1920 and 1940, ratios for high status, immigrant, and low status categories fell 15.5, 18.8, and 20.5 percent, respectively. Rates of reduction were roughly even in each of the two decades, and only the Depression-induced financial drought in public education temporarily reversed the trend. On the other hand, the pupil-teacher ratio in black schools in 1940 was only 1.9 percent below the 1920 level, and all of the decline occurred in the latter 1930s. In fact, while the three white groups' ratios were dropping by 7.4 to 10.6 percent in the 1920s, the figure for black schools rose 6 percent.

In examining pupil-teacher ratio, we can discern three phases in the interwar period. For the 1920s, racial favoritism must have accounted for the different patterns that black and white schools followed. Ratios for all three white sets fell, despite the fact that enrollment in one (high status) soared 50.5 percent, while the other two categories (low status and immigrant) lost students. Between 1930 and 1935, when a funding crisis wounded education, enrollment trends—not race—were decisive. The two groups with growing numbers of pupils (high status and black, up 8.7 and 20.7 percent, respectively) suffered from higher pupil-teacher ratios; immigrant and low status schools, which lost 14.7 and 20.4 percent of their enrollments, had relatively stable ratios. Changes in the final quarter, 1935-40, were similar for all groups. All ratios fell considerably, with the high status set leading the way. Neither race nor enrollment trends affected the ratio. The figure for black schools fell for the first time, despite continued population gains.

Although pupil-teacher ratio data do not reveal a clear and consistent pattern of racial discrimination, in other areas blacks experienced more definite deterioration. School financing provides one such example. To determine funding levels, I matched budgets with enrollments, giving money allocated per pupil in four categories of schools. I omitted capital improvements, since they fluctuated drastically and would therefore distort the results (the distribution of new school buildings is treated later in this chapter). It is clear that authorities budgeted fewer dollars per child for ghetto schools than in any white group in every year surveyed except 1925, when the black set ranked first (see first part of table 2). Moreover, the relative position of black schools worsened between 1920 and 1940. They began the period just three cents per student behind immigrant schools and only 6.3 percent lower than the most generously financed category. Twenty years later, however, ghetto institutions were $11.41 below their nearest rival and 23.6 percent under the appropriations leader. Whereas the Board of Education increased its per pupil allocations to immigrant and low status white schools over time, children in black schools got less in 1940 than they did ten to fifteen years before. School buildings reflected an area's age and economic condition, and black, immigrant, and low status categories did about the same here. That low status and immigrant institutions had the best pupil-teacher ratios and the most ample budgets during the 1930s suggests that racial factors shaped discretionary distribution of school resources far more than economic status.

Each school's non-capital budget had three categories—salaries, supplies, and plant operation and maintenance. Salaries for principals, school clerks, and teachers consumed nearly three-fourths of the budget for the typical elementary school. Since most schools had one principal and one clerk, funds mainly went for faculty pay. Rankings for instructional salaries in table 2 are nearly identical to those for total appropriations. Low status and immigrant schools placed first and second, respectively, in the latter part of the period. High status schools were best in 1920 but fell to third during the Depression. And black schools were worst again, except for 1925 when a low pupil-teacher ratio enabled them to narrowly outdistance their white competitors. Black schools were further behind their peers for salaries in 1940 than they had been in 1920. Whereas the three white groups each showed gains in salary funding from 1925 to 1930 and 1930 to 1940, black schools lost ground just as consistently over these years.

The two variables that determined per pupil spending on salaries were the number of teachers within each school and how much money they earned. Salary schedules for elementary instructors depended upon years of teaching experience. In 1920, the Board of Education computed salaries on a beginning annual base of $1,200, with $100 annual raises to a maximum of $2,000 in the ninth year. Primary teachers got $25 below and junior high instructors earned $100 above the basic rate. In 1922, the school board approved a new schedule giving beginners

Table 2
Per Pupil Budget Appropriations at Selected Chicago Public Elementary Schools, 1920-40

Group	1920	1925	1930	1935	1940
Total Appropriations					
High status	$52.56	$76.22	$91.74	$62.65	$86.50
Low status	50.08	78.69	95.32	73.13	98.48
Immigrant	48.98	75.69	93.72	69.97	94.55
Black	48.95	81.30	86.23	60.71	75.09
Appropriations for Instructional Salaries					
High status	$44.27	$59.98	$61.54	$46.19	$64.50
Low status	42.21	60.45	63.80	53.93	69.94
Immigrant	41.70	59.35	64.35	51.81	68.67
Black	41.18	61.42	59.27	45.27	58.98
Appropriations for Plant Operation and Maintenance					
High status	$ 6.93[a]	$13.73	$24.24	$14.81	$19.60
Low status	6.28[a]	15.55	24.88	17.37	25.46
Immigrant	5.73[a]	13.66	22.92	16.40	23.06
Black	6.41[a]	17.26	20.70	12.76	13.53
Appropriations for Books and Classroom Supplies					
High status	$ 1.36[b]	$ 2.51	$ 5.96	$ 1.65	$ 2.40
Low status	1.59[b]	2.69	6.64	1.83	3.08
Immigrant	1.55[b]	2.68	6.45	1.76	2.82
Black	1.36[b]	2.62	6.26	2.68	2.58

[a]Budgetary information is for plant operation only.
[b]Budgetary information is for classroom supplies only.

Sources: Chicago Board of Education, *Annual Directory,* 1920-21, pp. 51-184; 1925-26, pp. 59-195; 1930-31, pp. 65-230; 1935-36, pp. 64-218; 1940-41, pp. 52-203; Chicago Board of Education, *Proceedings,* July 2, 1920, pp. 1826-2089; Apr. 22, 1925, pp. 1130-1404; Jan. 14, 1930, pp. 1173-1486; Jan. 17, 1935, pp. 614-950; Jan. 10, 1940, pp. 674-1010.

$1,500 and veterans with nine or more years of service $2,500. Annual increments of $125 linked these two levels, and the board ended salary distinctions in the elementary pay scale based on grade taught. The 1922 schedule continued for the remainder of the interwar era.[6]

Teachers were not distributed on the salary scale in the same fashion in each neighborhood (table 3). Under the salary schedule implemented in 1922, black schools consistently had a smaller proportion of highly paid teachers than any of the three sample white groups. Near the bottom of the salary ladder, a significant change occurred over the years. In 1925, the percentage of instructors at the lower salary categories was nearly equal among the black, immigrant, and low status groups. During the 1930s, however, as the proportion of faculty members earning under $2,000 declined in each white category, starting teachers became increasingly common within the ghetto. This occurred because the substantial growth in black enrollment combined with the general reduction in pupil-teacher ratios to boost the number of faculty positions in black elementary schools by nearly 44 percent. Beginning teachers rather than instructors from other institutions filled most of these new jobs.

Teacher preferences also explained the figures in table 3. An instructor could attempt to leave her present assignment by applying for a transfer to any of ten different schools. When a position became available at a requested school, the teacher at the top of the waiting list could fill it. Transfer decisions reflected home-to-work distance, principals' conduct and reputations, and the social-class composition of school districts. As John A. Winget, a University of Chicago doctoral student who investigated teacher transfers in Chicago, wrote, "Newly appointed teachers are assigned to existing vacancies in the schools in underprivileged neighborhoods and they characteristically seek transfers to 'better neighborhoods.'" Winget compiled data on white female elementary instructors who applied for transfers in 1947-48, and his evidence shows that while the socioeconomic status of a school's attendance area affected the transfer request rate, race was an even more powerful variable. Whereas 5.4 percent of the teaching force in white schools ranking in the top third in socioeconomic status asked for a transfer, 11 percent at the bottom third SES schools wanted to switch jobs. In black schools, however, one-fifth of the teachers were transfer applicants in the year Winget studied.[7]

Most commentators believed that the high proportion of beginners and the smaller share of veterans in ghetto schools meant less-effective instruction. One teacher asserted that the high turnover rate at her predominantly black school fostered disorder among pupils and low morale among the faculty. She explained, "The new teachers only expect to be there a year so they don't care. When you know that you are going to be some place a long time, . . . you plan and work to make the place better." Frazier Lane of the Chicago Urban League concurred.

Table 3

Distribution of Annual Teachers' Salaries
at Selected Chicago Public Elementary Schools, 1925 and 1940

Group	Faculty Positions	$2500 or more		$2000-2499		Less than $2000	
		Number	Percentage	Number	Percentage	Number	Percentage
1925							
High status	605	332	54.9	182	30.1	91	15.0
Low status	2067	966	46.7	477	23.1	624	30.2
Immigrant	1949	905	46.4	505	25.9	539	27.7
Black	188	67	35.6	69	36.7	52	27.7
1940							
High status	763.8	639.9	83.8	44.8	5.9	79.1	10.3
Low status	1279.1	847.9	66.3	102.0	8.0	329.2	25.7
Immigrant	1324.0	930.8	70.3	102.5	7.7	290.7	22.0
Black	937.0	465.0	49.6	110.0	11.8	362.0	38.6

Source: Chicago Board of Education, *Proceedings*, Apr. 22, 1925, pp. 1130-1404; Jan. 10, 1940, pp. 674-1010.

"The high turnover of white teachers in our schools," Lane stated in 1939, "results in inferior training of our children."[8]

Salary distribution alone did not determine the results in table 2. Pupil-teacher ratios also shaped per student spending. In 1940, for example, low status and immigrant sets ranked first and second in per pupil allocations despite their middling position in instructor experience. The smaller number of children for each faculty member explained this showing. When ghetto schools led the three white categories in per student funding of salaries in 1925, the lead derived from the group's low pupil-teacher ratio, since it had the least experienced and lowest salaried faculty of any category.

Operation and maintenance of the physical plant was the next largest budgetary item. Repairs, electricity and coal, miscellaneous supplies, and salaries for engineer-custodians, firemen, and janitors accounted for an average of one-fifth to one-fourth of the typical school budget between 1925 and 1940. During these years, our four groups' rankings for operations were nearly the same as for teachers' salaries and total spending (table 2). Black schools, after placing first in 1925, fell to last for the rest of the period. Whereas each of the three white groups made a substantial recovery in the late 1930s, the improvement in operations and maintenance funding in black schools was negligible. And though each white group received more dollars in 1940 than it had in 1925, ghetto schools' funding for this category skidded 21 percent. Moreover, black institutions did more poorly in operations budgets than they had done in salaries appropriations. While the Board of Education allocated 16 percent less for salaries per pupil in black schools than in low status schools in 1940, the comparable gap between the two groups for operations and maintenance was 47 percent.

Why did black districts do so badly? Contrary to what one might suppose, the shortage of operations funds for black schools did not stem from variations in the ages of classroom buildings. A study of 1940 operations and maintenance budgets by building age revealed little or no relationship between per capita spending and date of construction for either white or black schools. At every level of building age, white schools received far more generous funding than black ones. Immigrant and black schools had similar median ages, yet the allocations in the latter set were less than three-fifths of the former. Did the poor showing of ghetto schools result from lower salaries for workers who ran the physical plant? Although per capita appropriations for maintenance employees were considerably lower in black schools, a comparable gap existed between black and white schools for repair work, supplies, and utilities. Thus, racial bias, not maintenance salaries or building age, placed the black ghetto behind both well-to-do and poor white districts in funding of plant operations.[9]

Books and classroom supplies constituted the third budget category. These items claimed about 3 percent of the funds for a typical school, except in 1930 when they took nearly 7 percent. Despite their small share of appropriations, books and academic supplies were important to teachers and students alike. A number of faculty members who served in ghetto schools during the 1930s recalled that they received insufficient supplies and old textbooks that had previously been at other schools. But although black schools placed third in four of five years surveyed, they trailed low status and immigrant areas by modest margins (table 2). And in 1935, a year blacks fared poorly in other categories, the ghetto unaccountably led all white groups. Unlike other budget categories, high status sections were behind black schools in books and supplies funding. Parent-teacher associations in high status neighborhoods sometimes bought equipment for local classrooms, and these purchases may have lifted the group out of last place in total spending.[10]

We have seen that for relatively fixed variables such as age and quality of school buildings, the ghetto ranked below well-off communities and the city as a whole but did about as well as heavily immigrant sections and slightly better than low status white districts. But in areas that were apparently more susceptible to administrative discretion, black schools performed more poorly than any white group. In 1920 and 1925, blacks enjoyed the best pupil-teacher ratio of any group studied. Thereafter, however, the ghetto lost so much ground relative to white communities that by 1940 it ranked last. In the budget process, the Board of Education treated ghetto schools even worse. Owing to their less experienced faculty and to a relatively deteriorating pupil-teacher ratio, black schools trailed three white groups in per pupil appropriations for teachers' salaries in 1920, 1930, 1935, and 1940. The ghetto did well in per capita funding of operation and maintenance early in the period, but by 1930 it had dropped to last in this department, too. In 1940, total per pupil allocations in the typical black grade school were more than 20 percent under those in the average immigrant or low status white institution.

Perhaps size of school enrollments—not race—explained appropriations and staffing practices in Chicago. Between 1920 and 1940, enrollment totals at many schools changed considerably. For example, the gain in black population between the wars raised the median student body at black schools from 750 to 1167, a 56 percent increase. Meanwhile, enrollment declines in low status and immigrant districts lowered the median size of these schools about 35 percent, from 1173 and 1181, respectively, to 760 and 770. (High status schools experienced a moderate decline in per school enrollment.) On the eve of World War II, half the twenty-four black elementary schools had 1,200 students or more, but only 4 to 18 percent of the selected white schools were so large. Five black schools had more than 2,000 pupils each, but of 114 white institutions surveyed, only one was that big. The size distribution of black schools had become nearly identical to that of low status and immigrant schools twenty years before.[11]

Did the higher median enrollment in black schools explain their smaller share of the system's resources? As we see in table 4, in immigrant and high status districts, as enrollment rose in a school, so did the pupil-teacher ratio. While this pattern also existed in the ghetto, the relationship here was weaker, with the ratio increasing only slightly for each enrollment increment above 600 students. Moreover, at given enrollment levels, there was sometimes considerable variation in ratios among the four groups of schools. Population differences were most significant for high status areas. They had the highest ratio at four of six enrollment levels, and only their moderate median size saved them from having the largest overall pupil-teacher ratio. At black institutions, school size affected pupil-teacher ratios but not enough to explain the ghetto's lowly standing. Even if black schools had been smaller, they still would have had higher pupil-teacher ratios than the immigrant or low status categories.

Futhermore, an examination of per capita appropriations in relation to school size (see table 5), gives little support to the thesis that black schools were underfinanced because of their larger enrollments. First of all, the number of children in a school was not always inversely correlated with the amount of funds it received. Though per capita salaries were inversely related to school size in high status and immigrant areas, this was not the case in low status and black districts. Only operations and maintenance budgets were consistently linked to school population figures. Second, the relationship between number of students and budget allocations was weaker in the ghetto than it was in white districts. Size was significant in ghetto school appropriations for operations and maintenance alone. Finally, although size and spending were sometimes related and though black schools were larger, the high enrollments of ghetto institutions did not account for their skimpier budgets. At four of five enrollment levels, overall appropriations for black schools lagged behind all three white groups. Thus, if ghetto children had attended smaller grade schools, the Board of Education still would have set fewer dollars aside for their education than it did for white children in other parts of Chicago.

To summarize, neither enrollment size nor building age nor aggregate

Table 4
*Pupil-Teacher Ratio by Size of Enrollment
at Selected Chicago Public Elementary Schools, 1940*

Enrollment	High status		Low status		Immigrant		Black	
	Schools	Ratio	Schools	Ratio	Schools	Ratio	Schools	Ratio
1-399	3	31.80	2	32.37	3	29.48	0	—
400-599	4	32.48	10	30.83	10	30.19	3	31.79
600-799	5	33.93	22	33.28	15	33.59	1	35.11
800-999	10	36.33	13	35.14	9	34.77	5	35.66
1000-1199	6	37.29	6	35.00	5	34.88	3	36.30
1200 or more	5	39.00	2	34.26	9	36.49	12	36.32
Total	33	35.91	55	33.37	51	33.92	24	35.95

Source: Chicago Board of Education, *Annual Directory,* 1940-41, pp. 52-203.

population trends explained the ghetto's deteriorating or inferior status in resource allocation. Black youngsters and their disadvantaged white counterparts attended classes in buildings of approximately equal quality. But the large gap in funding that developed between blacks and low status whites could only have resulted from racial bias. In a large institution like the Chicago public schools, discrimination stemmed not from any one official or policy directive but from a variety of individual decisions. White teachers who transferred out of ghetto classrooms, administrators who allocated staff and money, and Board of Education members who supervised the system each helped make ghetto schools unequal as well as separate.

School overcrowding was yet another problem for black Chicagoans between the world wars. Matching classroom accommodations with student enrollment was a vexing task, for administrators had to balance many factors, most of which were beyond their control. Seating capacity depended upon previously erected facilities, new construction money, curricular needs, and class-size standards. Demand for space fluctuated with birth rates, immigration to and emigration from the city, length of pupils' stay in school, reliance on private education, and neighborhood change. When more children than local schools could hold lived in an area, officials could not always simply shift pupils to another district. Overcrowding frequently engulfed so many schools that even massive transfers might not bring the nearest empty seats within walking distance. Even when nearby buildings had space available, transfers or boundary changes could touch off racial, ethnic, or religious conflict. For instance, a district superintendent on the city's West Side once reported that he could not fill unused rooms because "the Jewish children will not, if they can possibly evade it, come to a school where Bohemian children predominate." Even in the absence of ethnic or color prejudice, authorities disliked moving youngsters from one school to another because it confused the public and sometimes provoked charges of favoritism. Administrators therefore usually preferred to cope with overcrowding without changing a school's attendance area.[12]

One way to deal with overflow enrollments was to rent facilities and adapt them to classroom use. Since the nineteenth century, the Board of Education had rented "churches, barnes [*sic*], club-houses, grocery stores, amusement halls, and almost anything else with a roof above it which doesn't leak." While the proportion of students attending classes in such quarters was apparently lower during the interwar years than it had been earlier, rented classrooms were still necessary in some parts of Chicago. For example, in 1941, some children assigned to Doolittle School, which had 1,782 seats for 2,500 pupils, learned their lessons in

Table 5
Per Pupil Budget Appropriations by Size of Enrollment at Selected Chicago Public Elementary Schools, 1940

			Enrollment				
Group	1-399	400-599	600-799	800-999	1000-1199	1200+	Total
High status							
Salaries	$ 80.21	$ 60.17	$ 69.52	$65.64	$64.37	$58.72	$64.50
Supplies	2.51	2.23	2.40	2.46	2.42	2.35	2.40
Operations	25.66	20.45	22.81	20.78	17.36	17.08	19.60
Total	108.38	82.85	94.73	88.88	84.15	78.15	86.50
Low status							
Salaries	$ 70.73	$ 73.78	$ 70.86	$65.73	$66.61	$69.57	$69.94
Supplies	2.70	2.96	2.99	3.54	2.91	2.71	3.08
Operations	43.96	30.87	27.70	24.07	20.43	22.38	25.46
Total	117.39	107.61	101.55	93.34	89.95	94.66	98.48
Immigrant							
Salaries	$ 73.61	$ 69.23	$ 71.98	$68.87	$65.69	$64.37	$68.67
Supplies	2.56	2.99	2.92	2.97	2.93	2.53	2.82
Operations	30.74	31.75	28.08	20.75	20.18	17.82	23.06
Total	106.91	103.97	102.98	92.59	88.80	84.72	94.55
Black							
Salaries	—	$ 62.26	$ 58.06	$58.78	$55.23	$59.18	$58.98
Supplies	—	2.80	2.33	2.44	2.32	2.62	2.58
Operations	—	24.41	17.02	18.68	14.94	11.95	13.53
Total	—	89.47	77.41	79.90	71.59	73.75	75.09

Sources: Chicago Board of Education: *Annual Directory,* 1940-41, pp. 52-203; *Proceedings,* Jan. 1
1940, pp. 674-1010.

the meeting room of a recently completed federal housing project. A second, more common way to ease seat shortages was the portable school. As their name suggested, portables could be moved to districts needing additional classrooms and installed on playgrounds or vacant lots. Portables made school accommodations more flexible, for officials could readily add or remove the units as enrollments fluctuated. "School populations are ever changing," Board of Education president James B. McCahey explained in 1937. "The portable building gives us needed extra capacity while permanent needs are shaping." Introduced in 1905, portables numbered over 500 in the early 1920s. Thereafter, their numbers gradually declined, except for a temporary increase in the early thirties, and just seventy-eight remained in use throughout the city by 1938.[13]

Portables had a reputation for being unpleasant and unhealthy. Coal stoves heated the units, but they required periodic attention from teachers or students and did not warm the rooms evenly. A black journalist reported in 1936, "Students pointed out that those who sit near the huge stove get too much heat for comfort and concentration on their studies while those in the more distant parts of the room find it advisable to wear sweaters or other light garments for warmth." Furthermore, the portables, which youngsters called "dog houses," were poorly constructed. During one winter, the mother of a first-grader who attended class in a portable stated that "the children of his room gather to one side so that the snow will not blow through the old fashioned windows on them." Portables sometimes lacked modern blackboards and lighting fixtures, and when children needed a toilet, they had to go outside either to a regular building or to another portable. A reporter who visited the latter's "damp, dismal, smelly compartments" concluded that "the sanitary facilities are neither sanitary nor facilities in the technical sense."[14]

Their unsavory features made portables quite unpopular among the public. One black woman termed "those terrible portables . . . a menace to the health of the child and teacher." During the mid-thirties, blacks in Lilydale on the Far South Side blamed the movable units for tuberculosis among their children. In 1934, parents in Oakland, a white neighborhood on the South Side lakefront, attributed several pneumonia deaths to the despised portables. By this time, school officials, too, saw more harm than good in the wooden structures. In 1936, McCahey labeled the units "unsightly and inefficient" and admitted that "they penalized the needier students—the very ones who most needed healthy school conditions. Anemic, undernourished bodies in the draughty portables were easy prey to ever present disease germs." Two years later, a Board of Education report on the structures asserted, "Heating in them is not uniform, ventilation is nil, resistance to vermin is defective and the toilet facilities [are] mean and squalid."[15]

The third and most frequent method of coping with overflow enrollments within a district was to alter the scheduled school day in order to intensify building use. Several different plans accomplished this goal. Whereas children on regular schedules were in class from 9 a.m. to noon and from 1 to 3 p.m., students at the double school attended either from 8 a.m. to noon, or from noon to 4 p.m. Each classroom thus had two different groups of children per day and two different teachers as well. Instead of a five-hour school day, pupils at double schools were in session just four hours daily. An even more drastic plan was the double division or half-day division. Under this system, which was most common in the primary grades and was used on a class-by-class basis rather than by an entire school, children attended either from 9 a.m. to noon or from noon to 3 p.m. Pupils thereby lost 40 percent of the standard school day. Each room had two faculty members throughout the day, and they alternately conducted classes or helped their colleague.[16]

The rotary school was still another adaptation to large enrollments. Buildings on this plan used special-purpose rooms, such as gymnasia, assembly halls, and manual-training facilities, as homerooms for regular classes. Students moved from one room to another during the day, using space vacated by groups in gym or household arts. The rotary school system neither changed starting and finishing times nor deprived youngsters of hours in class. Its addition to seating capacity, however, was limited to the number of special rooms in a school building. Variations of these makeshift plans also existed, with some institutions operating a series of staggered shifts. Lack of precision in labeling makes it difficult to keep track of the changes. During the 1920s, "platoon plan" designated both the rotary and double school systems and by the late 1930s, "double shift" was sometimes used to mean both double schools and double-division classes.[17]

From the first years of the twentieth century into the mid-1920s, classroom overcrowding plagued many white districts in Chicago but was rare in black neighborhoods. Although the black population was growing, the number of black children of school age was relatively small. Moreover, the exodus of whites from the South Side helped prevent school crowding there. In the two wards with the largest numbers of blacks, no children attended school on half-day sessions in 1910. The six schools with the greatest concentration of black students had 805 vacant seats and no pupils in portables, rented buildings, or half-day sessions. Before World War I, overcrowding was worst on the immigrant-filled West, Southwest, and Northwest Sides. In 1914, one district superintendent testified that fifty-seven portables were in use at nine West Side schools, with some classes meeting in basements and hallways.[18]

During the early 1920s, overcrowding reached extreme levels in many white areas. Total public school enrollment in Chicago, which had already grown from 304,106 in the fall of 1910 to 410,768 in September, 1920, rose to 521,786 by September, 1926. Although the Board of Education finished twenty-seven additions and new buildings for elementary and high school students in white districts between 1920 and 1924, these projects were unable to house the unprecedented enrollment increases. Severe classroom seat shortages were the result. Between September, 1920, and September, 1924, the number of public elementary pupils attending portables, double schools, and half-day divisions jumped from 28,142 to 86,247, or 27 percent of all grade school students. Shortages were almost exclusively located in white neighborhoods of Chicago. In October, 1922, for example, twenty-eight elementary and fifteen high schools were operating on irregular schedules to accommodate excess enrollments. Of these forty-three institutions, only two elementary schools (Doolittle and Douglas) were predominantly black. Double schools at the elementary level were most common in immigrant areas on the West and Northwest Sides, while altered schedules in high schools were scattered throughout the city.[19]

School overcrowding and the Board of Education's response to it generated controversy among white Chicagoans in the mid-1920s. In 1923, an organization of club women from Hyde Park, Woodlawn, and South Shore denounced the staggered-shift relay system found in high schools, asserting, "We believe that dismissing the children at all hours of the day while many of their parents are working or are away from home, exposes them to the most injurious influences and is destructive of the morals of the community as a whole." The following year, a Near North Side alderman introduced a resolution in the City Council condemning portables. Parents in affluent neighborhoods like West Ridge and Hyde Park protested half-day sessions and other by-products of overcrowding. The attempt of school superintendent William McAndrew (1924-27) to implement the platoon system, a variation of the previously described rotary school, heated the atmosphere still further. Developed in Gary, Indiana, the platoon system used special-purpose classrooms more intensively and shifted some student time from academic subjects to manual training, art, and assembly programs. Organized labor, teachers' groups, and the City Council opposed the plan, which Margaret Haley of the Chicago Teachers Federation termed "the factory system carried into the public school." Critics charged that the platoon system undermined quality education by placing production-line efficiency above academic achievement.[20]

The overcrowding controversy among white Chicagoans, although intense, was short-lived. In the late 1920s, pupil enrollment and seating capacity in white areas began to become better balanced. On one hand, a surge of construction eliminated the need for double and rotary schools in many districts. Between 1925 and 1928, Board of Education contractors completed seventy-seven new schools and additions in white sections. The annual average of nineteen finished projects nearly quadrupled the pace of the previous five years. Meanwhile, enrollment growth began to diminish. Whereas the annual increase in total public school population had averaged 18,500 from 1920 to 1926, over the following five years the yearly gain averaged only 5,000. In fact, elementary enrollment grew by just 1,600 between 1926 and 1928 and declined thereafter. Overcrowding still occurred in high schools and in some white elementary districts, but it was not a severe citywide problem for the rest of the interwar period. Meanwhile, the platoon system, rendered unnecessary by reduced enrollment gains, received its death warrant when Mayor Thompson drove McAndrew out of office after returning to City Hall in 1927.[21]

While overcrowding and its remedies were capturing the attention of white Chicagoans, classroom shortages were not a problem in most of the black ghetto. Significantly, the black press criticized segregation and antiquated facilities in the 1920s but rarely, if ever, mentioned school overcrowding. To be sure, black enrollment was growing rapidly. As stated in chapter 2, Negro school attendance in Chicago rose from 12,299 in 1920 to 33,856 in 1930, with about nine-tenths of the children enrolled in the public schools. But the departure of whites from blocks in and near areas of black settlement left vacant seats in classrooms for black students to fill. In addition, from 1925 through 1930, the Board of Education completed one new school (Shoop) and six additions in the ghetto. Accordingly, overcrowding was not serious in black districts for most of the decade. Just one black double school existed in 1920 and two in 1922. Although there were six in 1923, the number of double schools in black districts fell back to two in 1925 and remained unchanged for the next three years.[22]

Eventually, however, steadily increasing enrollments in the ghetto began to overwhelm school accommodations. Whereas there had been hundreds of extra seats in classrooms with sizeable black enrollments before World War I, these seats were taken by the early part of the Depression. When George Strayer and his associates surveyed school facilities in September, 1931, they found 168 vacant rooms in sixty-eight elementary buildings scattered throughout the city. Only four rooms in two schools were in predominantly black areas, Smyth on the Near West Side and Shoop in Morgan Park. Not a single school in the South Side ghetto had a surplus classroom. Many of these schools, however, had too few classrooms, and they were among the 167 Chicago elementary schools with a total shortage of 601 rooms. While the number of double schools at the elementary level in Chicago had fallen to between ten and twenty by 1931, the number of black elementary double schools had increased to four. As for high schools, while Phillips had 1,500 more pupils than seats, it was not unique. Twenty-two of the twenty-four public high schools lacked sufficient classrooms. The average deficiency was 1,674 seats, with seven schools having shortages of 2,000 to 5,300. In sum, by the early 1930s, the pattern of overcrowding had changed considerably. Whereas black districts formerly had fewer seat shortages than white neighborhoods, by 1931, black high schools were as likely and black elementary schools were more likely to be overcrowded than comparable white institutions.[23]

School population trends that began in the late twenties gathered momentum during the next decade. The decline in the number of white pupils was the most striking development. Public school enrollment, which reached an interwar peak of 547,057 in September, 1931, dropped steadily to 478,295 in the fall of 1940. Robert Havighurst estimates that the number of whites in the public system slipped 15 percent between 1930 and 1940, slightly exceeding the 13.2 percent loss in overall white school attendance in the city. The high school population, which had risen sharply until 1932, began to level off by the mid-thirties. The loss of white students, however, was concentrated in the elementary grades. Enrollment here fell from a high of 429,080 in 1928 to 315,045 in 1940, a decline of more than one-fourth. Reductions in both the birth rate and the number of people moving into the city accounted for the change. Enrollment losses did not occur evenly throughout white Chicago, however. The low status and immigrant areas identified earlier in this chapter had enrollment declines of 34.7 and 30.4 percent, respectively, between 1930 and 1940, but high status districts had a 1.3 percent gain. Nonetheless, the net result was less overcrowding for white children. By the mid-1930s, double schools were becoming rare in white neighborhoods. Although the Board of Education did convert several white institutions to double-shift schedules, this was usually done temporarily while officials were replacing old buildings with new ones. By the end of the period, only one white school in the city (Madison, in South Shore) operated on double shifts.[24]

Meanwhile, an entirely different pattern took shape in the ghetto. As mentioned in chapter 2, black school attendance in the city gained nearly 50 percent between 1930 and 1940, climbing from 33,856 to 50,670. At least nine-tenths of these youngsters enrolled in the public schools. While many of the new black students were Chicago-born children of migrants who had arrived from the South since 1915, others numbered among the 37,000 blacks who came during the Depression decade. In 1939, administrators surveyed twelve ghetto schools and discovered that more than one-fifth of the pupils had moved to Chicago from the South in the previous five years.[25]

Several features of ghetto life increased enrollments above levels predictable from the total black school-age population. First, blacks relied on the public schools more heavily than whites, many of whom attended church-related institutions. According to one study, 92 percent of the black Chicagoans in school in 1940 were enrolled in the public system, as compared with 72 percent of the whites. Second, since black teenagers had a difficult time finding jobs, especially during the Depression, they tended to remain in school longer than their white peers. In 1940, a Works Projects Administration report stated that the percentage of black youngsters attending school was higher than the figure for the foreign-born or for native-born persons of foreign or mixed parentage. The 1940 census showed that 45 percent of non-white Chicagoans age 17 through 19 attended school, as compared to 41 percent of the whites, a difference which increased enrollment at ghetto high schools. A third factor that caused black school overcrowding was the ghetto's high population density. Although during the Depression the number of black residents increased, the size of the ghetto did not. According to St. Clair Drake and Horace Cayton, black areas on the South Side had 90,000 people per square mile, while nearby white sections had only 20,000 residents per square mile. The impact of residential overcrowding was evident in ghetto classrooms.[26]

Moreover, black enrollments were growing faster than the supply of new facilities. The financial catastrophe of the Depression nearly halted school construction in the city during the early thirties. In 1931 and 1932, the Board of Education did manage to complete four elementary buildings, but each was in an exclusively white neighborhood. No schools were finished in 1933. In that year, the Roosevelt administration awarded the Chicago public schools the first of several Public Works Administration grants. A combination of federal grants and loans which reached more than $5,600,000 by December, 1936, enabled the school board to resume an active construction program. But while building funds poured into the city from Washington, the black ghetto got only a trickle. Of sixty-six projects completed between 1934 and

Table 6
Pupil Enrollment and Seating Capacity
at Selected Black Schools, 1939-41

School	Date	Enrollment	Capacity	Space shortage
Burke	1939	1,851	1,180	671
Carter	1940	1,600	1,100	500
Colman	1939	1,449	700	749
Doolittle	1939	2,243	1,620	623
Douglas	1939	2,562	1,740	822
Farren	1939	2,061	1,660	401
Felsenthal	1939	1,537	940	597
Forestville	1939	3,564	2,620	944
McCosh	1939	1,606	1,340	266
Willard	1940	2,600	2,000	600
Du Sable High	1941	4,000	2,400	1,600
Phillips High	1941	3,600	1,500	2,100
Total		28,673	18,800	9,873

Sources: *Chicago's Schools,* 6 (Oct., 1939), 3, and 6 (Feb., 1940), 4; *Chicago Daily News,* July 30, 1941, Newsclipping Series, Box 11, Chicago Teachers Union Papers, Chicago Historical Society; "Notes on 1940 School Budget at Hearings of January 10, 1940," Mary Herrick Papers, Chicago Historical Society.

1940, just seven were located in black districts. Four were additions to existing buildings; the others were Du Sable High, Dunbar Vocational, and a grade school in Lilydale. The proportion of new or enlarged facilities blacks received equalled their share of the system's total enrollment. But in view of the ghetto's needs, the Board of Education was miserly with the black community.[27]

By 1940, the black belt was the only area of Chicago with sustained school overcrowding. Although overall pupil-teacher ratios were declining, residents in a number of black districts complained of large classes. One mother reported in 1938 that classes at Colman Elementary averaged forty-five pupils. Three years later, the executive secretary of the Citizens Schools Committee stated that Doolittle had forty-six to fifty-four students per class in the grades and sixty to seventy in the kindergarten. The population of ghetto schools far exceeded the available space, as table 6 demonstrates. Authorities provided for the overflow mainly by altering schedules. Double schools were becoming rare in white neighborhoods, but the number in the ghetto climbed from four in 1931, to seven in 1936, and to thirteen in 1940. By the latter date, all but one double-shift school in the city were predominantly black. According to George McCray, three-quarters of the children at black elementary schools on the South Side spent 20 to 40 percent fewer hours in class than did their counterparts in white areas. To make matters worse, overcrowding seemed to be becoming permanent. In 1940, A. L. Foster, executive secretary of the Chicago Urban League, complained, "My own boy, in the seventh grade, has never gone to school a full day."[28]

Overcrowded schools crippled the ghetto by seriously damaging the quality of public education. Principals often had to use assembly halls or other ill-suited accommodations as regular classrooms. After visiting Du Sable High in 1938, a reporter noted, "Classes are now held in assembly halls, store rooms, lunch rooms, corridors, special gymnasium, and ante rooms to the faculty lavatories." Even where children occupied conventional classrooms, their academic progress suffered in overcrowded buildings. Youngsters in double schools and half-day divisions had three or four hours of school daily instead of the normal five. As one parent put it, "This condition . . . robs the children of adequate education to which every child is entitled." Instructors could neither give additional assistance to the many pupils with learning difficulties nor provide average and above-average students with the learning opportunities they needed. "The child is not in school long enough to assimilate the requisite knowledge," a black journalist explained. "In such an undesirable situation reading habit, attention, concentration and discipline are lost. The learning process is interrupted." The playwright Lorraine Hansberry illustrated the effects of the double shift when she recalled her student days at Ross Elementary. The teachers lacked time for all the standard subjects, so they often neglected mathematics. "One result is that—to this day—I cannot count properly. I do not add, subtract or multiply with ease," Hansberry wrote. "The mind which was able to grasp university level reading materials in the sixth and seventh grades had not been sufficiently exposed to elementary arithmetic to make even simple change in a grocery store."[29]

School overcrowding also hurt both youth and the community as a whole by offering double-shift students too many chances to get into trouble. Observers pointed out that the shift system made it easy for pupils to become truants. A white woman's club officer testified, "Any child on the street at any hour of the day can explain his presence by saying, 'I went to school this morning,' or in the morning, 'I go to school in the afternoon.'" Even youngsters who were dutiful about attending classes had, in the words of the civic leader Irene McCoy

Gaines, "a half day in school and a half day on the street." Children from households that had no adult home during the day spent their afternoons or mornings without supervision. Half-day sessions, grumbled one South Sider, allowed boys and girls "time to learn all kinds of devilment." Children barred from school by seat shortages passed their time on street corners, in adult entertainment establishments, and in unchaperoned apartments. "We have seen dozens of boys in gangs traveling the streets for want of anything else to do," a black newspaper columnist reported. "Naturally they get into mischief." Journalists, Urban League personnel, and PTA leaders blamed shortened school hours for the ghetto's high incidence of youth crime. As Alderman Earl B. Dickerson asked rhetorically in 1941, "Is it any wonder that our juvenile delinquency rate is one of the highest in the country?"[30]

Finally, double schools and half-day divisions took their toll on faculty members, too. The hurried pace, large classes, and makeshift facilities discouraged instructors already inclined to leave black districts. A South Side parent wrote in 1938 that overcrowding "creates an unfair burden for the teachers who are handicapped with a too heavy teacher load and insufficient time to emphasize the mastery of reading, writing and other school subjects, because they cannot reach that number of children on a half-day schedule." The *Defender* was even more emphatic. "The double shift is contrary to sound educational practice, especially where the teaching load is so excessive as to make effective instruction and individual attention prohibitive." Reporting the huge seat shortages at Du Sable High School, the paper concluded, "It is obviously impossible for teachers to do effective work under such revolting circumstances. In fact they cannot teach at all in an atmosphere that is repugnant to teacher and pupil alike." Overcrowding undoubtedly helped demoralize black instructors and push white ones out of the ghetto and into neighborhoods that would provide a better chance for job satisfaction.[31]

By the eve of World War II, the community that had praised the local schools a generation earlier was brimming with anger and disillusionment. "Every time I think of children going to school in double shifts I get mad," a black woman exclaimed in 1940. "Don't our children need as much time in school as the white ones?" A month earlier, George McCray inquired, "What answer does the thoughtful Chicago citizen have as he faces this criminal neglect and segregation of Negro children in overcrowded, part-time public schools?" A *Defender* journalist wrote, "You wonder if the board of education is not willfully negligent or if it is not actually conspiring to retard the progress of this community." Black migrants who hoped to enhance their family's educational opportunities by moving North must have regarded the Chicago schools during the

Depression with mixed emotions. In 1938, a resident of the Douglas district, calculating that pupils on double-shift schedules were in class for fewer hours than children in the rural South, asked, "I want to know what it is all about. Why have these folks come here to get better schooling?" No one answered her question.[32]

NOTES

1. *Chicago Defender,* Sept. 28, 1912, p. 1, Apr. 19, 1913, p. 4, June 17, 1914, p. 1, Sept. 11, 1915, p. 8, Mar. 22, 1924, sec. 1, p. 3, July 12, 1924, sec. 1, p. 5.

2. Charles S. Johnson, "Source Material for Patterns of Negro Segregation: Chicago, Illinois" (working memorandum for Gunnar Myrdal, *An American Dilemma*), p. 4; *Defender,* Dec. 23, 1939, p. 8.

3. City of Chicago, *Journal of the Proceedings of the City Council,* Jan. 2, 1923, p. 1627, June 24, 1931, pp. 490-91; *Defender,* Mar. 21 and 28, 1936, pp. 1-2, Apr. 4, 1936, pp. 1, 17, Apr. 18, 1936, p. 7, June 13, 1936, p. 15, Sept. 16, 1936, p. 22, June 18, 1938, p. 18, Dec. 10, 1938, p. 2. For events in the Lilydale, Phillips, and Ross districts, see chapter 5.

4. George D. Strayer, *Report of the Survey of the Schools of Chicago, Illinois* (New York, 1932), IV, 13-15; Mary Josephine Herrick, "Negro Employees of the Chicago Board of Education" (M.A. thesis, University of Chicago, 1931), pp. 93-108; Chicago Board of Education, *Annual Directory,* 1940-41, pp. 54-203; Charles Predmore, "The Administration of Negro Education in the Northern Elementary School," *School and Society,* 39 (June 9, 1934), 753.

5. Homer Davis, *Chicago Building Survey* (Chicago, 1924), pp. 67-70; Strayer, *Report,* IV, 16-20.

6. Chicago Board of Education, *Proceedings,* Feb. 11, 1920, pp. 1312, 1315, June 14, 1922, p. 1160, Mar. 11, 1925, p. 842.

7. John A. Winget, "Teacher Inter-School Mobility Aspirations: Elementary Teachers, Chicago Public School System, 1947-48" (Ph.D. diss., University of Chicago, 1952), pp. 134, 138-77, 198-217; Edward E. Keener, interview, Chicago, Nov., 1969; Earl B. Dickerson, interview, Chicago, Dec., 1969. See also Howard S. Becker, "Role and Career Problems of the Chicago Public School Teacher" (Ph.D. diss., University of Chicago, 1951), pp. 183-84, 190, 195, 307. Winget's findings actually understate the transfer rate in black schools, since he counted only white female teachers applying for transfers.

8. Ruth Dunbar, "Memo re Negroes in Education" (unpublished paper, n.d., Chicago Sun-Times library); Miriam Wagenschein, "'Reality Shock': A Study of Beginning Elementary School Teachers" (M.A. thesis, University of Chicago, 1950), p. 36; *Defender,* June 3, 1939, p. 6, Dec. 23, 1939, p. 8.

9. Board of Education: *Annual Directory,* 1940-41, pp. 52-203; *Proceedings,* Jan. 10, 1940, pp. 674-1010.

10. Samuel B. Stratton, interview, Chicago, Oct. and Nov., 1969; Ethel M.

Hilliard, interview, Chicago, Nov., 1969; Mary Herrick, interview, Chicago, Nov., 1969; Dunbar, "Memo re Negroes in Education."

11. Board of Education, *Annual Directory,* 1920-21, pp. 51-184, 1930-31, pp. 65-230, 1940-41, pp. 52-203.

12. Board of Education, *Proceedings,* Oct. 14, 1914, pp. 338-39.

13. *Chicago Tribune,* Oct. 11, 1896, pp. 41-42, Sept. 26, 1937, Pt. 3, p. 9W; Jean Everhard Fair, "The History of Public Education in the City of Chicago, 1894-1914" (M.A. thesis, University of Chicago, 1939), pp. 27-28; *Defender,* Dec. 6, 1941, p. 26; Mabel P. Simpson, "Leaders Make Recommendations for Help for Negro Schools before School Opens This Fall" [1941], Mary Herrick Papers, Chicago Historical Society; Henry Evert Dewey, "The Development of Public School Administration in Chicago" (Ph.D. diss., University of Chicago, 1937), p. 49; Board of Education, *Proceedings,* Mar. 27, 1929, p. 1139; Board of Education, *Chicago Public Schools,* prepared for National Association of Public School Business Officials, Oct. 10-14, 1938, p. 24.

14. *Tribune,* Sept. 11, 1932, sec. 7, p. 2SB; *Defender,* Feb. 8, 1936, pp. 1, 3, Feb. 22, 1936, p. 10.

15. *Defender,* Sept. 19, 1936, p. 7; *Hyde Park Herald,* Feb. 2, 1934, p. 1; *Tribune,* Sept. 12, 1936, p. 15; Board of Education, *Chicago Public Schools,* p. 65.

16. Board of Managers, Chicago Woman's Club, "Even a Portable May Be Better Than Half-Day Divisions, Double Schools, and Staggered Shifts," April 4, 1939, Mary Herrick Papers; Board of Education, *Annual Directory,* 1940-41, p. 204; *Chicago's Schools,* 5 (Apr. 1939), 1; Margaret L. Hancock, "Graphic Representation of Various Types of Organization Found in Chicago's Elementary Schools" [1945], Mary Herrick Papers; Davis, *Chicago Building Survey,* p. 8.

17. Davis, *Chicago Building Survey,* p. 9; Harold Boyne Lamport, "A Study of School Building Needs in a Section of Chicago" (M.A. thesis, University of Chicago, 1923), pp. 57, 59; Chicago Woman's Club, "Even a Portable May Be Better"; George S. Counts, *School and Society in Chicago* (New York, 1928), pp. 116, 178; *Proceedings of the City Council,* Nov. 24, 1926, p. 4776.

18. The six black schools used here were Colman, Douglas, Farren, Keith, Moseley, and Raymond. Board of Education, *Proceedings,* July 20, 1910, p. 19, Apr. 20, 1910, p. 772; Allan H. Spear, *Black Chicago: The Making of a Negro Ghetto, 1890-1920* (Chicago, 1967), p. 15; Board of Education: *Annual Report,* 59 (1912-13), 168-69; *Proceedings,* Oct. 14, 1914, pp. 337-40.

19. Board of Education: *School Facts,* 1 (June 18, 1930), 4; *Annual Report,* 1940-41, pp. 537-38; *Annual Directory,* 1940-41, pp. 29-203; *Proceedings,* Oct. 11, 1922, pp. 630-31, Mar. 27, 1929, p. 1139.

20. Board of Education, *Proceedings,* Mar. 7, 1923, p. 1192; *Proceedings of the City Council,* Feb. 13, 1924, p. 1864, Nov. 24, 1926, p. 4776, Jan. 28, 1928, p. 2066; *Tribune,* Sept. 30, 1928, pp. N1, N5; *Hyde Park Herald,* Sept. 7, 1928, p. 1; Raymond E. Callahan, *Education and the Cult of Efficiency* (Chicago, 1962), pp. 128-47; Lawrence A. Cremin, *The Transformation of the School: Progressivism in American Education, 1876-1957* (New York, 1961), pp. 154-60; Counts, *School and Society,* pp. 99, 116, 177-83; *Chicago Schools Journal,* 5 (Mar., 1923), 280.

21. Board of Education: *Annual Directory,* 1940-41, pp. 29-203; *Annual*

Report, 1940-41, pp. 537-38; *School Facts,* 1 (June 18, 1930), 4; Mary J. Herrick, *The Chicago Schools: A Social and Political History* (Beverly Hills, Calif., 1971), pp. 165-72.

22. Robert J. Havighurst, *The Public Schools of Chicago* (Chicago, 1964), p. 54; Board of Education, *Annual Directory,* 1940-41, pp. 29-203; Chicago Commission on Race Relations, *The Negro in Chicago: A Study of Race Relations and a Race Riot* (Chicago, 1922), p. 244; Board of Education, *Proceedings,* 1919-28.

23. Strayer, *Report,* IV, 24-29, 35.

24. Board of Education, *Annual Report,* 1940-41, pp. 537-38; Havighurst, *Public Schools,* p. 54; U.S. Department of Commerce, Bureau of the Census, *Fifteenth Census, 1930: Population,* II (Washington, 1933), pp. 743, 1147; U.S. Department of Commerce, Bureau of the Census, *Sixteenth Census of the United States, 1940: Population,* IV, Pt. 2 (Washington, 1943), p. 629; Strayer, *Report,* IV, 46-48; Board of Education, *Annual Directory,* 1930-31, pp. 65-230, 1940-41, pp. 52-203, 1936-37, p. 217; Board of Education, *Proceedings,* Feb. 26, 1936, p. 978, Nov. 5, 1936, p. 276, Jan. 13, 1937, p. 505, Apr. 20, 1938, p. 1423, Sept. 28, 1938, p. 240; "Background Material for Recommendations of Education Commission of Mayor's Committee on Race Relations, 1945, re districting and use of school facilities," Mary Herrick Papers.

25. *Fifteenth Census: Population,* II, 743, 1147; *Sixteenth Census: Population,* IV, Pt. 2, 629; Havighurst, *Public Schools,* p. 54; Otis Dudley Duncan and Beverly Duncan, *The Negro Population of Chicago: A Study of Residential Succession* (Chicago, 1957), p. 34; *Tribune,* June 4, 1939, sec. 1, p. 18.

26. Havighurst, *Public Schools,* p. 54; St. Clair Drake, *Churches and Voluntary Associations in the Chicago Negro Community* (Chicago, 1940), p. 168; *Sixteenth Census: Population,* IV, Pt. 2, 629; St. Clair Drake and Horace R. Cayton, *Black Metropolis: A Study of Negro Life in a Northern City* (New York, 1945), p. 204; *Defender,* Sept. 16, 1939, p. 6.

27. Board of Education: *Annual Directory,* 1940-41, pp. 29-203; *Our Public Schools* (Chicago [1937]), p. 39; *Chicago Public Schools,* pp. 67-72; *Proceedings,* Sept. 28, 1936, p. 179, Oct. 20, 1937, p. 246, Jan. 12, 1938, p. 1060, Nov. 30, 1938, p. 414, Aug. 20, 1939, p. 115, Oct. 4, 1939, p. 239, Sept. 6, 1940, p. 142.

28. *Defender,* June 18, 1938, p. 18; Simpson, "Leaders Make Recommendations"; Board of Education, *Proceedings,* 1931-40; Commission on Intercommunity Relationships of the Hyde Park-Kenwood Council of Churches and Synagogues, "The Negro Problems of the Community to the West" (typewritten report, Chicago, 1940), p. 16; Board of Education, *Annual Directory,* 1940-41, p. 204; George F. McCray, "Jim Crow Goes to School," *The Record Weekly,* Dec. 9, 1939, Chicago Teachers Union Papers, Newsclipping Series, Box 10, Chicago Historical Society; *Chicago's Schools,* 6 (Feb., 1940), 4.

29. *Defender,* June 4, 1938, p. 2, June 18, 1938, p. 18, Nov. 5, 1938, p. 1; Robert Nemiroff, ed., *To Be Young, Gifted and Black: Lorraine Hansberry in Her Own Words* (Englewood Cliffs, N.J., 1969), pp. 35-36.

30. Stenographic Report of Public Hearing on the Proposed 1941 Budget of the Board of Education of the City of Chicago, Jan 10, 1941, pp. 40, 119-20, Mary Herrick Papers; Alonzo J. Bowling, "Report on Chicago Schools," Jan., 1939, in "The Negro in Illinois," Illinois Writers Project;

Chicago's Schools, 5 (Feb.-Mar., 1941), 1; *Defender,* May 17, 1924, sec. 1, p. 14, June 4, 1938, p. 2, Jan. 14, 1939, p. 1, Sept. 21, 1940, p. 4, Feb. 22, 1941, p. 6.

31. *Defender,* June 4, 1938, p. 2, June 18, 1938, p. 18, Oct. 22, 1938, p. 1.

32. *Ibid.,* June 4, 1938, p. 2, June 25, 1938, p. 18, Dec. 23, 1939, p. 8, Jan. 13, 1940, p. 14.

CHAPTER FOUR

Home, Community, and Classroom

MANY BLACK CHICAGOANS during the 1910s and early 1920s viewed schooling as the key to individual and group advancement. Newspaper headlines proclaimed, "Education Most Important Thing in Life," and editorials announced, "Education is the secret of all successes." In 1919, the founders of the *Chicago Whip* asserted, "The masses are beginning to hunger for the only permanent and effective remedy to cure and prevent human ills — education." Black publicists regarded academic training as a weapon in the unending struggle among races and ethnic groups. "Watch your Irish and Hebrew competitors," the *Defender* admonished its readers in 1921. "When they miss out in the day school you will find them in night school or business school." A journalist added, "The Caucasian race rules because it uses brains, not brawn." According to these leaders, education was also the pathway to personal success, for society was a color-blind meritocracy in which the deserving prospered. *Defender* publisher Robert Abbott advised, "That time-worn cry that there is no room at the top for an educated black man or woman is all rot. Push, energy, brains and plenty of them tell." At the start of the interwar period, the gospel of success through education was popular among both old settlers and migrants. In 1920, a Phillips High School student told a classmate, "You better stay in school while you can. . . . if you get an education there ain't no chance for the white people to take it away."[1]

By the 1930s, however, this optimism had waned. To be sure, the Great Depression washed away much of black Chicago's romanticism about the powers of schooling. But two permanent developments also shattered the earlier boundless faith in public education. First, between 1915 and 1930, the ghetto matured, and its many social problems handicapped black education. Second, the school system itself shortchanged ghetto children. Not only was black education segregated, overcrowded, and inadequately funded by the 1930s, but within the classroom instructors often treated black children badly and steered them into courses that reinforced their race's lowly position in society. Classroom racism, overburdened families, and ghetto social ills combined to make black schools poor vehicles for upward mobility.

Home and family accounted for so much of students' aspirations and academic performances that any account of ghetto education would be incomplete without attention to black households. Perhaps the tendency for teachers and administrators to stress students' home backgrounds was partly an effort to avoid responsibility for failures in the classroom. Nevertheless, poverty, disease, overcrowding, and transiency left such indelible marks on black schools that even educators' best efforts could not have erased their impact.

Low-paying jobs and unemployment kept most black Chicago families in poverty between the wars. Despite the economic growth of World War I and the 1920s, black workers remained concentrated in menial occupations that offered few opportunities for advancement. Although only one of every seven white workers in Chicago in 1930 toiled in unskilled labor or domestic or personal service, nearly three-fifths of black jobholders were employed in these categories. The Great Depression was even more devastating in black Chicago than it was in white neighborhoods. Early in 1931, three-fifths of the black women and four-ninths of the black men were unemployed. Four years later, whereas 13.7 percent of all Chicago families were on relief, 46 percent of the black families were receiving public assistance. As late as 1940, more than 36 percent of the black labor force either earned a living from government relief projects or was out of work entirely. Studies of individual black school districts further documented the desperate conditions in the ghetto. At Keith Elementary and at Phillips Junior High in the early thirties, nearly half the children came from families relying on public aid or private charities. In 1939, the principal of Smyth School on the chronically impoverished Near West Side reported, "A great majority of the families are supported by relief or WPA. The number of privately employed parents is negligible." Because fathers and mothers fortunate enough to have jobs usually were servants, porters, and laborers, even many working families could barely meet their basic needs.[2]

Although children growing up in homes plagued by poverty and unemployment did not always do poorly in school, they did enter the classroom with certain disadvantages. Low-income families could not afford the toys and games, books and magazines, travel, and other luxuries that expanded a child's horizons. Moreover, adults demoralized by demeaning jobs or by fruitless searches for work found it difficult to summon the strength to inspire their children to excel in school. Finally, youngsters surrounded by hardship might doubt that schooling was a way to escape the slums. Everyone knew of the college-educated red-caps and the girls who finished high school only to become maids and laundry workers.

Typical ghetto families were not merely poor; they were relatively un-educated as well. Among black Chicagoans eighteen years of age or older in 1934, only a quarter of the men and a third of the women had gone be-yond the eighth grade. While this was better than the city's white immi-grants did, blacks trailed far behind native whites, half of whom had more than an elementary education. Whereas whites born in the United States had a median 9.3 years of schooling, the figure for black adults was only 7.5 years. In just one predominantly black census tract, locat-ed in West Woodlawn, did the median grade completed exceed the city-wide level for native whites. While some parents who had scant schooling themselves showed little interest in it for their children, even mothers and fathers who wanted their youngsters to do well academically could rarely provide the appropriate help. As the principal of Smyth Elementary put it in 1939, "We cannot depend upon parental cooperation because even those parents who wish to co-operate do not usually know how." This principal was among several observers who noted that lower-class blacks tended to rely on physical punishment to solve educational prob-lems. One southern migrant beat his daughter because she was unable to read. "She was doing very well in kindergarten," a social agency reported in 1930, "but ignorant himself, he was determined she should have 'learnin' and he thought she was merely stubborn."[3]

Poor, ill-educated households had relatively little reading matter. At Keith Elementary in the thirties, nearly half the children questioned reported having fewer than ten books at home, and almost three-fifths said that they did not borrow books from school or public libraries. While a majority of pupils did receive a daily newspaper in their homes, only three in eight came from families with magazines available. Where reading was not a routine activity, children were more likely to progress slowly in school. Before beginning classes, these youngsters would not have learned the relationship between spoken and written language derived from the simplest illustrated storybooks. Moreover, girls and boys who had not become familiar with books during their preschool years would take longer to master the structure or patterns of the printed page. A lack of reading in the home could also have more lasting effects. The child who did not see parents and brothers and sisters reading regularly would have good reason to regard reading as a classroom task unrelated to what one did outside the schoolhouse. Such a boy or girl would not start out viewing reading as enjoyable or useful and, as a result, would be less apt to be an able student.[4]

Poverty and ignorance also impaired the health of many ghetto children. Residents of Chicago's South Side, like those in black communities elsewhere, suffered from pneumonia, venereal disease, and other ailments far more often than did whites. For example, the South Side led the city in tuberculosis cases during the 1930s; in 1939-41, the TB death rate of Chicago blacks was more than five times that of local whites. Nutrition was another problem. Pupils often skipped meals, and those they ate contained too many sweets and starchy foods and not enough milk, fresh fruit, and fresh vegetables. Schools tried to repair some of their students' dietary deficiencies through a penny lunch program introduced at three inner-city schools in 1910-11. Officials extended the service to seventy-four schools throughout Chicago by 1937, including many black ones. The economic crisis of the Depression intensified chronic nutritional deficiencies. In October, 1930, a South Side teacher reported that one-third of Moseley's students could not afford lunch. "There are a number every day who tell us there is no food in the house," she wrote. Many pupils, she added, were "anemic and under-weight from lack of nourishment." In Moseley and in other ghetto districts, faculty members, local businessmen, and other individuals raised funds to buy lunches for poor children. Though both the penny lunch and voluntary efforts helped relieve some suffering, many black youngsters continued to be hungry and malnourished. Under such conditions, children's classroom performance faltered, despite the best intentions of teacher and student.[5]

Housing problems also reduced academic achievement in black schools. Blacks' residential confinement to the ghetto produced acute overcrowding. Frequently, two families "doubled up" or shared a single household, while in other cases people took in lodgers to help defray expenses. Often owners divided older homes or apartments formerly occupied by whites into smaller units, such as the notorious one-room "kitchenettes." Where many people lived in a small space, youngsters lacked quiet and privacy. Children in such homes could not do schoolwork or educational projects of their own without distractions or interference. In 1940, a teacher at Keith Elementary described the consequences of ghetto housing for her pupils. "Even at home these little people are uncomfortable," she wrote. "Families of ten are often crowded into three rooms. . . . As a result [the children] are nervous, insecure, and always on the defensive—ready to fight." Transiency was another housing problem that left its mark upon black schools. Within census tracts half or more Negro in 1934, 39 percent of the families had lived at their current address less than one year and 53 percent for less than two years. In one black Chicago elementary school, only slightly over half of the pupils enrolled in September, 1924, were there the following June. When parents moved from one school district to another in search of cheaper, larger, or better-maintained housing, their children faced personal and academic adjustments that could hurt their classroom performance. One observer asserted that students who switched schools did poorer work, adding, "In most cases transient children require a maximum of personal attention wherever they enroll." Where a large proportion of a class's membership changed within a school year, it was difficult for teachers to provide students with continuity in subject matter or teaching style.[6]

Children from broken families found poverty, poor education, overcrowding, and transiency even more difficult to handle. Whereas 13 percent of native white families had no father in the household according to the 1930 census, about 20 percent of the city's black families were fatherless. As studies of individual black school districts revealed, however, broken families were more common when school-age children were involved. In the early 1930s in Keith Elementary and Phillips Junior High samples, four of every nine children did not live with both parents. At Du Sable High in the mid-thirties, one-third of freshmen questioned lived with neither parent or without their father. While experts differed over the impact of single-parent households on children, many feared that the situation created psychological and educational handicaps for many boys and girls.[7]

One such difficulty, which existed in both single-parent and two-parent households, was lack of adult supervision in many homes. During the 1920s and 1930s, between 40 and 50 percent of black women with school-aged children held jobs outside the home. While in some instances, a relative or another adult was present during the day to provide guidance, this was not the case in numerous households. Educators believed that lack of adult supervision impaired children's home life and school progress. For one thing, parents whose jobs monopolized their time during the day could not arrange conferences with teachers at school. About 1920, some instructors in black neighborhoods complained that frequently they "could get no co-operation from the mother, as she was never free to come to school to talk over matters affecting the child." Moreover, school-age children of working parents often had to care for themselves and for younger brothers and sisters as well. One mother who left home at 6:30 each morning to work at a laundry had her son and daughter stay out of school on alternate days to look after younger children in the family. With both parents absent, boys and girls were left with the responsibility for waking up on time, getting their own breakfasts, and arriving at school at the assigned hour. Referring to a seven-year-old who came to school late each day, a teacher explained, "His mother went to work early every morning and left him and his brother to get up and get to school unaided." While many youngsters cared for themselves reliably, contemporaries argued that the independence of black urban youth was not salutory. A 1932 account of ghetto young people concluded, "Too many Negro children are deprived of that parental guidance and care which the normal home should provide and their training apart from the formal education of the public schools is secured away from home in the questionable atmosphere of the city streets." Numerous boys and girls, the writer worried, received "a fortuitous education in the chance contacts of poolrooms and dance halls, speakeasies and gambling houses."[8]

That many of black Chicago's children were also immigrants from the South compounded their other economic and social handicaps. Thrust into a different culture, these newcomers often had difficulty adjusting to northern classrooms. Since migrant children in Chicago schools were used to the deference demanded of them by southern racial etiquette, they were sometimes shy and hesitant around whites. As early as 1906, Fannie Barrier Williams had noticed the difference between Chicago natives and "these timid little recruits from below the Ohio." The former were sure of themselves and interacted freely with white classmates. Not so for southern youngsters: "Their timidity and fear growing out of their inherited reverence for a white complexion is very pathetic," Williams observed. "There is little or no spirit of self-assertion." During World War I, an instructor at Farren Elementary confirmed that southern pupils "have a distinct and decided fear of the white teacher and it's up to the teacher to change this fear into respect." A black woman who had arrived in Chicago during the war at age twelve recalled years later her "inferiority complex" upon beginning school in a mostly white neighborhood. She remembered, "Sometimes in class I refused to answer questions that I really knew and also refused to participate in any sort of class discussion." Some children, on the other hand, compensated by lashing out at teachers or classmates. A Negro faculty member explained that the black migrant met resentment from both whites and longtime black residents. "No wonder he meets a word with a blow," she concluded.[9]

While most youngsters made the necessary psychological adjustments after living in the North for several years, overcoming weak academic backgrounds could take much longer. Since compulsory education laws were poorly enforced in the rural South, and since families needed sons and daughters to work on the farm, many southern children who came to Chicago had not attended school regularly. Youngsters who lived far from school or lacked money for clothes and supplies often missed classes. Furthermore, in black schools of the South, terms were short, teachers poorly trained, and buildings ill-equipped. Thus, even children keeping pace in Alabama or Georgia were undereducated by northern standards. Accordingly, the majority of southern pupils who enrolled in the Chicago schools were demoted, ususally by two to four grades. These children, who were overage for their grade in school, usually attended regular classes, where they received little individual attention and advanced only a year at a time, never reaching the norm for their age. The twelve-year-old second-grader or the seventeen-year-old eighth-grader was out of place socially and found the content of lessons inappropriate. These pupils sometimes became unruly, and more than a few dropped out of school as soon as possible.[10]

Some schools made special arrangements for southern migrants. During the early 1920s, Phillips High operated a prevocational department for students of secondary school age who were behind in their studies. Pupils took elementary courses and received training in typing, bookkeeping, cooking, woodworking, and mechanical drawing. At several elementary buildings, small ungraded rooms provided an opportunity for personalized instruction and rapid progress. At Doolittle, many of the teenagers in an ungraded room were illiterate when they first arrived, but within a year, they were doing fourth- to sixth-grade work. A teacher at Forestville, which maintained a similar program, explained, "Once they get started they learn very rapidly and often catch up to the proper grade if they are not too old when they start school." Instructors proudly reported many success stories. At Doolittle, a twelve-year-old boy who could not read or write when he came read sixty books the next year. A delighted teacher testified, "One big girl of thirteen, when she arrived from the South, pretended to read with her book upside down, but in a little more than a year she was doing sixth-grade work."[11]

Children of the ghetto were, in many ways, victims of circumstance. They were not to blame for the poverty, malnutrition, transiency, and family dislocation they so often endured. But these same burdens seemed to make some youngsters run afoul of authority, join gangs, use drugs, become sexually active, and commit petty crimes. Such behavior, which contemporaries labeled juvenile delinquency, undermined the public schools in several ways. Since youthful misadventures were more exciting and immediately satisfying than anything the schools could offer, children involved in such activities regarded life on the streets as more important than their studies; for them, formal education became peripheral or irrelevant. Sometimes, in the case of vandalism, theft, and attacks on students and teachers, the schools became direct targets of youthful crime in the ghetto. As with home and family conditions, juvenile delinquency showed that the schools were in some respects the captives of outside forces and had less power to shape their environment than educators would have liked.

School authorities and sociologists alike believed that truancy was "the first step toward initiation into a career of crime," as Superintendent of Schools William H. Johnson put it in 1937. In Chicago, while truancy was greatest among inner-city boys twelve to fifteen years old, blacks had far higher rates than whites. A study of the 5,159 males who appeared in juvenile court on truancy charges between 1917 and 1927 revealed that truancy was more than twice as frequent in the South Side ghetto north of Thirty-ninth Street as in comparably located white areas. In one Near West Side district in the late 1920s, investigators found thirty-five illiterate school-age blacks who had never enrolled in classes since moving to Chicago from the South. Blacks were seriously concerned about the truancy problem. In 1922, after a Negro journalist saw a number of black children in the downtown Loop during the school day, he declared, "Parents who allow their children of school age to run wild are responsible almost entirely for the thievery so common among the boys of the Race, and the average maintained by our boys in the lists of arrests for petty crimes is high." In 1938, a teacher worried, "Many children have so few hours in school due to the crowded condition of certain schools that they can ill afford to lose a single day except for a very good reason." The black press often accused parents of indifference about their children's school attendance. But the same newspapers also claimed that Board of Education truant officers enforced compulsory education laws more vigorously among whites than blacks. Because of the increasing number of double-shift schools in the ghetto and the lack of parental supervision in many black households, truancy continued unabated throughout the interwar period.[12]

Children who skipped school often became involved in stealing, personal violence, property damage, sexual activities, and other varieties of "incorrigibility." Like truancy, these offenses were rare in outlying parts of Chicago and most common in older, inner-city neighborhoods; among such areas, the South Side ghetto was the juvenile delinquency leader. Sociologists using juvenile court and probation officers' records in the 1920s learned that the portion of the black belt north of Thirty-ninth Street had the highest delinquency rates in the city for both boys and girls. Within the ghetto, however, delinquency was unevenly distributed, decreasing as one moved southward to the somewhat more prosperous areas into which blacks had recently moved.[13]

Sexual activity by ghetto teenagers was one diversion from school that disturbed black community leaders. In 1921, authorities apprehended several youths in the Webster Elementary district after what a journalist described as "a persistent campaign in the debauching of young girls." During the 1930s, one South Sider reported that Phillips High students utilized nearby rooming houses as "bawdy houses . . . a haven for indiscreet actions." School officials and civic leaders tried to prevent the installation of jukeboxes in apartments and houses near Phillips where "school children are induced to participate in questionable activities." Although attempts to halt teenage sex were futile, adults had good reason for concern. Statistics based on 1928-33 data showed the South Side black belt with the highest illegitimate birth rate of any section of the city. Moreover, World War II figures set the venereal disease rate among black Chicagoans twenty-five times above the number for the city's whites.[14]

Marijuana and alcohol were also more attractive than homework for some children. During the late 1930s, school authorities began to denounce marijuana usage among South Side pupils. In 1937, Chicago police conducted raids on "pleasure flats" and "dope dens" where students from several elementary and high schools gathered to buy "the dangerous dope weed." Authorities linked marijuana to truancy and narcotics and worried that use of the hallucinogen was increasing. The chief of the police narcotics unit asserted that "the sale of the drug cigarette is greater now than it ever was and has not only invaded homes and amusement spots but the high schools as well." Liquor also had its users among ghetto students. During prohibition, some pupils patronized speakeasies located near Phillips High. School officials, however, persuaded classmates to report where alcohol was served, enabling police to raid the "questionable resorts." In the late 1930s, parents and administrators in several ghetto districts tried to prevent stores near schoolhouses from selling liquor to pupils. A mother complaining about a grocery store near Doolittle Elementary pointed out that the sale of alcohol corrupted even students who did not drink. The availability of liquor, she said, "attracts loiterers whose profanity and unbecoming conduct has been heard and seen by children on their way to and from school."[15]

Unlike alcohol and marijuana, vandalism and theft frequently meant direct assaults on the schoolhouse. Some youths who destroyed or damaged school property were retaliating against indignities and frustrations they felt the school had inflicted on them. For other vandals, the school was merely a conspicuous, convenient, and vulnerable target for the daring deeds that won them status among their peers. No comparative vandalism data by school district exist for the interwar period, but the entire system did suffer considerable damage. From 1926 to 1931, the Board of Education spent an average of $147,000 annually to replace glass, most of it broken intentionally. Press reports suggest that black areas on the South and West Sides had serious vandalism problems, especially during the Depression. In 1932, authorities at Phillips High counted 300 panes of glass broken in three months. Nine years later, student government officers at Webster complained that vandals had smashed ninety-four window panes during summer vacation. While windows were the most popular target, unknown persons sometimes injured shrubs or broke into classrooms, pouring ink on books and throwing papers in toilets. Vandalism aroused indignation and inspired publicity campaigns, but neither succeeded in restraining the youngsters blamed for the crimes. The fact that McCosh Elementary, which served the well-educated, home-owning section of West Woodlawn, had a Damage Prevention Club in 1938 suggests that vandalism was not merely a consequence of poverty. Theft, the most common form of juvenile delinquency, victimized schools, teachers, and students alike. At Phillips and Englewood high schools in the mid-1930s, instructional materials, athletic equipment, and typewriters disappeared. The most vivid memory a former instructor at Douglas Elementary had of her school was the petty thievery there. Classroom supplies and teachers' purses vanished if not secured by lock and key.[16]

Although theft was the most frequent type of youthful crime, personal violence was more spectacular and, accordingly, more publicized. The South Side had high assault and homicide rates, and black children who attacked others were behaving like some adults around them. Defiance of student monitors, quarrels over small amounts of money, and other arguments and insults might culminate in assaults with knives, guns, or clubs. Following a stabbing at Willard Elementary in 1927, the eleven-year-old assailant informed police that his victim "called him a bad name which reflected greatly upon his dead mother, and he just could not stand it, and had cut her." Three years later, a fourteen-year-old girl fatally stabbed a schoolmate, age eleven, after the pair disagreed about why twenty cents was missing. In 1931, six teenagers were wounded in a gun duel between boys at Phillips High. The black press blamed school officials for such episodes, while parents demanded greater police protection. Although the latter might have prevented outbreaks at school buildings, the ready availability of deadly weapons and the culture of violence that called for drastic solutions to personal conflicts were the real causes of such incidents.[17]

Although vandalism, theft, and personal attacks were often individual acts, they could also be the work of youth gangs. Gangs flourished in most inner-city areas and were not limited to any one race or ethnic group. Most successful where other institutions were weak or unappealing, the gang, according to the contemporary sociologist Frederic Thrasher, "fills a gap and affords an escape." Typically, youth gangs coalesced from informal play-groups based on a local territory—a street corner, schoolyard, or pool hall. Here close personal relations and common experiences created gang allegiances, and conflicts with rivals and police strengthened them. Gangs thus aroused fierce, though not always permanent, loyalties among their members and increased their power by terrorizing victims and bystanders. In 1927, a black journalist described how "gangs of baby bandits" enforced silence: "Through their expert spy system in operation in some of the South Side schools, tab is kept on the unfortunate boy who has fallen victim to their banditry. If he tells, word is sent at once to the gang leader who issues the order to 'get him.' The boy knows from the experiences of other victims of the gangsters what it will mean if he talks, so he keeps quiet and the gangsters continue their unmolested reign of terror and intimidation." Even when police arrested gang members and charged them with crimes, the youthful terrorists frequently escaped conviction. Since victims and witnesses feared reprisals, they often refused to testify in court. In addition, gangs used political influence to avoid punishment.[18]

During the 1920s and 1930s, gangs disrupted ghetto schools by either converting or attacking hall monitors and student leaders and by threatening and assaulting pupils, teachers, and administrators. The bands of youthful criminals also caused much of the truancy, vandalism, and theft at black schools. In 1934, a teacher enumerating the achievements of South Side gangs asserted, "Robberies, theft, pocket-book snatching, fighting, gang wars, destruction of property are in constant practice." On the eve of World War II, a black reporter credited gangs with "robbing, assault and battery on school children, stabbing, shooting, and other acts of rowdyism and vandalism and general misbehavior." The "Twiddlers," "Sneakers," "Hornets," "Dragons," and "Gunners" inflicted injury and death by their knife and gun wielding in and around schoolyards. One enterprising Englewood High senior even carried a pistol in the hollowed-out pages of his dictionary. Some casualties resulted from fights between groups of gang members, while in other cases selected individuals or uninvolved observers became victims of gang attacks. In an incident in 1926, a sixteen-year-old tried to halt "a gang of street urchins who were molesting girls after school." A fellow known as "Devil" rewarded the boy by stabbing him near the heart. In 1931, a father asserted that his son had "his clothes cut to shreds and his face and body lacerated and bruised as the result of an altercation

Although the caption on this 1933 editorial cartoon suggests that Chicago blacks might yet fend off these symbols of segregation, the visual message was more pessimistic; Jim Crow already had a secure grasp on the local schools. The cartoon and all of the following photographs are from the *Chicago Defender*.

ASK MAYOR FOR SCHOOL BOARD MEMBER

Formal, dignified, and politically weak, a delegation of black civic activists visits Mayor Anton J. Cermak (third from left) in February, 1933, to repeat the long-standing call for black representation on the Board of Education. Cermak, a Democrat, snubbed the plea of a predominantly Republican voting bloc.

AN EXAMPLE OF WASTE OF TAXPAYERS' MONEY

Bitterness and determination to protest filled blacks passing the abandoned construction site of a new South Side high school. Work here began in 1931 but ceased when the Depression depleted the school system's finances. Federal loans enabled the project to resume, and New Phillips (soon renamed Du Sable) High finally opened in 1935.

Du Sable High School (1935) taught blacks that modern facilities could be inadequate, too. Ill-equipped and vastly overcrowded from the start, the school became the focus of a protest movement begun about 1938 and led by recent graduates and Urban League staff members.

Oakland Elementary School, completed in 1903 in a white neighborhood, was by the 1920s and 1930s on the east edge of the ghetto. Oakland was racially integrated until 1926, when the Board of Education gave the white portion of its district to another school. The building's massive formalism, typical of schools of the period, conveyed order and authority.

DUNBAR VOCATIONAL SCHOOL HOLDS OPEN HOUSE

Largely excluded from Washburne Trade School, blacks seeking vocational training could attend Dunbar Vocational School (1937). While some of its offerings, such as the sheet metal and electrical shop class above and the home economics class below, overlapped those at Washburne, overall Dunbar demonstrated that separate instruction was not equal.

Lilydale Parents Picket Dangerous Firetrap Portables

A boycott, picketing, and arson climaxed the protest against unpopular portable classrooms (seen in the background here) in the Far South Side black enclave of Lilydale in 1936. This stable, cohesive community, isolated from the rest of black Chicago, proved that militant direct action could win better school facilities.

A DREAM COMES TRUE; DR. BOUSFIELD SWORN IN

After more than thirty years of unsuccessful lobbying, black Chicagoans celebrated in October, 1939, when City Clerk Ludwig Schrieber swore in Midian O. Bousfield (left) as the first black member of the Chicago Board of Education. But during Bousfield's two and one-half years on the board, blacks criticized him for failing to speak out on behalf of their concerns.

with a gang of hoodlums at the Forestville playground who tried to take his baseball away from him."[19]

Petty theft and extortion were also gang specialties. Members robbed newsboys, took children's lunch money, and snatched their clothing. In 1940, a journalist declared, "The theft of overcoats, shoes, and gymnasium suits in the schools is getting to be almost a common thing." Youths were quick to imitate older outlaws' methods of acquiring regular incomes. The assistant principal of Du Sable High revealed, "Already gangs of older boys are formed in the community to 'shake down' school boys for 'protection' against the things they threaten to do to them." Police detectives told a court hearing in 1940, "Du Sable students must pay a 'protection' fee of 75 cents to the gang leaders. Failure to do so usually results in a shooting or cutting."[20]

Youth gangs sometimes attacked school officials and teachers as well as students. In 1924, daily newspapers reported about "colored 'bad men'" at Phillips High who beat and shot at the assistant principal after he threw them out of a dancing class. The administrator identified his assailants as part of the Prairie Avenue Gang, one of several groups often involved in disturbances at Phillips. Six years later, young gunmen fatally shot the director of playground activities at Oakland Elementary School. Instructors who tried to stop gang activities might become victims of violence themselves. In 1940, the *Defender* stated, "In one or two places, women teachers were pushed up against the walls and threatened if they tried to have the boys arrested." The same year, a black newspaper columnist disclosed that within a several-week period, "Boys have thrown acid on a high school teacher . . . and still another teacher who had the temerity to take a gun away from a pupil was forced to return the gun at the point of a knife." The journalist claimed, "Young hoodlums think nothing of entering the schools on occasion and actually running the classes."[21]

Instructors in gang-infested neighborhoods felt isolated and angry. In 1929, two leaders of a black elementary teachers' club expressed their frustration about their unruly students: "They have a general antagonistic attitude toward everything pertaining to the school. . . . Every teacher who has had to come in contact with this group knows that they come into the system with the attitude, 'Well, here I am, teach me something if you can.' Every effort to instill in them a little common decency and good citizenship is met with a resistance of the worst sort." Another instructor commented, "More time is spent in enforcing the simple habits of control than anything else." Faculty members believed that they stood alone in enforcing discipline and received little support from parents or administrators. In one incident, a teacher who physically punished a student was transferred to another school for violating regulations. Without the right to use corporal punishment, faculty members felt hard pressed to maintain order. "The business of telling a teacher that 'you will get yours' is a common thing," stated the elementary teachers' club leaders. "The teacher has to accept it. It seems that in our districts the teacher is not regarded nor treated any better than a door mat."[22]

Proposed solutions to the South Side's gang problem reflected a lack of consensus about the relative importance of home and school in influencing ghetto youth. Some blacks blamed the public schools for gang violence. A critic writing in the *Defender* denounced instructors who taught only academic subjects but omitted moral training. He announced, "A short period each day in which children could be told the values of being ladylike and gentlemanly and the resultant harm in being boisterous and uncouth would bring results." This observer concluded, "The main responsibility is the teachers'." Others, however, maintained that the family alone could prevent antisocial behavior. Predictably, "A Teacher" charged "the working parents, the uninformed parents and the careless parents" with a "lack of necessary home training." A Phillips High graduate agreed, "The blame should not be put on the executives of the school, but on the parents of the homes from which the students come."[23]

Blacks also disagreed about whether suppression or social reform was the best way to deal with youth crime. A pair of Negro instructors advised, "If a few more of these hoodlums were clubbed our teachers would not have such a disagreeable job imparting ideals of good citizenship into the heads of these smart upstarts who are pulling down the race." Many South Side residents called for more vigorous law enforcement to stifle trouble. For example, in 1935, the *Defender* decided, "This is a job for the police. . . . More police are needed and police who have the courage and can command respect enough to bring order out of chaos." But since youth crime continued even in the wake of police crackdowns, other observers argued that improving ghetto social conditions was the way to overcome gang power. In 1924, a Juvenile Protective Association report blamed youth crime on inadequate recreation and housing. The following year, a Boys' Club leader advised, "The only way to break up the gang . . . is to provide them with a constructive outlet for their energies." In 1940, YMCA officials claimed that vocational education and better social workers could curb gang popularity, while a black editor contended that poverty and discrimination were the seeds from which gangs grew. He stated, "Boys and girls who can find no jobs because their skin is of a different color from that of other

Americans will inevitably solve their personal problems in a destructive manner." This approach, however reasonable, was unsatisfying to victims of gang terror. As one exasperated father wrote, "I would appreciate very much if you would tell me if it is better to preach to them the injustices done them by unemployment because of color, or pack a .38 on my hip just as a precaution."[24]

Although ghetto poverty, instability, and delinquency were forces from outside the classroom which hurt children's academic progress, in important respects the public schools also limited their pupils' horizons. In teachers' day-to-day dealings with children and in the way educators classified and trained students for jobs, the schools too often failed to challenge the racism that narrowed black lives. Public education, instead of being a ladder of upward mobility for ghetto youth, actually mirrored and reinforced the social order that subjected black Chicagoans. Classroom racism went hand-in-hand with the overcrowding and underfunding that characterized a segregated school system.

White faculty members in ghetto schools were by no means uniformly hostile toward black children. Some displayed little or no prejudice and instead recognized pupils' accomplishments and encouraged their ambitions. The black press occasionally singled out white principals and teachers for praise, lauding one as "a firm friend of colored folk" and another as "one of the true friends of the Colored Race in Chicago." When the principal of Farren Elementary left his post in 1926, he drew compliments for "his fair, impartial treatment and keen personal interest." The *Defender* thanked the head of Willard School in the early 1930s for her "reputation for fair dealings" and asserted that she "not only is a prepared, efficient person, but one that is intensely interested in the welfare and intellectual progress of the children of the community."[25]

Evidence, however, suggests that among most white teachers, negative feelings about black students outweighed confidence and sympathy. Part of the difficulty was not race but social class. Instructors who understandably preferred to work with children whose home environments prepared them to learn rapidly in school often became disenchanted with and contemptuous toward students who did not have such backgrounds. As one observer of Chicago teachers noted, "Where the children come from a class background where the training is such as to make their attitudes toward school and education coincide with those of the teacher, the teacher has 'good' pupils; where this is not the case, she has 'bad' pupils." Black schools rarely offered instructors the fulfillment they might obtain from working with well-prepared students. One veteran of twenty years in a ghetto elementary school remarked, "These children don't learn very quickly. . . . It's hard to get anything done with children like that. They simply don't respond." The nonacademic orientation of many lower-class children created distance between teachers and pupils even where both were of the same race.[26]

In the ghetto, however, racial differences increased the gulf between faculty and students. Many white instructors believed that black people were inherently different and inferior. Coming from neighborhoods with few or no blacks, white teachers knew Negroes primarily as menials and as the familiar stereotypes of folklore and the mass media —African jungle savages, docile slaves, and violent slum dwellers. Although psychologists and sociologists in the 1920s and 1930s were beginning to reject the scientific racism of an earlier generation, the image of the lazy, rhythmic, slow-witted Negro still persisted in the minds of most whites. While some teachers changed their attitudes as a result of working in black schools, in many cases experience only reinforced earlier impressions. Accordingly, the myth of black inferiority flourished among white teachers in the ghetto. A majority of school personnel interviewed by the Chicago Commission on Race Relations felt blacks to be less able than whites. An elementary instructor asserted, "Colored children are restive and incapable of abstract thought; they must be constantly fed with novel interests and given things to do with their hands." At Moseley School, another teacher added, "The great physical development of the colored person takes away from the mental, while with the whites the reverse is true." One principal announced that blacks "shut down on their intellectual processes when they are about 12 or 14 years of age." "They cannot grasp the subject," an English teacher declared. "They do not understand as the white child does. They lack the mentality." Others alleged that black pupils were violent, immoral, and untrustworthy. A Phillips High faculty member complained, "Everything here that isn't tied or watched walks off. It didn't used to be this way before the colored came in so thick."[27]

With attitudes such as these, it is not surprising that racial insults from white teachers sometimes accompanied classroom instruction. In the early twenties, a physical education teacher at Englewood High called black students "coons" and urged them to switch to Phillips "where they belong." After a new principal arrived at Carter Elementary in 1930, her contempt for the school's children quickly angered the community. When she labeled a misbehaving girl a "nigger," the slur provoked a fight, a court hearing, and futile demands by local residents for the woman's removal. Several years later, she reportedly told a class, "If you fool with me I will send you back to the jungle where you belong." In yet another district, a parent charged that white teachers called pupils "ignorant blacks" and similar epithets. When faculty members hurled racial slurs, children might begin to question whether merit or achievement governed the educational process.[28]

Indeed, outside the ghetto in schools with black student minorities, there was much academic discrimination against black pupils. A black woman who had been a student at Englewood characterized her school as "a hate center," and added that teachers did not call on her for recitation. A girl who attended Hyde Park High in the mid-1930s said, "While at high school I always knew that I wasn't wanted. There was lots of discrimination. The teachers get it out by giving low marks." A black instructor accused some white faculty members of denying promotion to minority students for racial reasons. She fumed, "In the Chicago system a teacher is supposed to be a teacher regardless of color, but in practice there is a dead line drawn." Such bias against black children was a clear sign of how unwelcome they were in many predominantly white districts.[29]

Whereas black pupils outside the ghetto may have faced low grades and nonpromotion, within black schools white faculty members apparently made fewer academic demands. In 1922, the Chicago Commission on Race Relations reported, "Accordingly they are given handicraft instead of arithmetic, and singing instead of grammar." When a black teacher at Forestville Elementary in the 1930s expressed dismay that her students knew neither the alphabet nor arithmetic tables, the children explained that their previous instructor had not required them to learn such things. She recalled, "The worst cases I had came from children who had been pampered by white teachers." White faculty members confirmed that lower standards prevailed in black schools. "If you want to take it easy and not work too hard, you teach at a school like Du Sable or Phillips," a high school teacher said. "Down at Du Sable they just try to keep the kids busy and out of trouble. They give everyone in the room some kind of little job—one takes care of this, another takes care of that." "You don't have to work so hard in that kind of a school," another instructor explained. "Not so much is expected of you. They don't think that you'll get through the work in the required time. The children can't work that fast. So you can take it a little easier." From time to time, the black press complained about low standards in ghetto classrooms. In 1930, the *Defender* declared, "It is also said that many are yearly graduated who have not mastered the grades."[30]

Unfortunately for children of the ghetto, black teachers sometimes had color prejudices as well. The average Negro instructor in Chicago was lighter-skinned than the typical ghetto resident. The difference was most pronounced in the more desirable high school positions and early in the interwar period when Negro teachers were few. An instructor who began her career around 1920 described most of her early Negro colleagues as "light brown" or "medium fair." The light complexion of Negro teachers was no coincidence, for the elite who furnished most of their race's professionals were often fair-skinned. Furthermore, light color was an asset in finding a job, since whites were more tolerant of Negroes who looked "white." The early Negro teachers at Phillips High illustrate the role of color in precedent-breaking appointments. The first known Negro woman to teach in a Chicago public high school, Ida Taylor, was not only a well-qualified graduate of Chicago Normal College and the University of Chicago but was also attractive, by white standards, and fair. After she did well at Phillips beginning in 1921, the school's principal reportedly asked her to "get another nice, light-skinned colored girl" to join her on the faculty. By 1927, the number of Negroes on the Phillips faculty had grown to sixteen.[31]

Although light skin helped the professional advancement of Negro faculty members, it could cause ill-feeling between teacher and student. From time to time, blacks accused some of their race's instructors of color discrimination, charging them with favoring lighter children and neglecting or insulting black pupils. "The pure blooded, black children are seldom if ever the recipients of kindly counsel, or special favors, or justifiable considerations," asserted *Defender* publisher Robert Abbott in 1935. Abbott, who was dark himself, declared, "We can neither understand nor appreciate Race teachers who manifest no interest in, no sympathy and no consideration for those children of ours who show no physical sign of racial admixture." Parents occasionally confronted instructors about alleged cases of color bias. In one classroom conference concerning a girl who was doing poorly in school, an angry parent exclaimed, "You colored teachers just don't like Mattie Lou 'cause she's black and ain't got good hair!" The *Defender* concurred, "We resent it and decry it the more when Race teachers, who should be the last ones to exhibit aversion to their kind, practice the most objectionable form of partiality on the basis of color."[32]

When black students turned from their teachers to their textbooks, they found little relief from racism. An examination of twenty-seven history texts used in the Chicago public schools during the 1920s and 1930s clearly reveals the lowly role black people occupied in the curriculum. In these books, blacks hardly ever thought, said, or did anything on their own. For example, none of these books mentioned any black organization, institution, or social movement except for Tuskegee Institute, which was discussed in just one volume. Although several of the texts took a biographical approach, black individuals were rarely included. Only three of twenty-seven had a place for Booker T. Washington; Robert R. Moton and, surprisingly, Harriet Tubman and Nat Turner appeared in two books. For the most part, blacks were merely the objects of white action, primarily during slavery and Reconstruction. However, since the authors who said the most about blacks were in general blatantly racist, it was probably just as well that they received so little attention in the schoolbooks of the interwar period.[33]

Africa represented the origins of black people, but Africa and its civilizations were all but invisible in the texts examined. Several of the titles traced mankind from the ancient world to colonial America; though they offered extensive accounts of Egypt, Greece, Rome, and medieval Europe, black Africa was simply a target for European explorers. Children reading Grace Vollintine's *The American People and Their Old World Ancestors* or Reuben Post Halleck and Juliette Frantz's *Our Nation's Heritage: What the Old World Contributed to the New* could only conclude that Americans had no African ancestors and that Africa contributed nothing to the New World. Omission, however, was the best that blacks fared, for when textbooks did depict Africans, they described people with whom no self-respecting student could identify. Lorraine Hansberry, the future playwright who entered a South Side elementary school about 1936, later remembered, "In school in the lower grades, primitive peoples, hot, animals, mostly negative, how good it was we were saved from this terrible past." When, about 1960, a number of prominent blacks recalled how their schoolbooks had depicted Africa, one saw "horrid pictures of cannibals and savages," while another remembered "wild, pagan, hopelessly inferior, heathen-looking animalist types."[34]

A number of the American history texts used in Chicago during the 1920s and 1930s did not describe slavery per se but instead treated it only as a cause of sectional conflict leading to the Civil War. Those authors who did cover slavery, however, disapproved of it while at the same time denigrating the slaves themselves. Though writers usually mentioned the hard work, harsh punishments, and broken families, they treated such unpleasant aspects in a briefer and less lively fashion than their more vivid accounts of bondsmen being "cheerful at their work" and devoted to their masters. The only two color illustrations of slavery, for example, were a depiction of Uncle Remus telling white children stories and a painting of dancing, clapping blacks entitled "A good time on a plantation." According to Thomas M. Marshall's *American History*, "Although he was in a state of slavery, the negro of plantation days was usually happy. He was fond of the company of others and liked to sing, dance, crack jokes, and laugh; he admired bright colors." In *The Story of Our Nation*, by Eugene C. Barker,

William E. Dodd, and Walter P. Webb, historians from the University of Texas and University of Chicago, slaves hardly ever worked at all but instead spent their time celebrating slave weddings, dancing, telling white children stories, and reveling in "happy gaiety." *Leaders in Making America* by Wilbur Fisk Gordy had no black leaders but did describe white youngsters going "to hear the negroes tell quaint tales and sing weird songs" and "old colored 'mammies'" who were "very fond of 'Massa's chillun,' and liked to pet them and tell them stories." Henry William Elson's *History of the United States of America* stated that slaves were "wholly wanting in morals" and assured its readers that "the slave was a happy creature. This was due to the inherent quality of the race, and to the fact that he had no care of his own, no anxiety for the morrow." And Mary G. Kelty, who wrote *The Growth of the American People and Nation,* told pupils that blacks were better off as slaves in America than they had been when enslaved in Africa.[35]

Reconstruction was the other episode in which blacks invariably appeared in American history texts of the interwar years, and the schoolbook version of southern history from 1865 to 1877 was as offensive to blacks as the treatment of slavery. Nearly every account of Reconstruction was a copy from a single mold, that of the Dunning school of historiography which dominated white scholarship of the time. Children learned that blacks responded to freedom with idleness, begging, and foolish expectations of forty acres and a mule. As James Woodburn, Thomas Moran, and Howard Hill declared in *Our United States,* "Many Negroes who had been faithful, hard-working slaves soon became good-for-nothing loafers." Worse yet, these loafers quickly became puppets of "rascally politicians" and "mean and dishonest white men" who arrived from the North and "plundered and injured the South without mercy," according to *Our Nation Grows Up* (Barker, Dodd, and Webb). Along with carpetbagger domination came "Negro Rule in the South," a period in which illiterate "ignorant Negroes [who] were unfit to rule" undertook "an orgy of extravagance, fraud and disgusting incompetence," in the words of David Saville Muzzey. Soon, however, southern whites "took advantage of the negro's superstitious nature" (Muzzey once more) and regained control. Textbook authors were more explicitly partisan in their judgments about Reconstruction than they had been about slavery. Woodburn, Moran, and Hill announced, "It was a mistake to impose Negro suffrage on the South before the Negroes were ready for it . . . ," and Henry William Elson, who termed Reconstruction "drastic" and "merciless," advised, "A study of it enlists our sympathies with the South."[36]

Though black people vanished from post-1877 American history in most textbooks, a few writers treated freedmen in the post-Reconstruction South. Of these, Charles and Mary Beard's *History of the United States,* the sole deviant from the Dunning story of Reconstruction, and Woodburn, Moran, and Hill's *Our United States* provided nonracist accounts of the period. The Beard volume dealt in a nonjudgmental fashion with disfranchisement, the rise of the Solid South, segregation, and the decline of blacks in the skilled trades. Woodburn, Moran, and Hill, whose treatment of Reconstruction was decidedly anti-black, had a full section on Hampton and Tuskegee, mentioned black gains in literacy, property owning, business, and the professions, and named five prominent blacks as "men of distinction." This section, however, was unique in its focus on blacks themselves. More typical was Ruth and Willis Mason West's *The Story of Our Country,* which alleged that "most Negro leaders" endorsed the separate-but-equal principle. Elson's *History of the United States* proclaimed: "The great curse of the race today is, not the want of a free ballot, but the want of ambition to *do* something and to *be* somebody. Vast numbers of the southern blacks are of the listless, aimless class who aspire to nothing, who are content to live in squalor and ignorance." Elson asserted that the southern black would achieve political equality "only when he makes himself an equal force in civilization. And perhaps this may never be, for nature has done more for his pale-faced brother than for him." Elson defended segregation, for "nature seems to have drawn a line between the races that man has no power to obliterate." Lest students worry about the fate of Dixie's blacks, the author assured his readers that except for the lack of the vote, southern law did not discriminate against Negroes. Elson stated, "The negro is quite safe and his happiness quite secure under the white man's government" and concluded, "The rule of the white man is essential to southern progress."[37]

History books by no means enjoyed a monopoly on racism. *Community Life and Civic Problems,* by Howard Copeland Hill of the University of Chicago Laboratory School, told pupils: "Indeed, one of the chief causes of the lack of progress among the backward peoples of the earth is the fact that their wants are limited largely to their bodily needs. The famous negro leader, Booker T. Washington, tried constantly to make the members of his race dissatisfied with their one-room log cabins so that they would change their shiftless ways and become industrious citizens." In 1936, the Chicago NAACP branch succeeded in suppressing grade-school drawing books that depicted the black man as an animal-like brute. Two years later, the *Defender* protested, "The words 'sambo,' 'pickaninny,' and 'darky' appear too often in textbooks dealing with children's literature and folklore."[38]

While black Chicagoans did not regard biased textbooks as being as urgent a problem as double-shift schools, some did object to the harm racist classroom materials inflicted. Blacks explained that such books increased racial prejudice among whites. The *Defender* complained in 1938, "In the present set-up our money is being used against us to teach other people to ridicule and hate us." Nannie Jackson Myers, an NAACP member who took an interest in schoolbook bias, added, "The Chicago school system perpetuates ideas of racial inferiorities and breeds interracial ill will by using texts whose authors are either misinformed or prejudiced." Such books also injured black pupils by teaching them that whites alone were achievers and shapers of society and that blacks were a people without a positive past. The pioneer black historian Carter G. Woodson criticized "the miseducation of the Negro" in a 1931 essay. "The thought of the inferiority of the Negro is drilled into him in almost every class he enters," Woodson asserted. "To handicap a student for life by teaching him that his black face is a curse and that his struggle to change his condition is hopeless is the worst kind of lynching."[39]

During the 1920s, textbook bias in general became an issue in local politics. In William Hale Thompson's 1927 mayoral campaign, he claimed that Chicago's schoolbooks were unpatriotic and pro-British. Thompson vowed, "While I am mayor, I do not propose to have the school children taught that George Washington was a rebel and a traitor." "Big Bill" also demanded that textbooks feature the contributions to America of the Irish, Poles, and Germans—all groups with substantial voting strength in the city. Black Chicagoans believed that schoolbook racism was an equally deserving target for attention. The city's leading black newspaper remarked, "While the city authorities are interesting themselves in driving King George III out of the text books, the Defender suggests that a thorough housecleaning be in order." Instead of a clean sweep, however, the city's textbook collection received only a light dusting. Nannie Myers sent a fourteen-page letter to Board of Education officials, complaining about Hill's *Community Life and Civic Problems*. Myers criticized Hill's "blanket indictment of an entire race as shiftless," and the *Defender* agreed, stating, "He includes the Race among 'backward peoples,' forgetting that science knows nothing of backward peoples, recognizing only backward individuals." School authorities yielded readily. An assistant superintendent called the offensive passage in Hill's book "absurd, in bad taste, and clearly out of place in a high school text." Conceding that the book selection committee acted carelessly in approving the volume, the Board of Education persuaded the book's publisher to delete the sentence mentioning Booker

T. Washington and to change a condescending reference to an African to "a primitive tribesman." Local blacks congratulated themselves on this victory, even though it left the underlying pattern of textbook racism undisturbed.[40]

Intelligence testing was another way in which the schools helped subordinate blacks instead of liberating them. Developed by the French psychologist Alfred Binet in his work with mentally deficient children, the IQ test was first employed on a large scale during World War I, when the United States Army used the results to classify and assign over 1,700,000 men. Educators and psychologists quickly realized that intelligence testing could enhance the schools' efficiency by making it possible to identify pupils with special learning needs, group students of similar abilities, and channel children into jobs appropriate to their mental capacities. The testing movement spread rapidly during the 1920s, with most large school systems sorting their pupils according to IQ scores. For example, in 1924, the Chicago schools' Bureau of Standards and Statistics reasoned that since students with low IQ scores should plan on unskilled jobs and those with high scores would enter business or the professions, pupils' high school programs should reflect these separate paths. The study concluded, "The very inferior group would be advised to take the technical or commercial courses of the simpler type and omit the study of foreign languages."[41]

Although intelligence testing had an aura of scientific objectivity, it was nevertheless controversial. White critics, such as the Chicago Federation of Labor, attacked the IQ and educational tracking as undemocratic, since it threatened upward mobility for working-class children. Warning against "the acceptance of distinct and more or less permanent class divisions among the people," the CFL accused the testers of reviving "the ancient doctrine of caste" and pressing "the brand of inferiority. . .upon all productive workers." Blacks, too, found the popularity of the IQ disturbing. Blacks' lower median scores confirmed many testers' belief in racial inferiority. And if black students were inferior, scientific efficiency might dictate that they receive a different kind of education, perhaps even a segregated one.[42]

Black educators attacked intelligence tests and the ways in which they were used. Noting that pupils at Keith Elementary had below average IQs on vocabulary and reading tests but rated normal on a nonlanguage exam, Maudelle Bousfield, Chicago's only Negro principal, concluded that children's "intelligence" depended on the measuring tool employed. Other blacks pointed out that the poor rapport between white testers and black children would lower scores, especially of southern migrants who had learned to conceal their abilities and emotions from whites. Adding that northern Negroes had higher median IQs than whites from some southern states, blacks like the Du Sable High School psychologist Albert Beckham contended that the tests reflected differences in schooling, home life, and cultural opportunities rather than innate intelligence. As Horace Mann Bond, a black educator who did research on the IQ issue as a University of Chicago graduate student, declared, "The conclusion cannot be escaped that the Army Intelligence tests were excellent measures of environment and educational experience." Black critics protested that the IQ had become a powerful weapon against their race. Bond, for example, described an episode in a Chicago high school in which a teacher humiliated a dark-skinned girl by citing the findings of Princeton University's Carl Brigham that blacks and immigrants trailed native whites in mental capacity. Calling the tests "funds for propaganda and encouragements for prejudice," Bond wrote sarcastically, "We are now able to fortify our prejudices with a vast array of statistical tables, bewildering vistas of curves and ranges and distributions and the other cabalistic phrases with which we clothe the sacred profession of Psychology."[43]

Like the IQ movement, the Chicago schools' vocational education efforts complied with existing social patterns instead of challenging them. As surveys during the 1920s and 1930s disclosed, black children in Chicago had high aspirations for future employment. Half the black eighth-graders responding to a quiz about future job plans in 1921 named professions such as teaching, nursing, medicine, and dentistry. The remainder divided between skilled jobs (auto mechanic, dressmaker) and clerical work. Nearly three-fifths of the Du Sable High freshmen listing vocational choices in a survey given about 1935 chose nurse, teacher, or stenographer. "The ambition and vision of these negro children demands the active support of the employing public," a member of the school system's vocational guidance bureau commented. She urged that whites give blacks "a chance on the basis of their education and personal ability to enter those chosen fields and to stand or fall on their merits as individuals."[44]

Employers, however, largely ignored such appeals. Despite gains during World War I and the 1920s in semiskilled industrial jobs and in government employment, black workers remained primarily on the lowest rungs of the job ladder. Few obtained the professional, business, clerical, or skilled occupations black students sought; instead, ghetto workers continued to be overconcentrated in unskilled labor and domestic and personal service. Employment barriers were so rigid that St. Clair Drake and Horace Cayton used the metaphor of the "job ceiling" to describe blacks' situation. Black graduates consequently faced disappointment when looking for work that utilized their schooling. As a black university student reviewing the plight of his younger brothers and sisters put it, "Public sentiment in the city which educates them to aspire sees well that their aspirations are crushed." A sympathetic journalist described the fate of the job-hunting black young person: "He is strong enough to overcome the first few rebuffs he receives, but when every attempt proves a failure, . . . he stops and wonders if there is something radically wrong with him, or with the world." The Depression pushed prospects for ghetto youth below their previously low levels and deepened their despair. As one observer said in 1938 of the black graduate, "Friendly faces encouraged him to strive for an education. Cold countenances rebuff him when he asks for a job." A *Defender* columnist mourned for black high school seniors in the 1930s, since "the door of hope is actually shut squarely in their faces." A 1941 survey of Du Sable High graduates found a wide gap between goals and achievements. Although half the sample desired jobs in the arts, professions, or trades, just 7.3 percent of the young people secured work in these areas.[45]

How should the schools have responded to the job ceiling? If educators ignored racial bias in employment and prepared each black child to fulfill his or her potential, they would produce disillusioned graduates unable to use their training. Moreover, each pupil educated to be an accountant who instead became a Pullman porter represented wasted school resources to efficiency-minded administrators. If, on the other hand, the schools trained black students only for available jobs, this would dash youthful aspirations, discourage children from remaining in school any longer than legally necessary, and violate the tenacious myth of equal opportunity. The dilemma was indeed vexing.

Although a survey of northern high schools during the Depression found nearly three-quarters of the educators agreeing that they should "attempt positively to dispel racial prejudice so as to provide a wider range of occupational opportunities" for blacks, the historian David Tyack concluded that in reality "most [educators] appear to have accepted the racism of unions and employers as a fact they could do little about." As one New York City school official put it, "Isn't a girl better off as a seamstress making a living than as a stenographer not making one?" The same attitude apparently prevailed in Chicago classrooms. A black senior at Englewood High in the 1920s told her counselor that she wanted to teach. "You can't be a teacher. There's no place you can teach," the adviser replied erroneously. A black elementary instructor recalled urging her ghetto students to aim for post office jobs, since they were available. When asked why she did not encourage her pupils to break employment barriers, she answered, "It was useless to even think about it." On the eve of World War II, representatives of the North Central Association of Colleges and Secondary Schools and the state Department of Public Instruction examined the Chicago schools and issued a veiled critique of the system's response to discrimination. "In planning the educational program for any racial group," they warned, "care must always be taken not to provide a program of such a nature that it tends to fix or determine the social and economic status of the group." Citing new openings for blacks in the professions, the experts recommended that the city's schools broaden their training as new opportunities arose.[46]

The Chicago public schools' vocational education programs showed how educators dealt with the job ceiling. Vocational or industrial education has had a mixed legacy since it gained popularity among reformers before the Civil War. It appealed to educators wanting to diversify schooling and make it more practical. Businessmen seeking orderly, well-trained workers found industrial education attractive, as did blacks and immigrants wanting to learn useful skills. In the late nineteenth and early twentieth centuries, compulsory education and child labor laws lent increased urgency to the movement, as educators developed programs for children they regarded as unsuited for traditional academic courses. Events in Chicago mirrored national trends. Under Superintendent Ella Flagg Young, the city high schools introduced two-year courses in electricity, machine shop, carpentry, accounting, stenography, and mechanical drawing, and by 1920, most elementary schools offered cooking, sewing, and manual training. Industrial education, however, sparked heated controversy. Between 1913 and 1917, the Illinois legislature considered and three times defeated the Cooley Bill, which would have authorized separate school systems for academic and vocational students from seventh through twelfth grades. Supported by business interests, the bill angered organized labor, which warned that the plan would restrict social mobility.[47]

Some leading black Chicagoans supported industrial education, claiming that it was more practical than the traditional curriculum. Robert Abbott, who learned the printer's trade at Hampton Institute and was on friendly terms with Booker T. Washington, asserted, "There is no question but what a boy or girl who learns to do things with his hands as well as his brain is better fitted for life's struggle." Abbott's *Defender* declared, "Education is no education if it does not give the person a livelihood, or rather give them an earning power." Even college-bound students should acquire a skilled trade to help earn tuition and to provide an alternative if higher education did not lead to

an appropriate job. Amid the despair of the Depression, the Chicago
Urban League held assemblies at eleven black schools to promote vocational education. Meanwhile, black journalists continued to insist that
students learn barbering or one of the building trades "because they offer a means of livelihood."[48]

During the interwar decades, however, the vocational training program of the Chicago schools was hardly the liberating force that black
spokesmen like Abbott claimed it was. Washburne Trade School was
the city's major public vocational institution. Established in 1919 as a
special continuation center for students under sixteen who had left regular schools, Washburne soon developed extensive trades instruction
programs and offered formal apprenticeships, besides maintaining its
continuation role. Federal funds authorized by the Smith-Hughes Act
of 1917 paid for half the cost of faculty salaries. Although pupils living
anywhere in Chicago were technically eligible to attend Washburne,
blacks rarely enrolled. Labor unions, which supplied much of Washburne's equipment, determined who could use it, and blacks did not
qualify. In 1940, a group of black residents told their ward committeeman, "It is learned that courses in Electrical Engineering, Steamfitting,
Plumbing and Carpentering are only made available to boys whose
fathers or other next of kin were or are at the present time members of
the American Federation of Labor in some one of these 'Locals.'"
About the same time, a study by the National Technical Association
reported that auto mechanics, air conditioning, heating, welding, and
sheet-metal work were also on the list of restricted courses. Since the
craft unions in question barred Negroes from membership, black
students could not train in these fields at Washburne.[49]

Blacks bitterly assailed discrimination at the trade school, arguing
that it was unfair for black taxpayers to support a public institution that
enforced union color barriers. A local NAACP officer stated, "The
unions ought not to be given the right to control the schools. It is simply
a public school matter." At the annual school board budget hearing in
1940, Alderman Earl Dickerson demanded that the Board of Education
stop funding Washburne if racial bias continued. Most black spokesmen, however, simply recommended that Washburne sever its union
connections. Irene McCoy Gaines, who headed the Chicago Council of
Negro Organizations, a federation of clubs and civic groups organized
by the Chicago Urban League, stated the goal that "all vocational opportunities directed by the Board of Education may be given to all of
the City's children seeking these courses, regardless of race, color or
creed, or the social status of their parents."[50]

The school board did not change policies at Washburne, however, and vocational training for blacks remained segregated. Most black pupils seeking such courses took whatever was available at their regular elementary and high schools. In 1937, officials supplemented these offerings by establishing Dunbar Vocational School in the heart of the South Side ghetto. Dunbar offered courses in nursing, commercial cooking, commercial art, dressmaking, millinery, beauty culture, tailoring, drafting, cabinetmaking, and sheet-metal work. A basic academic program supplemented instruction in the trades. Although the school's enrollment grew from 55 students during its first year to 450 in 1940, blacks did not regard Dunbar as adequate compensation for exclusion from Washburne. Since many Dunbar pupils had not completed the normal grade for their age, Dunbar was a vocational center rather than a high school. Therefore, even though most of the students were of high school age, they could not transfer credits earned at Dunbar to a high school. Alderman Dickerson, who headed a study of Dunbar in 1940, declared, "No school should exist in any community that does not offer a transferrable credit." A year later, the Citizens Schools Committee agreed that Dunbar's curriculum should be revised to meet high school standards. Blacks were also unhappy that the state of Illinois refused to recognize Dunbar as a trade school, thus imperiling certification of its graduates. Questioning a witness about Dunbar's beauty culture program in a 1941 state investigation, Dickerson asked, "And did you know that when they have done their work there, when they have finished the prescribed course they are unable to get a license, pass the state examination, did you know that?"[51]

Dunbar also shared some of the financial shortcomings and other inequities that characterized black schools in general. Although authorities apparently intended Dunbar to be a black analogue of Washburne, its budget was much smaller. In 1940, teachers' salaries per pupil at Dunbar were 17 percent lower ($86.62, compared to $101.53 at Washburne), and appropriations for books and supplies per pupil were less than half the amount spent at Washburne ($6.01 compared to $12.84). Total instructional expenses per Dunbar student thus lagged 23 percent behind those at the white trade school. Since Dunbar had full-time students, whereas at least seven-tenths of Washburne's enrollment was part-time, the actual gap in resources was even larger than these figures suggest. Although Dunbar occupied a new building, a Citizens Schools Committee delegation that toured it reported that it was designed for elementary use and was ill-suited for vocational purposes. A member of the Dickerson probe in 1940 pronounced Dunbar "unworthy from the standpoint of buildings, equipment and personnel, to bear the name of trade school." The following year, Benjamin A. Grant, another black alderman, termed Dunbar "a 'No Man's Land,' in which no appreciable results have been attained comparable with the great amount of effort expended." Grant joined other critics of the school administration in calling for a four-year vocational high school for blacks equal to Washburne.[52]

When officials announced such a project on the eve of World War II, their plans disappointed those who hoped that the schools would at last begin to challenge the job ceiling. School board president James Mc-Cahey allegedly informed black leaders that South Side schools would, in a reporter's words, "train the students for jobs they are likely to get." And the conservative Midian O. Bousfield, first Negro member of the Board of Education, told a South Side audience in 1941 that since few blacks found work as accountants, bookkeepers, or stenographers, education in the ghetto should provide more training of janitors and food, laundry, and domestic workers. The black press did not accept this reasoning. A journalist proclaimed, "Civic leaders are determined that the Board of Education shall not insist that the school train only maids, butlers, cooks and waiters but follow the pattern of every other vocational school and leave the matter of employment to the individuals after they have received training." The *Defender* warned that different training for blacks would mean that "the fiction will be fixed that we are hewers of wood and carriers of water and nothing else." Such complaints apparently did not convince school officials. The outbreak of war, however, delayed construction of the proposed South Side trade school, so blacks were left with neither access to Washburne nor comparable facilities in the ghetto. The public schools' vocational programs for blacks posed little threat to existing patterns of employment discrimination.[53]

Determining exactly how home, community, and classroom influences combined to shape school achievement in black Chicago between the wars is probably beyond the reach of any investigator. First come the problems inherent in any study of academic performance. Teachers vary widely both in the kind and amount of work they expect and in the standards they require for a given letter grade. Students, too, enter classes with widely varying abilities, values, environments, aspirations, and levels of commitment. Next come the factors peculiar to the historical setting. Little useful evidence remains about pupil achievement in Chicago during the 1920s and 1930s. Moreover, the cultural forces at work strain in opposite directions. On the one hand, many blacks regarded education as important and approached the schools with high expectations. At the same time, though, classroom racism made it difficult for black children to fulfill their potential. In view of the lack of data and the nonmeasurable factors influencing school accomplishment, it may well be impossible to reach definitive conclusions about achievements of black pupils in Chicago.

Three types of information about black student performance exist: scores on subject-matter achievement tests, percentages of pupils failing to be promoted to the next grade, and rates of retardation (i.e., in a grade behind the norm for a child's age). Evidence from subject-matter achievement examinations is the most useful of the three, since it measures only student responses. During the mid-twenties, two such surveys showed blacks ranking far below native-born whites of "American" ancestry but doing as well or better than children of recent immigrant families. One study of over 2,400 sixth graders in twenty-one elementary schools asked students to identify civics terms such as "precinct," "tariff," "slums," and "divorce." White "American" pupils led by a wide margin over Jews, with blacks finishing slightly behind Jews, and Italians ranking last, far below blacks. Similar results came from reading achievement tests in which blacks from Keith and Forestville Elementary trailed native-born whites but scored higher than Italian children from the Near West Side and youngsters from the South Chicago steel mills district.[54]

Other evidence, however, gives a bleaker impression of black accomplishment. When students in the city's eight junior high schools took arithmetic and sentence-structure tests in 1926, all-black Phillips ranked last in each test for each grade. In math, Phillips pupils began and ended their junior high careers more than a half-year behind the citywide average. They fared even worse on the English test, beginning seventh grade a year behind their peers and finishing ninth grade two and one-half years behind. In the mid-1930s, when over seven hundred Du Sable High freshmen took tests measuring acquired language skills, their median score was a year and one-half behind the norm for their grade. If these results were typical, and if the exams tested what was required for school success, the average black student had a difficult time in school. Such tests are inexact gauges of classroom progress itself, however, since they do not distinguish what children learned in school from what they acquired elsewhere.[55]

The annual percentage of unpromoted pupils is a second type of information about children's school advancement. During the first half of the 1920s, one out of every eleven or twelve pupils in the city's public elementary schools was not promoted to the following grade each year. The Chicago Commission on Race Relations used a small sample of schools to compare failure rates of black, immigrant, and "white American" children. The Commission's data showed "white American" schools with relatively low failure rates, immigrant schools with the greatest incidence of failure, and blacks slightly better off than immigrants. However, a broader analysis of student failure during the 1921-22 academic year, using the same schools and groups that appeared in chapter 3, found blacks doing worse than every other group. Six institutions with at least four-fifths Negro enrollment had an average failure rate of 10.4 percent, well above the failure rates for high status (6.7 percent), low status (8.4 percent), and immigrant (8.7 percent) schools.[56]

If the 1921-22 results were typical, school failure was inversely related to social and economic status, and black children had a harder time advancing through the grades than other young Chicagoans. One might suppose that a pupil who failed a grade was deficient in ability or achievement. But since failure reflects a teacher's perception of how well a child performed, nonpromotion statistics are an imperfect guide to youngsters' classroom attainments. After all, the high incidence of failure in black schools fits poorly with reports of low standards. Perhaps if teachers had higher expectations of their students, they would have failed even larger numbers than they did. On the other hand, failure is not always a function of academic deficiency. Illness, transience, and teacher-pupil conflict often explain student failure. Unfortunately, we can do little more than speculate about the meaning of nonpromotion rates.

The third type of information concerns retarded pupils, children who were older than normal for their grade in school. As the title of *Laggards in Our Schools* (1909) suggests, educators often assumed that all children of a given age belonged in the same grade, and those who were not in the "proper" grade constituted a problem. Some worried about retardation because it apparently proved that the level of instruction was too difficult for many youngsters, while other experts stressed the increased costs school systems incurred when pupils repeated grades. In the Chicago schools, retardation was considerably more common among black children than among whites. As early as 1908, the Dillingham Commission on immigration disclosed that while 29 percent of Chicago's native white and 34 percent of its foreign-born students were retarded, 53 percent of the blacks were so classified. In 1922, the Chicago Commission on Race Relations found that while retardation rates had risen, blacks continued to do worse than whites. Whereas half the "white Americans" and immigrants at twenty-four selected schools were retarded, three-fourths of the black children were in a lower grade than normal for their age.[57]

Grade retardation among black students was not only more frequent but more severe as well. In the race relations commission survey, although two of every five retarded pupils in "white American" and immigrant areas were less than one year behind, just one in five of the retarded youngsters in mostly black districts was similarly situated. By contrast, while only about 5 percent of the overage children at "white American" and immigrant schools were three or more years behind, 24 percent of the retarded pupils at black schools were at least three years behind. Many black students were five or six years retarded, giving ghetto schools eleven-year-old first graders and eighteen-year-old seventh graders. During the mid-1920s, another study revealed the persistence of high black retardation. In predominantly black schools, twice as many children were two to five years over-age for their grade as in the city as a whole.[58]

What was the significance of the frequent and severe retardation among black pupils? Some observers thought it reflected the race's lower innate mental capacity. As *Crisis* remarked in 1928, "Retardation in colored school children has for years been considered a mark of their 'inferiority' and has been a resting place for all persons wishing to measure 'intelligence.'" However, a Chicago Commission on Race Relations survey of over 3,000 over-age pupils (table 7) made it clear that low intelligence was more likely to cause retardation among whites than among blacks. Whereas low mental ability accounted for nearly one-third of white retardation, it explained only about one-fifth of black retardation. As table 7 demonstrates, environmental factors caused most black retardation. Chief among these was the inadequate educational background of southern migrants. Poverty, weak instructional programs, inconvenient school locations, and short terms in the South accounted for many of the "late entrance," "family problems," and "irregular attendance" notations in school records. According to the race relations commission, "the great majority of the retarded Negroes were from southern states and . . . Negro children born in the North had, as a rule, no higher rate of retardation than the whites." Conditions of black life in Chicago also added to the list of overage students. Household transiency, family disruption, and child-care duties all helped to slow children's progress in school.[59]

Contemporaries stressed the negative effects retardation had upon both individual students and the school system. The boy or girl who was substantially over-age for his or her grade found it uncomfortable to sit in class with younger students. As one commentator noted, "Children who by experience are old but whose formal training is that of the young, present a disciplinary, as well as overage, problem." A juvenile probation officer pointed out that overage pupils, humiliated at having

Table 7
Causes of Grade Retardation, by Race,
in 24 Chicago Elementary Schools, ca. 1920

Cause	Overage Negroes		Overage Whites	
	Number	Percent	Number	Percent
Late entrance	564	38.3	187	12.0
Mental deficiency	312	21.2	510	32.8
Family problems	253	17.2	175	11.3
Illness or physical impairment	163	11.0	280	18.0
Foreign language	3	.2	217	14.0
Irregular attendance	167	11.3	161	10.4
Other	12	.8	24	1.5
Total	1,474	100.0	1,554	100.0

Source: Chicago Commission on Race Relations, *The Negro in Chicago: A Study of Race Relations and a Race Riot* (Chicago, 1922), p. 260.

to mix with younger classmates, sometimes became truant or delinquent. Since retarded students in large classes rarely received individual assistance, only the most highly motivated could ever reach the standard grade for their age. Nevertheless, in important respects, retardation was not the tragedy that experts believed. A 1928 study of one local school showed that although 71 percent of the blacks were over-age, more than half of this number had never failed a grade; they had started later or had other problems which delayed their progress. Indeed, blacks had a high rate of retardation partly because they were willing to remain in school beyond the compulsory age limit, even when they were "behind." The race relations commission contrasted blacks' tenacity with immigrants' eagerness to leave school and get a job. In both the 1920 and 1940 census, the percentage of black children age sixteen to eighteen (above the legal requirement) attending school was higher than the citywide figure. Rather than a sign of individual or racial failure, retardation represented both the considerable environmental handicaps burdening black children and their determined efforts to get an education.[60]

Although evidence about black pupil performance in interwar Chicago is fragmentary, it does tempt us into some speculation. Black students advanced through the grades at a slower pace than either youngsters from immigrant families or those from upper-status neighborhoods. Despite their high failure and retardation rates, however, it is by no means certain that blacks learned less than poor whites. While Phillips Junior High did rank last on the 1926 math and sentence structure exams, elementary civics knowledge and reading achievement tests in the mid-1920s showed black children doing better than those in most immigrant areas. If the latter findings were typical, black children learned more than their relative pace of promotion warranted, and some combination of teachers' perceptions and students' environmental difficulties explained the lag between learning and advancement in school.

The nature of that combination, however, is uncertain. As we have seen, racism infected teachers and textbooks and underlay intelligence testing and vocational training policies. One might expect that a group ignored or denigrated in the books it studies would lose self-esteem and become estranged from formal education. Similarly, since teacher-pupil rapport is an important part of successful learning, we might suppose that the attitudes and behavior of instructors in ghetto schools accounted for low achievements of black children. It thus seems reasonable to assume that classroom racism impaired the academic progress of black students. Yet proof that racism caused poor performance or slower advancement is lacking. For some people, adversity increases morale and inspires group and individual achievement. Blacks began the period after World War I with high aspirations and faith in schooling, but the ghetto was barren soil for mastering academic skills. Children from troubled families without traditions of formal learning were severely handicapped in the classroom. One can only conclude that the schools' racism combined in some indeterminate way with home and community disabilities to limit the educational attainments of ghetto youth. Classroom racism had other effects as well. In a perhaps unintended manner, the public schools prepared black children for the adult world, by acclimating them to the humiliation and restricted opportunities they would experience after graduation. By the 1930s, black Chicagoans had shed much of their traditional optimism about education and had begun to realize that the schools were simply part of the problem.

NOTES

1. *Chicago Defender,* June 8 and Oct. 19, 1912, p. 3, Oct. 10, 1914, p. 4, Jan. 2, 1915, p. 2, Apr. 13, 1918, p. 16, May 28, 1921, p. 16, June 25, 1921, p. 3, July 2, 1921, p. 16; *Chicago Whip,* Sept. 27, 1919, p. 12, Sept. 18, 1920, p. 2.
2. St. Clair Drake and Horace R. Cayton, *Black Metropolis: A Study of*

Negro Life in a Northern City (New York, 1945), pp. 214-32; Perry R. Duis, "Arthur W. Mitchell: New Deal Negro in Congress" (M.A. thesis, University of Chicago, 1966), pp. 14-15; Maudelle Brown Bousfield, "A Study of the Intelligence and School Achievement of Negro Children" (M.A. thesis, University of Chicago, 1931), pp. 16-17; Alicia Treanor Doran, "Retardation among Negro Pupils in the Junior High School" (M.A. thesis, University of Chicago, 1934), p. 47; Susan L. Gorman, "Character Education under Difficulties," *Chicago Schools Journal,* 20 (Jan.-Feb., 1939), 118.

3. Mary Elaine Ogden, *The Chicago Negro Community: A Statistical Description* (Chicago, 1939), pp. 94, 207-12; Chicago Commission on Race Relations, *The Negro in Chicago: A Study of Race Relations and a Race Riot* (Chicago, 1922), p. 263; Julia Hermine Lorenz, "The Reading Achievements and Deficiencies of Ninth Grade Negro Pupils" (M.A. thesis, University of Chicago, 1937), pp. 11-12; Gorman, "Character Education," p. 118; Juvenile Protective Association of Chicago, *Annual Report,* 1930, p. 9.

4. Lorenz, "Reading Achievements," pp. 11, 30-31; Bousfield, "Study of the Intelligence and School Achievement," pp. 14-16; Maudelle B. Bousfield, "The Intelligence and School Achievement of Negro Children," *Journal of Negro Education,* 1 (Oct., 1932), 390.

5. Drake and Cayton, *Black Metropolis,* pp. 204-5; Ogden, *Chicago Negro Community,* pp. 201-3; Doran, "Retardation among Negro Pupils," p. 45; Bousfield, "Study of the Intelligence and School Achievement," p. 23; Chicago Commission on Race Relations, *Negro in Chicago,* p. 264; Jean Everhard Fair, "The History of Public Education in the City of Chicago, 1894-1914" (M.A. thesis, University of Chicago, 1939), pp. 112-13; "The Chicago Schools," *School and Society,* 11 (Apr. 10, 1920), 433; Chicago Board of Education, *Proceedings,* Dec. 15, 1937, pp. 487-90; Gertrude Birkhoff to Raymond S. Rubinow, Oct. 3 and 24, 1930, Julius Rosenwald Papers, Box 26, Folder 7, University of Chicago Library; *Defender,* Oct. 10, 1931, p. 4, Nov. 14, 1931, p. 3, Nov. 21, 1931, p. 4, Dec. 20, 1930, p. 16, Nov. 8, 1930, p. 4, Jan. 24, 1931, p. 17, Mar. 26, 1932, p. 13.

6. Ogden, *Chicago Negro Community,* pp. 48-60, 70-73, 171-72; Lorenz, "Reading Achievements," pp. 11, 30; Anna E. Harmon, "Orienting First-Graders," *Chicago Schools Journal,* 22 (Sept.-Oct., 1940), 10; Don C. Rogers, "A Study of Pupil Failures in Chicago," *Elementary School Journal,* 26 (Dec., 1925), 276; Thomas J. Woofter, ed., *Negro Problems in Cities* (Garden City, N.Y., 1928), pp. 191-92; Margaret J. Synnberg, "Transiency —A Major Problem," *Nation's Schools,* 28 (Sept., 1941), 49-50.

7. Bousfield, "Study of the Intelligence and School Achievement," pp. 12-13; Doran, "Retardation among Negro Pupils," pp. 45-47; Lorenz, "Reading Achievements," p. 29; E. Franklin Frazier, *The Negro Family in the United States* (Chicago, 1939), p. 607; E. Franklin Frazier, *The Negro Family in Chicago* (Chicago, 1932), pp. 144-45.

8. Ogden, *Chicago Negro Community,* pp. 225-26; Chicago Commission on Race Relations, *Negro in Chicago,* p. 262; Woofter, *Negro Problems,* pp. 192-93; *Defender,* Mar. 8, 1930, p. 2; George Gregory, Jr., "The Harlem Children's Center," *Opportunity,* 10 (Nov., 1932), 341.

9. *New York Age,* Sept. 20, 1906, p. 5; Chicago Commission on Race Relations, *Negro in Chicago,* pp. 241, 248; W. Lloyd Warner, Buford H. Junker, and Walter A. Adams, *Color and Human Nature* (Washington, 1941), p. 194.

10. Chicago Commission on Race Relations, *Negro in Chicago*, pp. 239, 241, 264-65, 267; Louise Venable Kennedy, *The Negro Peasant Turns City-ward* (New York, 1930), pp. 196-99; *Defender*, Nov. 19, 1921, p. 15.

11. Chicago Commission on Race Relations, *Negro in Chicago*, pp. 267-68; *Broad Ax* (Chicago), Jan. 29, 1921, p. 1; *Defender*, Nov. 19, 1921, p. 15, May 27, 1922, p. 20, June 24, 1922, p. 15.

12. William H. Johnson, "The Problem of Truancy in the Chicago Public Schools," *School and Society*, 45 (May 15, 1937), 665; Clifford R. Shaw, *Delinquency Areas* (Chicago, 1929), pp. 33-52; Woofter, *Negro Problems*, p. 176; *Defender*, Oct. 14, 1922, p. 2, Nov. 19, 1938, p. 15, Sept. 6, 1913, p. 5, Sept. 20, 1913, p. 2, Oct. 3, 1914, p. 8, Sept. 11, 1915, p. 8.

13. Shaw, *Delinquency Areas*, pp. 53-54, 60-65, 74, 153; Ogden, *Chicago Negro Community*, pp. 99-101; Earl R. Moses, "Community Factors in Negro Delinquency," *Journal of Negro Education*, 5 (Apr., 1936), 220-27; Frazier, *Negro Family in Chicago*, pp. 204-19.

14. *Whip*, June 18 and 25, 1921, p. 5; Illinois Writers Project, "The Negro in Illinois"; *Defender*, Feb. 18, 1939, p. 4; Frazier, *Negro Family in Chicago*, pp. 179-203; Drake and Cayton, *Black Metropolis*, pp. 202-3, 589-95.

15. *Defender*, Mar. 14, 1931, p. 2, Jan. 23, 1937, pp. 1, 25, May 22, 1937, p. 1, May 20, 1939, p. 7, Apr. 27, 1940, p. 3, May 27, 1944, pp. 1, 5.

16. George D. Strayer, *Report of the Survey of the Schools of Chicago, Illinois* (New York, 1932), IV, 60; *Defender*, July 16, 1932, p. 11, Sept. 30, 1933, p. 15, Oct. 19, 1935, p. 20, Oct. 30, 1937, p. 10, Nov. 20, 1937, p. 24, Dec. 10, 1938, p. 22, Sept. 27, 1941, p. 16, Oct. 3, 1942, p. 3; Sylvia Bonheim, interview, Chicago, Sept., 1969.

17. *Defender*, Feb. 27, 1926, sec. 1, p. 3, Jan. 29, 1927, sec. 1, p. 3, May 3, 1930, sec. 1, p. 6, Jan. 31, 1931, pp. 1, 6, Nov. 21 and 28, 1931, p. 1, Nov. 2, 1935, p. 10, Oct. 31, 1936, p. 1, Mar. 2, 1940, p. 2.

18. Frederic M. Thrasher, *The Gang: A Study of 1,313 Gangs in Chicago* (Chicago, 1927), pp. 3-57, 452-86; *Defender*, Dec. 17, 1927, sec. 1, pp. 1, 6, Oct. 5, 1940, p. 2. The quotation from Thrasher is from p. 38.

19. Woofter, *Negro Problems*, p. 195; *Defender*, Oct. 3, 1925, sec. 1, p. 10, Nov. 27, 1926, sec. 2, p. 6, July 2, 1927, sec. 1, p. 12, July 23, 1927, sec. 2, p. 2, Oct. 22, 1932, p. 13, Apr. 7, 1934, p. 6, Aug. 11, 1934, p. 14, Aug. 24, 1940, p. 8, Oct. 5, 1940, p. 2; *Chicago Tribune*, Jan. 15, 1924, p. 22; *Whip*, Oct. 10, 1931, p. 12.

20. *Defender*, Oct. 5, 1929, p. 6, Sept. 28, 1935, p. 2, Apr. 13, 1940, p. 7, July 6, 1940, p. 24, Oct. 5, 1940, pp. 1-2; *Chicago's Schools*, 7 (Feb.-Mar., 1941), 1.

21. *Chicago Herald and Examiner*, Jan. 12, 1924, pp. 1-2, *Tribune*, Jan. 12, 1924, p. 1, Jan. 15, 1924, p. 22; *Chicago Daily News*, Jan. 12, 1924, p. 3; *Broad Ax*, Jan. 19, 1924, p. 1; *Defender*, Jan. 19, 1924, sec. 1, p. 4, Feb. 28, 1931, pp. 1, 5, Mar. 9 and Apr. 13, 1940, p. 7, May 11, 1940, p. 14, July 6, 1940, p. 24.

22. *Defender*, Mar. 9, 1929, sec. 1, p. 4, Aug. 11, 1934, p. 14.

23. *Ibid.*, May 24, 1930, p. 16, Feb. 7, 1931, p. 16, Dec. 5, 1931, p. 13, May 11, 1940, p. 14. See also *Defender*, Mar. 9, 1929, sec. 1, p. 4, Mar. 23, 1929, sec. 2, p. 2.

24. Juvenile Protective Association, *Annual Report*, 1924, p. 18; *Defender*, Nov. 28, 1925, sec. 2, p. 7, Mar. 9, 1929, sec. 1, p. 4, Oct. 5, 1935, p. 11, Mar. 2 and 16, 1940, p. 14, July 6, 1940, p. 24, Oct. 5, 1940, pp. 1-2, Oct. 12, 1940, p. 5.

25. *Crisis,* 14 (June, 1917), 91; *Broad Ax,* Aug. 16, 1924, p. 7; *Defender,* Feb. 6, 1926, sec. 1, p. 3, May 30, 1931, p. 17, Feb. 6, 1932, p. 17.

26. Howard S. Becker, "Role and Career Problems of the Chicago Public School Teacher" (Ph.D. diss., University of Chicago, 1951), pp. 43, 45-50, 79-83.

27. *Defender,* Oct. 4, 1924, sec. 1, p. 16; Chicago Commission on Race Relations, *Negro in Chicago,* pp. 248-49, 269, 438-40, 457.

28. *Defender,* Dec. 22, 1923, sec. 1, p. 3, Feb. 22, 1930, p. 3, Mar. 1, 1930, p. 2, Mar. 8, 1930, pp. 3, 7, Apr. 26, 1930, p. 5, May 10, 1930, p. 3, Nov. 30, 1935, p. 16, May 9, 1936, p. 16. See also *Defender,* Sept. 27, 1924, p. 1, Oct. 25, 1941, p. 16; Edith M. Stern, "Jim Crow Goes to School in New York," *Crisis,* 44 (July, 1937), 202.

29. Madeline R. Stratton, interview, Chicago, Oct., 1969; Charles S. Johnson, "Source Material for Patterns of Negro Segregation: Chicago, Illinois" (working memorandum for Gunnar Myrdal, *An American Dilemma*); *Defender,* Mar. 8, 1930, p. 2.

30. Chicago Commission on Race Relations, *Negro in Chicago,* pp. 438-39; Ethel M. Hilliard, interview, Chicago, Nov., 1969; Becker, "Role and Career Problems," pp. 53-54, 202; *Defender,* Feb. 22, 1930, p. 12.

31. Drake and Cayton, *Black Metropolis,* pp. 495-506; Warner, et al., *Color and Human Nature;* Annabelle Carey Prescott, interview, Chicago, May, 1973; *Defender,* Feb. 5, 1921, p. 2, Sept. 20, 1919, p. 6; Arthur N. Turnbull, interview, Chicago, Nov. and Dec., 1969; Frederick H. Robb, ed., *1927 Intercollegian Wonder Book, or, The Negro in Chicago, 1779-1927* (Chicago, 1927), p. 52.

32. Samuel B. Stratton, interview, Chicago, Oct. and Nov., 1969; Hilliard, interview; Becker, "Role and Career Problems," p. 312; *Defender,* Apr. 6, 1935, p. 16, Aug. 3, 1940, p. 13.

33. For a complete list of approved Chicago public school textbooks, see Board of Education, *Proceedings,* Aug. 9, 1933, pp. 69-107. The Center for Research Libraries in Chicago has an extensive collection of school textbooks, including those used in local classrooms. For a recent study of American history texts from the nineteenth century to the present, see Frances FitzGerald, *America Revised* (Boston, 1979).

34. Grace Vollintine, *The American People and Their Old World Ancestors* (Boston, 1930); Reuben Post Halleck and Juliette Frantz, *Our Nation's Heritage: What the Old World Contributed to the New* (New York, 1925); James A. Woodburn and Howard C. Hill, *Historic Background of Our United States* (New York, 1938); Henry Noble Sherwood, *Our Country's Beginnings* (Indianapolis, 1924); Harold R. Isaacs, *The New World of Negro Americans* (New York, 1964), pp. 162, 285.

35. Thomas M. Marshall, *American History* (New York, 1930), p. 342; Eugene C. Barker, William E. Dodd, and Walter P. Webb, *The Story of Our Nation* (Evanston, Ill., 1929), pp. 307-12; Wilbur Fisk Gordy, *Leaders in Making America* (New York, n.d.), p. 248; Henry William Elson, *History of the United States of America* (New York, 1923), pp. 557-58; Mary G. Kelty, *The Growth of the American People and Nation* (Boston, 1931), pp. 284-85, 300-301.

36. James Albert Woodburn, Thomas Francis Moran, and Howard Copeland Hill, *Our United States* (New York, 1935), pp. 492-93, 499-500; Rolla M. Tryon and Charles R. Lingley, *The American People and Nation* (Boston,

1927), pp. 488-90; Barker, Dodd, and Webb, *Our Nation Grows Up* (Evanston, Ill., 1932), p. 174; David Saville Muzzey, *History of the American People* (Boston, 1929), pp. 405, 408; Elson, *History*, pp. 799-800; Kelty, *Growth*, pp. 377-83.

37. Charles A. Beard and Mary R. Beard, *History of the United States* (New York, 1925), pp. 373-75, 382-89, 396-98; Woodburn, et al., *Our United States*, pp. 744-47; Ruth West and Willis Mason West, *The Story of Our Country* (Boston, 1935), p. 384; Elson, *History*, pp. 801-3.

38. Howard Copeland Hill, *Community Life and Civic Problems* (Boston, 1922), p. 333; Chicago Branch NAACP, "Your Civil Rights in Chicago," pamphlet, NAACP Papers, Branch Files, Box G53, Library of Congress; *Defender*, Mar. 26, 1938, p. 1.

39. *Defender*, Mar. 26, 1938, p. 1, Mar. 13, 1926, p. 1; Carter G. Woodson, "The Miseducation of the Negro," *Crisis*, 38 (Aug., 1931), 266.

40. George S. Counts, *School and Society in Chicago* (New York, 1928), pp. 275-84; *Defender*, Nov. 19, 1927, sec. 2, p. 4, Mar. 13, Apr. 24, and May 8, 1926, p. 1, May 22, 1926, sec. 1, p. 9; *Crisis*, 32 (July , 1926), 115; *Opportunity*, 4 (July, 1926), 231.

41. Daniel J. Kevles, "Testing the Army's Intelligence: Psychologists and the Military in World War I," *Journal of American History*, 55 (Dec., 1968), 565-81; David Tyack, *The One Best System: A History of American Urban Education* (Cambridge, 1974), pp. 204-8; E. E. Keener, *Mental Ability of High School Freshmen in Relation to Problems of Adjustment* (Chicago, 1924), pp. 5, 12, 18, 21.

42. Tyack, *One Best System*, pp. 214-15; Clarence J. Karier, "Testing for Order and Control in the Corporate Liberal State," in Karier, Paul Violas, and Joel Spring, *Roots of Crisis: American Education in the Twentieth Century* (Chicago, 1973), pp. 120-21; Counts, *School and Society in Chicago*, pp. 185-90; E. L. Thorndike, "Intelligence Scores of Colored Pupils in High Schools," *School and Society*, 18 (Nov. 10, 1923), 569-70; Morris S. Viteles, "The Mental Status of the Negro," *Annals of The American Academy of Political and Social Science*, 140 (Nov., 1928), 166-77; Herman G. Canady, "The Methodology and Interpretation of Negro-White Mental Testing," *School and Society*, 55 (May 23, 1942), 569-75; Horace Mann Bond, *The Education of the Negro in the American Social Order* (New York, 1966), p. 329.

43. Bond, *Education of the Negro*, pp. 316-21, 326-29; Charles H. Thompson, "The Educational Achievements of Negro Children," *Annals*, 140 (Nov., 1928), 193-208; Horace Mann Bond, "Intelligence Tests and Propaganda," *Crisis*, 28 (June, 1924), 61-64, and "Some Exceptional Negro Children," *Crisis*, 34 (Oct., 1927), 257; Stern, "Jim Crow Goes to School," p. 202; Albert Sidney Beckham, "Race and Intelligence," *Opportunity*, 10 (Aug., 1932), 241; Bousfield, "Intelligence and School Achievement," pp. 393-95.

44. Turnbull, interview; Mary J. Herrick, interview, Chicago, Nov., 1969; Lorenz, "Reading Achievements," pp. 12, 33; Letitia Fyffe Merrill, "Children's Choice of Occupations," *Chicago Schools Journal*, 5 (Dec., 1922), 156-57.

45. Richard R. Wright, Jr., "The Industrial Condition of Negroes in Chicago" (B.D. thesis, University of Chicago, 1901), p. 6; Louise de Koven Bowen, "The Colored People of Chicago," *Survey*, 31 (Nov. 1, 1913), 117; *Defender*, Aug. 23, 1913, p. 4; June 22, 1935, p. 8, Sept. 13, 1941, p. 6; Drake and Cayton, *Black Metropolis*, pp. 214-62; Theophilus Lewis, "Where Do They Go from School?" *Commonweal*, 29 (Oct. 28, 1938), 6.

46. Tyack, *One Best System,* pp. 221-25; Stern, "Jim Crow Goes to School," p. 202; Madeline R. Stratton, interview; Hilliard, interview; Chicago Board of Education, *Annual Report,* 1940-41, p. 169.

47. August Meier, *Negro Thought in America, 1880-1915* (Ann Arbor, Mich., 1963), pp. 85-99; Lawrence A. Cremin, *The Transformation of the School: Progressivism in American Education, 1876-1957* (New York, 1961), pp. 23-57; Sol Cohen, "The Industrial Education Movement, 1906-17," *American Quarterly,* 20 (Spring, 1968), 95-110; Chicago Board of Education, *Annual Directory,* 1920-21, pp. 62-184; Fair, "History of Public Education," pp. 79-80; Mary J. Herrick, *The Chicago Schools: A Social and Political History* (Beverly Hills, Calif., 1971), pp. 117-19; William R. Chenery, "Adulterated Education," *New Republic,* 4 (Oct. 23, 1915), 304-5.

48. *Defender,* Nov. 23, 1912, p. 3, Mar. 4, 1916, p. 8, May 24, 1930, p. 16, June 7, 1930, p. 13; A. L. Foster, *The Urban League and the Negro Community: The Eighteenth Annual Report of the Chicago Urban League* (Chicago [1932]), p. 19.

49. John A. Lapp, *The Washburne Trade School* (Chicago, 1941), pp. 23-29; Marjorie Lord Dunnegan, "Vocational Education at Dunbar," *Integrated Education,* 1 (June, 1963), 30; William J. Connors to Edward Kelly, received June 8, 1940, State of Illinois File, Chicago Housing Authority Papers, Chicago Historical Society; Hearings of Illinois State Commission on the Condition of the Urban Colored Population, Jan. 1941, p. 192, Committee on Fair Employment Practices, Record Group 228, National Archives.

50. Chicago Conference on Home Front Unity, *Home Front Unity* (Chicago, 1945), pp. 24, 28; "Notes on 1940 School Budget at Hearings of January 10, 1940," Mary Herrick Papers, Chicago Historical Society; *Defender,* Feb. 11, 1939, p. 16; Hearings of Illinois State Commission on Condition of Urban Colored Population, pp. 195-96.

51. Chicago Board of Education, *Proceedings,* Oct. 20, 1937, p. 246; *Defender,* Nov. 26, 1938, p. 7, May 27, 1939, p. 20, Sept. 16, 1939, p. 15, Mar. 16, 1940, p. 7, Oct. 12, 1940, p. 4, July 5, 1941, p. 3; Turnbull, interview; Mabel P. Simpson, "Leaders Make Recommendations for Help for Negro Schools before School Opens This Fall" [1941], Mary Herrick Papers; Hearings of Illinois State Commission on Condition of Urban Colored Population, p. 225.

52. Board of Education, *Proceedings,* Jan. 10, 1940, pp. 615-16; Board of Education, *Annual Directory,* 1940-41, pp. 53, 89; *Chicago's Schools,* 7 (Feb.-Mar., 1941), 4, and 7 (Apr., 1941), 2; *Defender,* May 28, 1938, p. 13, Oct. 12, 1940, p. 4, Mar. 22, 1941, p. 6, Dec. 6, 1941, p. 4; Simpson, "Leaders Make Recommendations."

53. *Defender,* Mar. 8, 1941, p. 2, Oct. 25, 1941, p. 28, Nov. 29, 1941, p. 4.

54. William Henry Burton, "The Nature and Amount of Civic Information Possessed by Chicago Children of Sixth Grade Level" (Ph.D. diss., University of Chicago, 1924), pp. 131-32, 191-94, 226, 260-61; Gertrude Whipple, "An Analytical Study of the Reading Achievement of Three Different Types of Pupils" (M.A. thesis, University of Chicago, 1927), pp. 1-2, 39-40, 66.

55. Board of Education, *Annual Report,* 1925-26, pp. 102-3; Lorenz, "Reading Achievements," pp. 12-15.

56. Rogers, "Pupil Failures," p. 273; Chicago Commission on Race Rela-

tions, *Negro in Chicago,* p. 271; Board of Education, *Annual Report,* 66 (1922), 74-76.

57. Tyack, *One Best System,* pp. 199-201; U.S. Immigration Commission, *The Children of Immigrants in Schools* (Washington, 1911), II, 548; Chicago Commission on Race Relations, *Negro in Chicago,* pp. 256-57.

58. Chicago Commission on Race Relations, *Negro in Chicago,* pp. 258-59; Woofter, *Negro Problems,* p. 175.

59. *Crisis,* 35 (July, 1928), 238; Woofter, *Negro Problems,* pp. 175, 184; Chicago Commission on Race Relations, *Negro in Chicago,* pp. 260-65; E. George Payne, "Negroes in the Public Elementary Schools of the North," *Annals,* 140 (Nov., 1928), 228-29; Don C. Rogers, "Retardation from the Mental Standpoint," *Chicago Schools Journal,* 9 (Apr., 1927), 302; Rogers, "Pupil Failures," p. 273.

60. Woofter, *Negro Problems,* pp. 175, 184-85; *Defender,* Apr. 6, 1929, p. 1; Ruth S. Jewell, interview, Chicago, Oct., 1969; Edward E. Keener, interview, Chicago, Nov., 1969; Chicago Commission on Race Relations, *Negro in Chicago,* p. 258; Ernest W. Burgess and Charles Newcomb, eds., *Census Data of the City of Chicago, 1920* (Chicago, 1931), pp. 33-34; U.S. Department of Commerce, Bureau of the Census, *Sixteenth Census of the United States, 1940: Population,* IV, Pt. 2 (Washington, 1943), p. 629.

CHAPTER FIVE

Black Activism and the Public Schools

BLACK CHICAGOANS were not merely passive observers as a segregated and unequal system of public education developed during the 1920s and 1930s. While less vital to blacks than jobs or housing, the public schools were nonetheless important both for their immediate benefits and for the future hopes they symbolized. Thus, it is not surprising that ghetto organizations were concerned about school problems. In this chapter, I will analyze black activism and the public schools in interwar Chicago through an examination of the strengths and weaknesses of the various groups that dealt with educational issues. I will also consider the goals and priorities blacks held regarding public education and show how these aims changed over time, and will describe the tactics blacks used in school controversies, analyzing the effectiveness of the methods employed. I hope the resulting account will not only enhance understanding of black urban education but also illuminate the values and dynamics of ghetto civic life between the world wars.

Like other communities, black Chicago in the 1920s and 1930s was an organized society with formal and informal networks binding residents to each other. Of the formally structured organizations, churches attracted the largest membership, but social clubs, fraternal orders, political groups, and, late in the period, labor unions all had their followings. Despite the ghetto's rich associational life, however, black civic action suffered from significant weaknesses. Many important black groups, such as churches, lodges, and social clubs, usually did not take part in civic action efforts. Like members of any community, most black Chicagoans involved in associational life found religion and socializing more interesting than community affairs. Whereas only a tiny minority of people in any setting are active in civic affairs, that segment was especially small in the black ghetto between the world wars. Black Chicago was a predominantly lower-class society, with a large share of its residents coming from the black peasantry of the rural South. The poor, ill-educated, and transient lower class lacked a strong sense of community awareness and had relatively low rates of membership in voluntary associations. Therefore, the ghetto's associational structure was primarily a product of its small middle and upper classes. Although these groups shared the common tie of color with the masses, business, professional, and white-collar activists frequently differed so much in style, values, and goals from lower-class blacks that there was only a tenuous link between ghetto civic associations and the bulk of the black population. In other words, the Urban League, NAACP, and other groups that worked on school issues were not mass movements but small elites. Their degree of representativeness depended on the ability of each organization's leaders to identify and articulate issues that had a mass appeal. As we shall see, this capability varied considerably from group to group.[1]

The Chicago Urban League was easily the most successful civic or-ganization in black Chicago during the interwar period. Founded in December, 1916, at the initiative of National Urban League officials, the CUL reflected its parent group's emphasis on employment, welfare services and referrals, and research into problems affecting urban blacks. The CUL's priorities and style, however, changed markedly be-tween the world wars. T. Arnold Hill, the Virginia-born social worker who served as executive secretary from 1916 to 1925, was a tactful dip-lomat adept at courting influential whites and deeply committed to the Urban League's belief in interracial conciliation. Under Hill's leader-ship, the CUL stressed job placement through cooperative relations with Julius Rosenwald of Sears and Roebuck, stockyards operators, and other businessmen and manufacturers who furnished its funds. Although it never repudiated this approach, the CUL moved in new directions under Albon L. Foster, an ex-YMCA social worker and former head of the Canton, Ohio, Urban League, who was CUL's exec-utive secretary from 1925 to 1946. Foster's belief in active protest and racial solidarity, the League's increasing attention to publicity, and un-rest among blacks stemming from rising joblessness combined to broaden the organization's scope and make it more militant by the late 1920s. Between 1927 and 1929, the CUL campaigned for clerical jobs for blacks in white-owned ghetto businesses, agitated for more park fa-cilities on the South Side, and joined the outcry against racially gerry-mandered school district boundaries in Morgan Park.[2]

During the Great Depression, the CUL moved even further from the approach Hill had taken during the early years. The economic collapse fueled discontent in the ghetto, and Communist initiatives on behalf of evicted families and relief recipients threatened to discredit established black organizations. Although the CUL maintained biracial leadership

and continued its social service programs, such as neighborhood beauti-
fication, disease screening, and individual casework, Foster asserted
that his agency was also "an aggressive, fighting organization." Between 1934 and 1940, the CUL battled to integrate public housing projects, took part in the lengthy struggle for public housing on the South
Side, and pushed for expanded job opportunities in federally funded
construction and work-relief programs. The CUL also established and
supported a number of groups that used their technically independent
status to carry protest beyond the limits traditionally associated with the
Urban League movement. For example, in 1937, Foster was instrumental in founding a Negro Chamber of Commerce that protested
white business domination of the ghetto and agitated for jobs for blacks
with local mass transit companies. The same year, Howard D. Gould,
director of the CUL's Industrial Relations Department, and Joseph
Jefferson, boys' work secretary of the Wabash Avenue YMCA and
later a National Youth Administration project director for the CUL,
started the Negro Labor Relations League. The NLRL, a small organization of young manual workers, used picketing and boycotts in its
drives for black branch managers for daily newspapers and black film
projectionists, milk drivers, and telephone operators in the ghetto.[3]

In addition to its activities in the jobs and housing fields, the CUL
under Foster was prominent in school issues of the 1930s. The League's
Interracial Commission worked to restore peace during the Morgan
Park High School branch dispute of 1934. The CUL also played a key
role in the drive to gain representation on the Chicago Board of Education. It was the CUL's leaders who revived the demand for a black
school board member in 1932 and 1933. Whites like CUL president El-
bridge Bancroft Pierce, a well-known attorney; CUL vice-president
Amelia Sears, Cook County commissioner and assistant superintendent
of United Charities; and Mrs. Emile Levy, member of the CUL Board
of Directors and the Chicago Woman's Club, joined Foster and the
CUL Interracial Commission head Dr. Arthur G. Falls in lobbying
Mayor Anton J. Cermak. Two years later, the CUL set in motion the
mass approach that ultimately made the campaign a success. The
League was also an important part of the anti-overcrowding movement,
assisting protests in individual school districts and participating in the
general ghetto-wide effort. As early as 1935, Frazier T. Lane, director of
the CUL's Civic Improvement Department, cooperated with PTA representatives in a committee to investigate and complain about double-
shift schools in black neighborhoods. At the 1939 Board of Education
annual budget hearing, Joseph Jefferson, by then a CUL employee, elo-
quently asked authorities to break the circle of poverty, overcrowding,

and juvenile delinquency by providing adequate school facilities. Lane testified about South Side school needs before a City Council committee in June, 1939, and Foster did the same at the Board of Education budget hearing in January, 1940. The following year, the CUL conducted several tours of ghetto schools for white civic leaders to dramatize educational conditions. The CUL concerned itself with other school matters as well. It held meetings with South Side principals to help combat juvenile delinquency and helped stop an effort in 1940 to oust the Du Sable High School principal, Chauncey C. Willard. Willard's opposition to the school administration stimulated a dismissal move by regular Democrats, but the CUL rallied support for the principal, whose honesty and firmness had won him the respect of South Side blacks.[4]

The CUL's preeminence among black Chicago's civic groups was based upon several different strengths. As already mentioned, its able leaders sensed the popular mood during the Depression crisis and adjusted their approach accordingly. But the CUL's responsiveness was by no means limited to the 1930s. Throughout the interwar years, the League earned the confidence of ghetto citizens by stressing the things that concerned them most. Its endeavors in employment, housing, education, and social services addressed the basic needs of ordinary people. During recessions of the 1920s and the Depression of the 1930s, the CUL fed the hungry and lodged the homeless. As Lovelyn Evans, a onetime *Chicago Whip* writer who was active in PTAs and women's clubs, said of the League, "They'd get out and work with the people." The CUL's support among white "people of good will," in Arthur Falls's words, was another asset which explained the agency's success. Men and women like Pierce, Sears, and Levy gave the CUL access to white political and civic leadership and this, in turn, enabled the League to accomplish its goals. White support also meant financial solvency. While the CUL did have lean years in the mid-twenties and early thirties, its funding was far more ample than other ghetto-based civic groups. As noted, Rosenwald and other white businessmen supported the CUL's operations during its early years. During the thirties, the Community Fund supplied half the annual budget. In the Depression year of 1935, Foster boasted that the League was in "very splendid financial condition," and the CUL's income nearly tripled between 1934 and 1940. In this period, the League administered projects for the NYA, the Works Progress Administration, and the city relief agency, all of which enabled the CUL to add staff and visibility on the South Side. For the scope of its programs, its rapport with the black masses, and its ties to prestigious whites, the CUL was unrivaled in black Chicago.[5]

The creation of the Chicago Council of Negro Organizations in 1935 was another example of the CUL's leadership in the civic life of the black ghetto. A federation of affiliated community groups, the CCNO was as much the child of the Urban League as were the Negro Chamber of Commerce and the Negro Labor Relations League. The CUL furnished office facilities and clerical assistance, and Albon Foster served as CCNO president until 1939, when women's club activist Irene McCoy Gaines succeeded him. As Foster wrote of the CCNO in the CUL's 1937 *Annual Report,* "While this is not an Urban League subsidiary, our contribution to its success is so substantial and its assistance to us so potent that we feel justified in mentioning a few of its accomplishments." Although the CCNO fulfilled a long-standing desire to coordinate the black associational structure, it was primarily an attempt by the established black leadership to compete with the Communists and to forestall the creation of a National Negro Congress affiliate in the city. The CCNO began with forty member organizations in 1935 and grew to sixty-five in 1937 and seventy-eight in 1940. Among its affiliates were nineteen civic groups, ten church organizations, ten social clubs, and a number of fraternities, sororities, professional societies, and labor unions. Foster's call for "mutual cooperation and solidarity" had found a receptive audience, for by the late thirties, the CCNO claimed to speak for 100,000 people, more than one-third of black Chicago's population.[6]

Like the CUL, the CCNO voiced the growing impatience of urban blacks and reflected the impact Communists had made on the black belt in the 1930s. The CCNO emulated the "Reds" by using aggressive rhetoric and direct action, as it staged marches, boycotted milk companies, and picketed movie houses to achieve the job gains also sought by the NLRL. The CCNO joined the CUL's agitation for public housing on the South Side, lobbied the state legislature for a bill against restrictive covenants, and denounced racial bias in AFL unions. School issues figured prominently on the CCNO's agenda as well. The campaign for black representation on the Board of Education was the group's first major project and one that it vocally and tenaciously carried to completion. In addition, the CCNO demanded action to remedy classroom overcrowding, called for placement of teachers without regard to race, and urged redistricting to reduce pupil segregation. The CCNO was an important addition to black Chicago's civic scene, as the school board campaign showed. Although it employed the militant tactics of the left, it attracted an older, more established following than the Communist party or the National Negro Congress. The CCNO was an umbrella organization, with the assets and problems such a structure entailed. Its size and inclusiveness made it a truly representative voice of the active black citizenry. On the other hand, the same breadth led the CCNO to raise more issues than it could thoroughly pursue, making its program somewhat unfocused and undisciplined. Moreover, the CCNO's diversity made it difficult to get unanimous agreement for projects. Since officers did not try to force reluctant member groups to support CCNO positions, frequently only part of the total membership favored a campaign. In fact, the CCNO selected the school board issue as its initial target partly because its disparate membership was united on the question.[7]

Unlike the CCNO and CUL, the Chicago branch of the National Association for the Advancement of Colored People did not attract widespread support even among civically active blacks. From its founding in 1910, the branch, like the NAACP itself, was a civil rights organization that worked for racial equality and integration through court litigation, lobbying, and publicizing injustice. In the beginning, the Chicago branch was white-dominated. Among the leading figures were Edward Osgood Brown, a judge and single-tax advocate who was president until 1921; Unitarian ministers Jenkin Lloyd Jones and Celia Parker Woolley; Jane Addams; and Julius Rosenwald, who furnished one-quarter of the chapter's budget between 1912 and 1914. Although during its first decade the branch opposed discriminatory bills in the Illinois legislature, tried to ban the film "The Birth of a Nation," and provided legal defense for blacks after the 1919 riot, it was generally weak and inactive. NAACP Great Lakes area organizer Robert W. Bagnall reported in 1918, "The Chicago Branch is dead. . . . The branch should be declared dormant and reorganized from the bottom up." Its program's limited appeal to blacks, lack of paid staff, and white control handicapped the local chapter from the start. As the *Broad Ax* remarked in 1913, "It is strange indeed that an association or combination, which is supposed to be gotten up in the interests of the Colored People, should be absolutely controlled in every particular by those belonging to an opposite race."[8]

Although blacks assumed important roles in the Chicago branch by the early 1920s and completely ran the chapter after Bagnall reorganized it early in 1925, the local NAACP still did not fulfill its friends' hopes for success. Blacks now controlled the organization, but they were attorneys, physicians, businessmen, and ministers, an elite with whom ordinary ghetto residents did not identify. Again and again in the 1920s and 1930s, national and local NAACP officials acknowledged the chapter's reputation as a "high-brow," "blue-stocking" group. Branch coordinator E. Frederic Morrow testified after visiting working-class black Chicagoans in 1938, "These people felt they weren't in the right social plane to be with us. . . . There are thousands of dollars in the shadow of the El, if we can get these folks to come down off their high horses and be with, if not of, those people there." As Morrow charged the following year, "There is a feeling that it is run by the lawyers for the lawyers." It was not only the branch's elite composition that prevented it from gaining mass appeal. The NAACP's civil rights platform was more attractive to upper-class blacks than to typical ghetto dwellers. While the CUL made jobs, housing, and emergency relief its chief priorities, the local NAACP devoted most of its energies to fighting segregation and discourteous treatment in movie theaters, restaurants, buses, and department stores and attacking restrictive covenants in white neighborhoods. In addition, the branch assisted the national office in campaigns to defend the Scottsboro boys and enact antilynching legislation. Such activities were laudable, but many blacks believed they benefited little from NAACP projects. For example, in a 1933 bid for public support, the branch cited its opposition to a proposed ban on racial intermarriage, bias at a travel bureau, and exclusion of blacks from polo matches at a state armory and from the Chicago Bar Association. Suggesting that the chapter broaden its efforts, Morrow wrote, "The legal fights the branch has waged here are commendable, but there are other matters that need attention that seem equally important, and certainly are to the teeming thousands who cannot find money to go to theaters, restaurants and taverns." Morrow, however, did not seem to realize that in this respect the Chicago chapter simply followed the program of the NAACP's national headquarters.[9]

The branch's conflict-prone leadership compounded its difficulties. During the early twenties, Charles Bentley and Morris Lewis were rival leaders of the chapter. Bentley, the Ohio-born, Chicago-educated dentist who had helped establish the Equal Opportunity League, the Niagara Movement, and the local NAACP, served from 1919 to 1925 as vice-president, a position of prime importance in light of the inactivity of presidents Brown and Harold L. Ickes. Lewis, an aide to former alderman Oscar De Priest, was branch secretary from 1922 to 1930. The energetic Lewis found Bentley passive. Bentley, on the other hand, resented Lewis for trying to seize control of the movement and for being closer to machine politicians and black churches and fraternal orders than to the biracial elite Bentley favored. Jealousies flared when Bentley publicly denounced Lewis's successful settlement of a bias case against a Chicago theater. Lewis became less involved in the group's affairs after he went to work for the *Chicago Defender* and the Federal Board of Conciliation in 1924. After the Bentley-Lewis period, the chapter's leading figures were Herbert A. Turner, a physician who was president from 1926 to 1932, and Archie L. Weaver, a postal worker and the branch's dedicated secretary, financial secretary, or executive secretary from 1926 to 1934. Like Bentley, Turner was relatively inactive, and he left office amid bitter quarreling with the new regime of Arthur Clement MacNeal. MacNeal, the fiery branch president from 1932 to 1937, had come to Chicago in 1919 after graduation from Yale Law School to co-edit the *Chicago Whip*. He had also assisted the chapter's defense of blacks accused in the 1919 riot. An energetic and outspoken individual, MacNeal vowed to "give no 'let-up' or consider any compromise or 'truce.'" Although the branch grew more lively under his administration, MacNeal nonetheless had serious shortcomings as a leader. His abrasiveness and combativeness involved him in personal clashes that drained the organization's limited strength. His emphasis on integration was shared by relatively few blacks in the 1930s, yet he was not interested in white support, as seen by his anti-Semitism and his attacks on the Rosenwald Fund.[10]

The Chicago NAACP's leadership problems, the limited scope and appeal of its program, and its image of social exclusivity helped keep it small, underfunded, and frequently inactive. Membership averaged about 1,500 but fluctuated drastically from a peak of 2,600 in 1931 to a low of 269 in 1932. Without the white support that gave the Urban League financial health, the branch's budget was only a small fraction of that raised by the CUL. While the chapter's funding also varied sharply from year to year, the annual average between 1926 and 1938 was about $2,800. Even these membership and financial statistics overstate the branch's viability, for throughout the interwar decades, it alternated between brief bursts of accomplishment and longer periods of suspended animation. In October, 1922, Mary White Ovington, chairman of the NAACP's Board of Directors, wrote that Bagnall "finds there is no National Association Branch in Chicago; that the Board has not met for many months. . . . " A little more than a year later, Lewis admitted, "N.A.A.C.P. matters here are at a very low ebb." Nor did the situation improve at the end of the decade. In 1930, a Chicago businesswoman complained to Acting Secretary Walter F. White, "With regard to the local branch it does not seem to function to any noticeable extent. You never hear of any of its activities, although there is plenty to be done." After MacNeal assumed the presidency, he told White, "For eight years the Chicago Branch has been more or less a paper and pencil organization. . . . " Despite MacNeal's efforts, by the end of the decade the chapter was once again becoming inert. Late in 1939, Morrow complained, "If the truth be told, there is really no branch in Chicago—merely a few individuals who keep an office open and use the name. As for activity, it is at a standstill."[11]

The Chicago NAACP did involve itself in school issues, but its contribution was quite different from the CUL, CCNO, and other black civic groups. The branch was of negligible importance in protesting overcrowding and in working for school board representation, the two most important educational concerns black Chicago had in the 1930s. Between 1933 and 1936, the branch interested itself to some degree in overcrowding and school facilities. In 1933, it called for the completion of New Phillips (Du Sable) High School, and two years later it waged a petition drive on behalf of needed renovations at Old Phillips. In addition, in 1935 and 1936, the branch planned broader campaigns aimed at overcrowded classrooms, but there is no evidence that they were carried out. Furthermore, the group played no part in the double-shift issue when it intensified between 1939 and 1941. Similarly, although MacNeal voiced support for a black appointee to the Board of Education in 1935, the branch was silent when the drive entered its critical stage over the next four years. On the other hand, integration was a more consistent concern of the Chicago NAACP. As mentioned in chapter 2, the branch successfully defended black transfer students at Parker High from ejection in 1923 and in 1937 overcame racial exclusion at the Bowen High prom. It also spoke against discrimination in the Sexton-Ross case and in the use of transfers for white pupils living in black districts. In addition, as we shall see, the chapter helped Morgan Park blacks resist elementary school segregation in 1926 and 1927. Nevertheless, the branch could have been more vigilant in its pro-integration efforts. A number of significant areas, such as faculty segregation, generated no action by the chapter. For example, in the Morgan Park High School branch affair of 1934, the CUL's Interracial Commission represented black interests, but the NAACP's participation came not from the Chicago chapter but by means of a telegram from Walter White in New York to Mayor Kelly.[12]

The founding of the National Negro Congress in 1936 was additional evidence of the Depression's deep impact on black civic groups both nationally and locally. Started by the Washington, D.C., attorney John P. Davis and the Howard University political scientist Ralph J. Bunche, the NNC sought to become a broad-based civil rights organization that would address a wide range of economic, political, and legal issues. The election of the Brotherhood of Sleeping Car Porters president A. Philip Randolph as NNC president illustrated the group's special interest in labor unionism and its attempt to establish a reputation for aggressive protest among the black masses of the urban North. Chicago supplied more than two-fifths of the delegates at the NNC's founding meeting, and a city chapter soon appeared. Like its parent organization, the Chicago Council of the National Negro Congress attracted young blacks, many of working-class backgrounds, who felt that the established civil rights associations were failing to provide the aggressive leadership that the economic crisis required. Charles Wesley Burton, a Presbyterian minister who had been vice-president of the local NAACP from 1926 to 1930, served as CCNNC president from 1936 until February, 1939. His successor, Dewey R. Jones, former managing editor of the *Chicago Defender* and Negro affairs official in the Interior Department, died three months after taking office and was replaced by Lillian Summers, a social worker with United Charities of Chicago. Whereas the CCNNC's presidents were liberal reformers, executive secretary Henry Johnson and financial secretary Edward L. Doty were union activists close to or part of the Communist party.[13]

Though its membership never exceeded 500, the CCNNC vigorously addressed issues of importance to black Chicagoans. It protested high rents, pressured transit and utility companies to hire more blacks, helped organize CIO unions in the stockyards, steel mills, and garment industry, and fought segregation at the Cook County Nurses' Home. Under George McCray, a former YMCA and WPA worker who succeeded Johnson as executive secretary, the CCNNC took an interest in public school conditions as well. The Chicago Council joined other groups in the campaign to place a black on the Board of Education, but it placed special emphasis on school overcrowding. In November, 1939, the Council established "Better Schools for Negro Children," a fact-finding and publicity committee headed by Eva T. Wells, who was prominent in the women's club movement. Two months later, Dean H. M. Smith of the Baptist Institute, a ministerial training center, represented the CCNNC at the Board of Education's annual budget hearing, where he attacked double-shift schools in the ghetto. McCray was especially active on the school issue, addressing meetings and writing articles and reports on the inadequacies of ghetto education.[14]

Despite its small size, lack of money, and conservative opposition, the CCNNC made a distinctive contribution to school protests of the late 1930s. McCray's reports on overcrowding were based on more research than those of other black organizations, and the group gave more attention than did most blacks to integration as a possible remedy for double-shift schedules. At the national level, however, the National Negro Congress failed to become a significant force in black America, despite its promising beginning. The NAACP remained aloof, fearing a competitor for publicity and scarce funds. The NNC's stress on union organizing precluded black business support, while churchmen and liberals who had participated at the beginning grew suspicious of the radical rhetoric and prominence of the Communists in the NNC. As moderates and liberals withdrew, the NNC became increasingly dependent upon Communists and CIO unions for funds and membership. Although Davis remained as executive secretary, Randolph quit the presidency at the third convention in 1940. Randolph and other critics charged that the Congress was no longer an independent voice of blacks but had become an ally of the white-dominated Communist party.[15]

The Negro women's club movement was yet another participant in school issues during the interwar years. The National Association of Colored Women began in 1896, and its affiliates flourished in Chicago, where Fannie Barrier Williams and Ida B. Wells-Barnett were leading figures prior to World War I. Around 1900, local clubs established the Colored Women's Conference of Chicago, which eventually gave way to the Chicago and Northern District Association of Colored Women (ACW). Based largely on an upper- and middle-class foundation, the ACW's seventy member clubs mixed charitable work and civic education with card games, teas, fashion shows, and dances. Women's clubs financed institutions for single women and the aged, day care centers, scholarship programs, and other community projects. For most of the interwar era, the ACW's school activities were more informational than protest-minded. In the late 1930s, however, the organization became more venturesome under leaders like Maude Roberts George, who was married to Albert B. George, Chicago's first Negro municipal judge, and Irene McCoy Gaines, a Florida-born, Chicago-educated social worker for the CUL, YWCA, and public relief agencies who was active in Republican politics and married to attorney and state representative Harris B. Gaines. The ACW joined the fight for a black school board member in 1935, when President Helen O. Brascher served on the committee that founded the CCNO. As one club officer put it, "It is time we are looking and working in behalf of our own." The movement remained a vocal part of the Board of Education campaign until its completion. Meanwhile, the ACW also began to attend to the ghetto's other major school priority—overcrowding. Members made fact-finding tours of several South Side schools, and at Board of Education annual budget hearings in 1940 and 1941 President Nannie N. Williams called for action to end double-shift schedules. Finally, the women's clubs assailed a variety of other "deplorable conditions under which children of the black belts must attend school," including high teacher turnover, inadequate classroom supplies and equipment, and transfers for white children living in black districts. The ACW was active in school protests mainly toward the end of the period, and it played a supporting rather than a leading role. Nonetheless, its participation in the Board of Education and overcrowding campaigns demonstrated that a portion of black Chicago's female leadership had mobilized for action on school problems.[16]

Organizations in individual school districts carried on some of the most effective civic action concerning public education. Of these groups, parent-teacher associations had great potential, since unlike the NAACP or CUL, PTAs focused primarily on the schools. The purpose of the PTA was to protect the interests of children and to "bring into closer relation the home and school that parents and teachers may cooperate intelligently in the training of the child." In Chicago in the mid-1930s, two-thirds of the schools had PTAs, and one or both parents were PTA members in about one-third of the eligible families. While nearly three-fourths of the teachers joined, they were usually inactive. Over 80 percent of PTA members were mothers, and they dominated the association. PTAs operated a wide-ranging program. They educated parents about child development, donated food and clothing to poor families, fought liquor sales and gambling, and bought supplies and equipment for their school. PTA teas, candy and bake sales, and entertainment events not only raised money for projects but attempted to strengthen the sense of community in local districts. PTAs also sometimes became lobbying forces, agitating for or against principals and teachers, working to secure improved educational facilities, and testifying on behalf of child welfare or school legislation at the local and state levels. In the late 1930s, PTAs from several black districts met with school officials to demand relief from overcrowding. In addition, representatives from Willard Elementary and Phillips High PTAs complained about South Side school conditions to the City Council Schools Committee in 1939, and a number of PTA leaders reiterated the protests at the Board of Education budget hearings in 1940 and 1941. Declared Lillian Wadell of the Burke PTA, "These half day sessions have forced out children into the streets and into undesirable companionships, while children of other communities are enjoying the fullness of their educational possibilities."[17]

Although in some cases PTAs in the ghetto were effective organizations, they shared certain weaknesses with other black civic groups. Like the CUL, NAACP, and the women's clubs, black PTAs were operated by active elites and were not mass organizations. A number of black-belt school districts had no PTAs. In the districts where they existed, PTAs were the province of an involved minority. In 1928, a survey of over 1,000 mothers and fathers in a black school district found just 89 who expressed interest in joining a PTA, and only ten came to the first meeting. A decade later, the situation was much the same. In 1939, Maude Roberts George claimed that no PTA in the South Side ghetto had enrolled as much as 10 percent of its eligible parents. Soon afterward, the *Defender* revealed, "Today in two elementary schools with a combined population of 6,000 pupils it is impossible to muster in

300 members for the Parent Teacher association." While PTAs tended to be more robust in middle- and upper-status neighborhoods where associational ties were stronger, even more favored districts, such as McCosh and Shoop, did not consistently support flourishing PTAs. "We don't have much of a parent problem down there," a teacher in one black school observed. "The PTA doesn't amount to very much and they don't have enough power to really make any trouble."[18]

Both parents and school personnel were responsible for the weakness of black PTAs. Some mothers and fathers stayed away because they felt uncomfortable about their own educational shortcomings, while others viewed schooling as the teachers' duty and believed that parents should not go to school unless asked to do so by an instructor. Faculty members interpreted such attitudes as apathy. "The parents in a neighborhood like that aren't really interested," a white teacher declared. "That's why the PTA doesn't amount to very much." Parents were "not overly interested in school," a black ex-teacher agreed. Many black parents were too busy for PTA meetings, which were often held during daytime hours. "Most of the parents work; in most families it's both parents who work. So that there can't be much of a PTA program," an instructor explained. "Especially because a lot of them work odd hours, work all night and sleep during the day so that they just can't make it at all." But parents were not wholly accountable for the weakness of PTAs. Though PTAs generally functioned as an auxiliary supporting principal and faculty, with articulate leadership and educational grievances, mothers could readily become vigorous critics of teachers and administrators. Accordingly, school personnel tolerated PTAs if they were deferential but tried to undermine them when they became too independent. One teacher berated parental involvement, "Especially when they have a PTA, you know. My, then they're just into everything." One former PTA leader recalled teachers misplacing meeting notices instead of sending them home with children, and a principal reportedly discouraged the PTA at his school because "parents were not sufficiently intelligent to confer with the teachers." In 1939, Frazier Lane of the Chicago Urban League advised blacks, "Strong parent-teacher organizations should be organized in our district, even in the schools where the principal tries to discourage such associations."[19]

Because PTAs frequently were unable to oppose school officials, protest activity often occurred outside the PTA framework. PTA guidelines required the association "to cooperate with the principal and the teachers" and "to abstain from encroaching on the administrative functions of the school." In addition, PTAs needed the cooperation of principals and teachers to communicate with parents and to hold meetings. Accordingly, PTAs occasionally became agents of the school administration opposing dissidents unhappy with classroom conditions. For example, in 1940, a group of Keith parents criticized the lack of a playground, gym, and assembly hall, denounced the double shift and supplies shortages, and called for the transfer of the principal, whom they accused of denigrating area residents. The PTA, however, came to the principal's defense and claimed to have collected 2,000 signatures on her behalf. The following year at Doolittle Elementary, the PTA president allegedly told parents not to complain about inadequate school accommodations. Because of such circumstances, parents engaged in school protests often formed ad hoc organizations, with or without the cooperation of the local PTA. Thus, Betsy Ross parents created the Fifth Ward Citizens Protective Association in 1933, Lilydale residents set up the Citizens Committee of Lilydale in 1936, the Parents' Community Club appeared in the Keith district in 1940 and the Wellstown Parents Civic Organization in the Doolittle district in 1941. As we shall see, these localized, special-purpose organizations sponsored the most militant school protest campaigns that took place in black Chicago between the wars.[20]

Black politicians were civic activists of a somewhat different breed from the ones we have described so far. While the CCNO, NAACP, and CCNNC emphasized verbal protest and had limited links with the black masses, the politician fashioned electoral majorities by distributing jobs and trading favors. Black Chicagoans acquired more political influence at an earlier date than did their counterparts elsewhere in the country. The rapidly growing and highly segregated black population combined with the city's ward system, intraparty factionalism, and relatively even balance between the two major parties to give the ghetto strategic importance. Disfranchisement in the South made Chicago blacks appreciate the value of the ballot. In 1930, whereas 68 percent of all eligible Chicagoans were registered to vote, 77 percent of the blacks were registered voters. Moreover, the fact that blacks were native-born citizens with relatively few children resulted in high voter turnout compared to total population. Blacks used this political power to gain jobs ranging from elective office and patronage and civil service posts in government to employment in politically protected gambling and drinking establishments. In addition, voting strength could sometimes bring better city services and more equitable treatment from police and the courts.[21]

For the first half of the interwar period, black politics was mostly Republican politics. Between 1919 and 1932, GOP candidates for major offices from mayor to president of the United States usually took between 76 and 93 percent of the black vote in Chicago. As mentioned in chapter 1, blacks were a key part of Mayor William Hale Thompson's organization. Since the Republicans were split into rival factions and since two-party competition was lively, blacks occupied a pivotal role. They helped launch Thompson's career and were responsible for his political survival on more than one occasion. This meant that black Republican leaders were independent figures rather than puppets of a white machine. During the 1920s, the two most prominent black politicians were Edward H. Wright and Oscar De Priest. Wright was born and educated in New York and entered politics shortly after coming to Chicago in the 1880s. He served two terms as Cook County commissioner (1896-1904) and became the city's first black ward committeeman (1920-27). Wright was an exceptionally able politician who was master in his own political house. Asked in a 1926 U.S. Senate hearing about the Crowe-Barrett faction in his ward, Wright replied, "Well, there is not any Crowe-Barrett group in my ward. . . . I am the group." More forceful and no less independent than Wright was Oscar De Priest. The Alabama-born De Priest worked as a house painter after he arrived in Chicago in 1889 but eventually became a wealthy real estate agent and investor. He rose through Republican ranks as county commissioner (1904-8), Chicago's first black alderman (1915-17), and the first black congressman from the North (1929-35). De Priest always stayed close to what he termed "the common herd" and earned popular respect for his commanding presence, outspokenness, and fearlessness. Like Wright, he defied Thompson and tangled with the Republican regulars when personal or racial considerations required it. Black politicians took some interest in school affairs during the Wright–De Priest era. They helped expand the black teaching force during the 1920s and secured physical improvements at South Side schools. For example, Alderman Robert R. Jackson, an ex-postal worker who served on the City Council from 1918 to 1941, and Alderman Louis B. Anderson, an attorney and a council member from 1917 to 1933, took credit for new school playgrounds and building additions in the ghetto. Unfortunately, black political independence and power was at its peak at a time when school facilities problems had not yet become severe.[22]

The thirties were politically unsettling for black Chicago. Blacks still voted Republican in most elections, albeit by sharply reduced margins, and Republicans still represented the ghetto in the City Council and state legislature for most of the decade. But new political coalitions were emerging. Anton J. Cermak, a Democrat, defeated Mayor Thompson for reelection in 1931, costing blacks their patronage jobs but paving the way for a Democratic bid for black support. In 1932, for example, the Democrats chose their party's first black ward committeeman. As noted in chapter 2, under Mayor Edward J. Kelly (1933-47), the Democrats courted the black vote with greater vigor. A black Democrat, Arthur W. Mitchell, was nominated and elected to Congress in 1934, useating De Priest. Kelly gave blacks the same mix of symbolic recognition and jobs that had helped build the Thompson machine two decades earlier. Kelly solved the Morgan Park High School branch controversy of 1934 to blacks' satisfaction, spoke at Du Sable High School dedication ceremonies in 1935, made Joe Louis honorary mayor, and permitted blacks to parade downtown prior to a Tuskegee-Wilberforce college football game. Kelly also slated more black Democrats for elective office and dispensed patronage to ghetto residents. Kelly's alliance with Alderman William L. Dawson (1933-39) was of foremost importance. Dawson, a Georgia-born attorney who had graduated from Fisk University and Northwestern University School of Law, was an independent Republican who had unsuccessfully challenged the Thompson organization. Kelly cultivated Dawson and other black Republicans and cemented the alliance in 1939, when, after Dawson lost his reelection bid, he switched parties and became Ward Two Democratic committeeman. In the mayoral election that year, blacks gave Kelly 60 percent of their votes, the first time in the decade their Democratic support had exceeded the citywide Democratic average. Meanwhile, New Deal relief programs and the Roosevelt administration's black appointments reinforced the mayor's efforts to convert ghetto voters. One black minister allegedly advised his congregation, "Let Jesus lead you and Roosevelt feed you!" The position of blacks in the Kelly Democracy, however, was different from the one they had occupied in the Thompson machine. Blacks were late arrivals, not founding partners, in the Democratic camp, and Kelly was so strong that blacks had less bargaining power with him than they had had with "Big Bill." As the political scientist James Q. Wilson wrote, the Democratic structure in the 1930s and 1940s was "tighter, more centralized, and less faction-ridden," which meant that black Democrats had less independence. Thus, when serious school overcrowding developed in the late 1930s, black Democrats had to operate within closely defined limits if they wished to retain the favor of the Kelly organization. Accordingly, though these politicians concerned themselves with patronage matters like admittance to Chicago Normal College and teacher assignments and transfers, they stayed far away from school protest.[23]

Between Kelly's inauguration and World War II, therefore, the only politicians who complained about school conditions were outside the regular Democratic organization. For example, Republican state representative Charles Jenkins, an attorney first elected to the legislature in

1930, was prominent in a movement demanding renovation of Old Phillips High School in 1936. Similarly, Republican and independent Democratic candidates for City Council and mayor in 1939 called for a black Board of Education member and attacked double-shift classes. The politician who was the school system's most imaginative critic, however, was Earl B. Dickerson, Democratic City Council member from 1939 to 1943. Born in Canton, Mississippi, in 1891, Dickerson moved to Chicago at age 15. He later graduated from the University of Illinois and in 1920 became the first black to receive the J.D. degree from the University of Chicago Law School. The following year, Dickerson opened a law office and also became general counsel for Liberty Life Insurance Company, a new firm that grew into one of the nation's major black-owned businesses; Dickerson was its attorney for thirty-four years. Like many other young lawyers, Dickerson became active in civic affairs and politics. In the 1930s, he served on the Chicago NAACP's Legal Redress Committee and Executive Committee and was Chicago Urban League vice-president and president. Unlike most blacks, however, Dickerson was a Democrat. He campaigned for Alfred E. Smith in 1928 and Cermak in 1931, and the Democrats rewarded him with an appointment as an assistant attorney general of the state of Illinois. In 1939, Dickerson won the Ward Two aldermanic election by upsetting incumbent Republican Dawson, the choice of Mayor Kelly. Dickerson forced the City Council Schools Committee, which had not met in six years, to hold hearings on classroom overcrowding and segregation on the South Side, and he was instrumental in advancing *Hansberry* v. *Lee,* the restrictive covenants case. Dickerson's pro-integration politics threatened Democratic unity, and his "silk-stocking" image and refusal to play the machine's game deprived him of patronage and limited him to one term in office. It is unlikely that Dickerson's fate escaped the notice of other black Democrats.[24]

Between 1920 and 1940, the goals and priorities of black activists concerned with school issues changed considerably. As I have shown in chapter 3, during the twenties educational accommodations for black children were fairly satisfactory. Although blacks called for additions or improvements to ghetto schools from time to time, the quality of school facilities was not low enough to become a source of discontent. Instead, black spokesmen, like their predecessors, placed greatest importance on defending the general principal of integration and agitating to save racially mixed schools when they came under attack. Black activists stressed that integrated schools were the only way to guarantee their children equal educational opportunities. The *Defender* declared in 1926, "Where there are mixed classes, there also are better classes, more and better equipment, and more thorough instruction." Several months later an NAACP officer maintained, "You can get no equality under a system that is invented to prevent equality." Enemies of segregation warned that while whites might promise to continue equal facilities when they introduced separate schools, they in fact rarely honored that commitment. Black activists rarely failed to point out that the South's dual school systems gave blacks only a fraction of the per capita appropriations that whites received. In 1922, Chandler Owen of the New York magazine *The Messenger* explained to a Chicago audience the connection between integration and equality:

> Where schools are segregated, Negroes generally have limited equipment. . . . Not so where the schools are mixed. Whenever new high schools are built they are built for all pupils, black and white. . . . we get the full advantage for Negro children out of the interest and concern of white parents for their own children. Herein lies the great argument for mixed and against segregated schools. . . . When all children sit in the same class rooms, what is taught one must be taught the other; the equipment of the white child must be the equipment of the Negro child, too; if a white child has a competent teacher, the Negro child has a competent teacher also.[25]

While equality accounted most for black activists' attachment to integration, they also believed that mixed schools conferred other tangible and symbolic benefits. Despite the substantial racial friction in Chicago's integrated schools, many asserted that the contacts between whites and blacks that occurred in mixed schools led to better race relations. Under separate education, a local journalist wrote in 1927, "the races are kept apart . . . and hatreds result." By contrast, declared black spokesmen, racial bigotry was less likely to flourish where children attended integrated schools. In 1926, the *Defender* proclaimed, "Nothing is better for both races than mixed schools where the children are given opportunities to know each other and dispel some of the prejudices they have which are based entirely upon ignorance." The *Defender*'s publisher, Robert Abbott, repeatedly insisted that integrated education curbed racial bias. "Contact is the one thing that will do more to break down prejudice than all other means," he affirmed. Abbott assured his readers that graduates of mixed classrooms were brighter and claimed that whites from such schools would uphold the rights of black people. Separate schools represented the hated South, and blacks' determination to keep southern ways out of the North also helped motivate the race's opposition to segregation. In 1923, Morris Lewis of the Chicago NAACP announced, "I am free to say that those who desire separate schools are invited to return at once to Alabama, Georgia, Mississippi, and Louisiana." Five years later, the *Defender* advised "traitors within the Race always willing to sell their birthrights for the proverbial mess of pottage" to "pack up and get back South as fast as they can accomplish the act." Furthermore, mixed schools symbolized acceptance of blacks as full-fledged members of the community. As one black concluded in 1928, segregation "is diametrically opposed to the principles upon which this country was founded. It is dangerous to the doctrines and practices of republicanism."[26]

The best example of black activists' devotion to integration during the 1920s was the Shoop-Esmond boundary fight of 1926-27. As we have seen in chapter 2, the Far South Side neighborhood of Morgan Park had a sizeable black minority of about 3,500. Residential segregation here was as extreme as it was elsewhere in the city. While two census tracts east of Vincennes Avenue (map 5) were 91 percent black in 1930, the Morgan Park Improvement Association and a businessmen's group had helped to keep the area west of Vincennes exclusively white. A black reporter noted in 1927, "It is an unwritten law that no members of our Race should be allowed to own or occupy land west of Vincennes Rd." Despite the separate housing pattern, both black and white children attended Esmond Elementary School, which was located in the white part of Morgan Park. Local blacks were dissatisfied with this arrangement, however. Since Esmond was overcrowded, some sixth-, seventh-, and eighth-graders had to go three miles to another school, and the long trip deterred some black pupils from continuing their education. Esmond's black students were also the victims of racial harassment. Although about 1920 a teacher told visitors that the faculty treated blacks and whites alike, she grouped the youngsters by race when her class played games. Four years later, a black reporter asked school officials "why all children of our Race had been herded into one room at the Esmond St. school, or why teachers in the school encouraged the white children in calling other students 'niggers.'" In 1922, the Chicago Commission on Race Relations reported, "The Negroes have repeatedly requested enlarged school facilities. They want a new building to be placed conveniently for their children." Whether blacks realized that conveniently located classrooms would probably be segregated is not known.[27]

Since Esmond had too many pupils and since blacks had called for their own accommodations, the Board of Education cooperated by installing three portables in the black part of Morgan Park in 1924. Blacks should hardly have been surprised to discover that they had traded the evils of white abuse for those of racial isolation. The portables were a branch of Esmond and had no attendance area of their own, en-

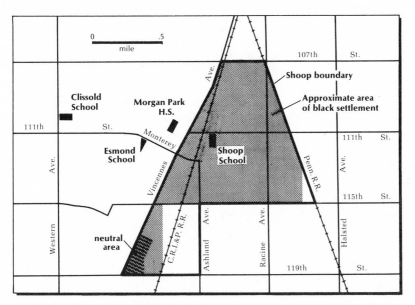

5. Shoop Elementary School District, 1926

Based on Ernest W. Burgess and Charles Newcomb, eds., *Census Data of the City of Chicago, 1930* (Chicago, 1933), and Chicago Board of Education, *Proceedings,* July 28 and Nov. 10, 1926.

abling a school administrator to order "all children of our Race to report to the portables, while white children were allowed to attend any school they chose." Suspicions about segregation grew when the same official asked blacks to help him find "good Colored teachers." In September, 1926, racial isolation became permanent when the Board of Education replaced the portables with a regular building. Since the western boundary of John D. Shoop Elementary School followed the Vincennes Avenue racial barrier, instead of the Rock Island Railroad to the east, Shoop was all-black and Esmond all-white.[28]

When Shoop opened its doors, a chorus of complaints arose against segregation. Among Morgan Park blacks active in the movement were John H. Simons, a realtor, and Carrie Taylor, who presided at meetings and headed a citizens' committee that coordinated the protest. The fact that only 130 residents signed an antisegregation petition suggests that Morgan Park's black community was either disorganized or sharply divided. The protest did not rely wholly on local support, however, since leaders of organizations based in the South Side ghetto rushed to defend mixed schools in Morgan Park. They included the NAACP's Morris Lewis, the CUL executive secretary Albon L. Foster, and George Arthur of the Wabash Avenue YMCA. These black men accused school officials of manipulating boundaries and transfers to segregate elementary education in Morgan Park. They alleged that administrators designed the Shoop district to include 848 of the area's 850 black pupils and argued that Esmond, which supposedly now had vacant rooms, was the most conveniently located building for children whose homes were between the Rock Island Railroad and Vincennes Avenue. Youngsters living here had to cross the railroad on their daily walks to and from Shoop, and this risk violated standard districting policy. The black petitioners contended that school officials used transfer permits to complete racial separation at the two schools. Authorities granted transfers to the few whites who resided in the Shoop district, no matter how close they lived to the schoolhouse, but blacks west of the railroad who wanted to enroll at Esmond could not obtain permission to do so. In an unusual case, a household containing children of both races sent the black to Shoop and the white to Esmond.[29]

The Board of Education quickly responded to the black grievants by offering them a partial concession. School trustees decided to make the southwest tip of the Shoop district neutral, thereby enabling pupils residing within the area to attend either Shoop or Esmond. This ruling, however, pertained to less than one-fifth of the territory between the railroad tracks and Vincennes. Otherwise, school administrators rebuffed the blacks. District Superintendent William Hedges announced that he favored racial segregation and promised to continue transferring white children from Shoop to Esmond. According to a black observer, board member Helen Hefferan suggested that "the Race citizens of Morgan Park ought to be satisfied with what they have and not bother about the transfer of other students." The *Defender* reported that some school officials "went so far as to state that the parents and citizens should be glad that they are in Chicago and able to enjoy having their children attend school." Authorities' responses angered black activists. "Regardless of the beauty of the buildings and its cost, nothing will make up for the segregation practiced in this community," Robert Abbott retorted. "The school is the cradle of democracy, but if segregation is allowed to enter there can be no democracy and justice when these youths of both races grow up."[30]

Regarding the Board of Education's position as unsatisfactory, Morgan Park blacks and the Chicago NAACP filed suit against the school board in May, 1927. The *Defender* reported: "The citizens have stated that they will fight the case to the United States supreme court if necessary in order that their children might not have to attend a segregated school and grow up feeling that they were inferior to the white child." The NAACP's attorneys were Henry W. Hammond, a young member of the chapter's Legal Redress Committee, and Edward H. Morris, a distinguished former state legislator and constitutional convention delegate who had helped organize the Equal Opportunity League in 1903. Hammond and Morris noted that before Shoop opened, children living between the Rock Island Railroad tracks and Vincennes Avenue attended Esmond School. When Shoop was established, officials ordered pupils in this area to the new school, forcing them to travel farther and to risk death or injury in crossing the tracks. The plaintiffs claimed that racial bias was the root of the problem: "The Board of Education and its Superintendent, and other officials and representatives have insisted that the Esmond School is a white school and that the Shoop School is a Colored School and that no Colored children . . . would be permitted to attend the Esmond School, no matter how near to it they lived, but that any white child living in the same district, no matter how close to the Shoop School, would be permitted to attend the Esmond School upon request." Since such discrimination violated Illinois law, the attorneys demanded that the court order redistricting to permit blacks residing near Esmond to go there instead of to Shoop. The petition also insisted that "Colored children [receive] the same accommodations and privileges at Esmond as white children receive." School board attorneys asked Circuit Court Judge Otto Kerner, father of a future Illinois governor, to dismiss the case on the ground that the blacks had been unable to prove that color bias had governed administrative policy. Hammond conceded that school board records did not refer to race but held that the results of school officials' actions provided evidence of discrimination. Kerner agreed with the Board of Education, and despite the blacks' vows to pursue the case, they never did so. Although a school board attorney promised that his employers would remedy any injustice, the Shoop boundary was not changed.[31]

The Shoop-Esmond case illustrated some of the difficulties with the NAACP's legalistic approach to the problems of northern urban blacks. At first glance, court litigation seemed a potentially fruitful tactic for integrationists. Illinois law banned racially separate public schools, and black activists could assume that a court of law would be less bigoted than the court of public opinion. Yet there were good reasons why the Shoop dispute was the only one in which black Chicagoans mounted a legal challenge to public school policies during the 1920s and 1930s. First, there was no basis in law through which blacks could overturn classroom segregation caused by housing patterns. This limited litigation to cases dealing with the ghetto's periphery or enclaves such as Morgan Park. Even here, however, the prospects for success were dim, for judges such as Kerner required evidence of intent to discriminate by school authorities. Since Board of Education records did not mention race, black attorneys could not prove officials' intent. In the eyes of the law, it was simply a coincidence if school district lines followed racial barriers in housing. Other segregating actions by authorities, such as manipulation of pupil transfers or teacher assignments, were no more likely than boundary cases to yield evidence to vindicate black plaintiffs. Furthermore, the courts offered even less hope for challenging the overcrowding and underfinancing that harmed black schools during the Depression. Statutes did not require equal educational facilities within a school system or protect children against double-shift schools. In any event, the Chicago NAACP was ill-suited to deal with the crisis in ghetto school accommodations because of its limited appeal and its emphasis on integration. As the Parker High transfer incident of 1923 and the Bowen High prom case of 1937 demonstrated, the local NAACP was more effective in school issues as a lobbyist than as a litigant.

The Shoop-Esmond boundary fight also revealed that blacks' commitment to racially mixed classrooms was weaker than NAACP rhetoric would suggest. Before World War I, some black Chicagoans favored separate schools (see chapter 1), and this was still true in the 1920s and 1930s. As indicated earlier, Morgan Park blacks had wanted their own school, and they gave only limited support to the protest against the Shoop-Esmond boundary. More than a year after the court case, the *Defender* reported, "The inability of factions of citizens to work in harmony on the issue gave victory to their opponents." Although the exact nature of disunity in Morgan Park's black community is unknown, it may have been geographic as well as ideological. Even if the NAACP had won its suit, only black students living between the railroad tracks and Vincennes Avenue would have gone to school with whites, while Shoop's enrollment would have still been predominantly if not totally black. Most of the community, in other words, stood to gain nothing tangible from the court case. Although integrationists were correct in their argument that mixed schools meant equal education, even in an enclave like Morgan Park, integration had become an abstract or theoretical matter for the great majority of black residents. As for the rest of Chicago, the black population was so large and housing so rigidly segregated that racially mixed classes were no longer possible on a wide scale. While black activists defended integration when whites insulted the race, as in the Morgan Park High School branch furor or the prom exclusion episodes, integration had become a symbolic issue, requiring an assertion of principle but having little relation to the experience of most black Chicagoans.[32]

Even though separate schools were the norm between the wars, only a tiny minority of Chicago blacks explicitly endorsed them as a positive good. Some support for segregation came from recent southern migrants who apparently felt threatened by the different character of interracial contacts in the North. In 1926, the *Defender* attacked "weak-minded, weak-kneed brothers, recent arrivals from Dixie's foreign shores, coming into the northland and asking that they be given separate classes in our schools." A second motive of those who favored formally segregated education was that it would enhance job opportunities for black teachers and administrators. In 1938, a letter to the *Defender* asserted that with separate schools, "Educated Negroes can get a chance to use their education for something beside running elevators and carrying luggage." Two years later, in an article entitled "Plea for More Segregation," a woman complained that in a formally integrated school system like that of Chicago, "well-trained Negro teachers must stay for years on the substitute list or get jobs in the South where separate schools provide openings for them." Such open endorsements of segregation, however, were rare and provoked charges about harming the race's children to gain material advances for a favored few. Accusing pro-segregation blacks of "Race treason," the *Defender* said of them in 1922, "They do not believe in the principle of the greatest good to the greatest number, but the greatest good to themselves regardless of the other ninety and nine." Abbott's newspaper advised, "There may be offered the frail argument that our teachers are not permitted to teach white children, but let us not sacrifice a high social principle, but to the contrary advocate with great vigor the right of the teacher to the fullest place in the school system."[33]

As the integrationist cause became reduced to the defense of "a high social principle," black activists began to stress improving education within the ghetto and increasing the ghetto's influence in the public school system. This change in emphasis was evident in the two main educational goals of black Chicagoans during the 1930s: the campaign for representation on the school board and the fight for more and better school facilities.

According to a 1917 state law, the mayor of the City of Chicago nominated school board members for five-year terms, and they took office following City Council confirmation. The eleven-member board, which served without pay, chose the superintendent of schools and approved the financial, personnel and educational decisions that the superintendent and his or her staff made. According to George S. Counts's analysis in the late 1920s, most Chicago school trustees were middle-aged business or professional men whose income and educational backgrounds were substantially higher than the city average. Although religious and ethnic blocs and organized labor customarily enjoyed representation on the Board of Education, until the late 1930s, the school board was all-white.[34]

Blacks argued that representation on the Board of Education would symbolize the race's status as a major interest group in the city. The *Defender* declared, "We are a part of the people of Chicago and are taxpayers. . . . Representation equal with other citizens of our government means mutuality and common respect." In 1939, the editors of *Opportunity,* the journal of the National Urban League, said of school board membership, "It is the recognition of the Negroes' right to participate in the councils which direct public education in one of America's great cities." Moreover, ghetto residents assumed that if a black sat on the school board, he or she would voice their concerns. In 1938, a group of black civic leaders declared, "Our interests cannot possibly be properly protected unless and until such an appointment is made." The following year, a newspaper reporter noted that the Chicago Council of Negro Organizations "believes with a member of the Race on the board, the pressing school problems of the south side will receive more attention." *Opportunity* added, "Sometimes the mere presence of a Negro on policy-making bodies of the city and state is sufficient to change the attitude of members of the body and to alter programs which might have been initiated with no thought of the interests of the Negro, and sometimes calculated to do him infinite harm." On several occasions, threats to the rights of black students in the public schools brought calls for a Negro on the Board of Education to prevent injustice.[35]

Black spokesmen were especially bitter that whereas they were excluded from the board, immigrants were not. "The Greek, the German, the Jew, the Irish, the Italian, the Pole, French and Spanish extractions are all represented on the Board of Education but not a colored citizen," complained a black journalist. The racial prejudice of white ethnics on the Board particularly galled the black press and stimulated nativism in the ghetto. The *Defender* thought it ironic that "foreigners who came to this country seeking an asylum" were "seeking to impose the oppression and disadvantages from which they fled upon the American black man." When a Bohemian-American banker on the board told a foreign-language newspaper in 1933 that he would try to exclude Near West Side blacks from a school attended by pupils from immigrant families, an outraged black reporter exclaimed, "The schools have been turned over to wreckers and immigrants. Now it is the native American child who must suffer while foreigners strut about prattling of their 'cultural superiority.'" In a similar vein, the *Broad Ax* once listed the names of eight black women whom it believed were worthy of serving on the school board. The paper affirmed, "They can all speak the English language correctly, which is much more than can be said in favor of some of the present members of that board, for they not only chop up the English language in a horrible manner but no true American can pronounce some of their names."[36]

Although the campaign for a black on the Board of Education became most intense in the 1930s, it had begun in the early part of the century. In 1907, black politicians asked newly elected Republican mayor Fred Busse for a school board appointment. The Busse administration allegedly promised "that a fair consideration will be given to any worthy Afro-American who may be commended to the Mayor," but nothing more occurred. Another black delegation renewed the request when Democrat Carter Harrison II returned to the mayor's office in 1911. Harrison supposedly pledged his intent to select a black but did no more than Busse. This was not surprising, since the black electorate was small and not yet important. Moreover, since racial tensions were rising, appointment of a black to the highly visible Board of Education would have been potentially costly for either Busse or Harrison. Instead, these mayors gave blacks less important posts in city government.[37]

As I have already pointed out, black political influence increased sharply during William Hale Thompson's three terms as Chicago's chief executive (1915-23, 1927-31). In fact, blacks received so many city jobs that Thompson's enemies called City Hall "Uncle Tom's Cabin" and played "Bye, Bye, Blackbird" during the 1927 campaign. Despite continued pleas for a black on the school board and Thompson's promise to make the appointment, however, "Big Bill" selected only whites. Since blacks had won so much other recognition under Thompson, the mayor may have believed that choosing a black for the school post would irritate white voters while adding nothing to his black following. Ghetto politicians who raised the question during the Thompson years were told, "The time is not ripe." Yet the mayor may have done more to satisfy black demands than the public realized. During his third term, rumors circulated that Thompson had offered a place on the Board of Education to his longtime ally, the Reverend Archibald J. Carey, Sr. Carey supposedly turned down the appointment in favor of a position on the Civil Service Commission, which dealt with municipal employment and police conduct, areas of special interest to blacks.[38]

Blacks accelerated their lobbying efforts after the Democrats captured control of City Hall in 1931. As already mentioned, the CUL sent a biracial delegation to Mayor Cermak to ask him to choose a black for the school board. In addition, white members of the Urban League persuaded the socially prestigious Woman's City Club to endorse several blacks for Board of Education membership. Although Cermak promised to comply with the request, as he had said he would do during his campaign, the new mayor did not keep his word. Cermak once remarked, "Bill Thompson didn't appoint a Negro, how in the world do they expect me to appoint one?" After Cermak was murdered in 1933, blacks stepped up their pressure on Mayor Kelly. The birth of the CCNO in 1935 was a turning point in the school board campaign, for the CCNO had a broad base and made the issue its top priority. The CCNO had the assistance of the *Chicago Defender,* the black women's club movement, and the United Alumni Association of Chicago, a federation of black college alumni clubs headed by the attorney and Republican party worker George W. Lawrence. Black activists asked Kelly why Chicago should be different from Philadelphia and Cleveland, other northern cities with black school board representation. They claimed that their loyalty to the mayor entitled them to a seat on the Board of Education, although they overstated the extent of black Democratic support. For instance, in 1937, the *Defender* declared that the mayor "has overlooked our group which is among his most loyal supporters." The following year, Abbott's paper was less gentle. "Black citizens of Chicago are beginning to believe their loyalty to the city administration on election day means nothing . . . in determining their recognition to public office." The *Defender* concluded, "They have followed the political lead of Mayor Kelly; they have supported his programs and policies; they have voted for the candidates that he presented without question, and they now feel that they should have representation commensurate with the support they have given his administration."[39]

The intensity of the school board campaign grew in 1939, a critical year in the ghetto's entry into the Kelly organization. White reformers had long been complaining about corruption and political favoritism in the public schools. To quiet these critics, particularly during the forthcoming municipal elections, in February Kelly created a Citizens Advisory Committee on Schools and announced that the seven-member group would help him make school policy and Board of Education selections. The "blue-ribbon" group included the head of Hull-House, several university professors, and one Negro, Midian O. Bousfield, a physician and businessman and husband of the first Negro principal in the city schools. Kelly, however, still had to face blacks' demand for a voice in governing public education. Led by the CCNO and the United Alumni Association, ghetto activists showered the mayor with telegrams, petitions, press releases, and visits to City Hall. In addition, they secured the support of five South Side aldermen (three of them white) and enlisted the aid of the predominantly white Citizens Schools Committee, which included two blacks on its list of Board of Education endorsements. In the spring city election campaign, Republican mayoral hopeful Dwight Green pledged to install a black on the school board if elected, and the party's City Council candidates in the black belt made the same promise. One, noting Kelly's failure to satisfy black aspirations, proclaimed, "It has been a standing shame that a quarter of a million of native-born patriotic Americans should never have been represented on the school board of their own city and I shall do everything in my power to remedy the injustice."[40]

At first, Kelly appeared to ignore the steadily increasing clamor. In May, his new advisory committee offered him five names, including Bousfield's, for two vacancies on the board. The mayor angered blacks by selecting two white men: a Brinks Express Company executive and an official of the Amalgamated Clothing Workers of America. "This is a great blow to the Negro race," declared a black club president. CCNO vice-president George W. Hutchinson added, "The justly warranted hope and desire of 250,000 Negro citizens to have one of their number represent them on the Chicago School Board have been blasted and their faith in the promises of officialdom greatly shattered." But when one of the newly chosen members resigned, Kelly fulfilled black demands by appointing Midian Bousfield. The mayor had already named blacks to the Civil Service Commission and the board of the Chicago Housing Authority, and the Bousfield selection was another sign of the political alliance he was fashioning with ghetto voters.[41]

The first Negro to serve on the Chicago Board of Education was born in Tipton, Missouri, in 1885. The son of a barber, Bousfield attended the Kansas City, Kansas, public schools and graduated from the University of Kansas in 1907. After earning his medical degree from Northwestern University, he interned at Freedmen's Hospital in Washington, D.C. Bousfield established a practice in Kansas City, emigrated to Brazil in 1911, and returned to the United States when life abroad proved unsatisfactory. Bousfield settled in Chicago and for several years was secretary of the Railway Men's International Benevolent Industrial Association, an independent midwestern union of dining-car waiters and cooks. During the 1920s, he became an executive of Liberty Life Insurance Company (Supreme Liberty Life after 1929), where he served as president, vice-president, and medical director. In addition, from 1933 to 1942, he was director of Negro health for the Rosenwald Fund. Besides his career activities, Bousfield was active in black civic and professional affairs. He had been president of the CUL and on the boards of the Wabash Avenue YMCA and the Provident Hospital. A president of the National Medical Association, Bousfield published articles on the medical training of blacks.[42]

Several traits made Bousfield a logical choice to be the first Negro on the school board. As one contemporary put it, he was "the fair-haired boy of the Rosenwalds," an important asset in a city in which Julius Rosenwald (a neighbor of Kelly) and the Rosenwald Fund were influential in the field of race relations. Bousfield's experience with Supreme Liberty Life demonstrated that he was a successful, respectable businessman. But unlike his Supreme Life colleague Earl Dickerson, Bousfield had always been conservative and had not brought up troublesome issues in public. "He wasn't raising any Hell," a former colleague recalled. While his wife's position in the school system may have helped him gain the appointment, his tall, light-skinned, distinguished appearance was a more weighty factor. As one former activist pointed out, Bousfield's fair complexion and refined style won him acceptance in circles that were closed to most black Chicagoans.[43]

Spokesmen for both races greeted Bousfield's installation enthusiastically. The *Defender* captioned a photograph of the swearing-in ceremony, "A Dream Come True." *Opportunity* asserted, "Those who are concerned with the progress of the American Democracy will be elated" by the appointment. Although the editorial writers of the *Tribune* ignored the selection, the *Daily News,* a critic of the school administration, was optimistic. Bousfield's choice, it editorialized, "should provide a measure of encouragement to those individuals and organizations who have battled and are battling to put the Chicago schools system on an educational basis instead of the basis of spoils politics." The newspaper predicted, "As the first Negro to serve on the board, it is to be expected that Dr. Bousfield will be particularly interested in the many problems relating to the status of Negroes in the schools." But white reformers' expectations quickly proved illusory. From the start, he supported schools superintendent William Johnson and Board of Education president James B. McCahey. Soon after his appointment, Bousfield voted against a motion to nullify the results of an allegedly corrupt principal's examination, explaining, "I would prefer to stay with the administration." Later, he helped defeat a proposal for a merit system for school administrators. In addition, Bousfield voted to retain Johnson and McCahey when they stood for reelection in 1940 and 1941, respectively. After the former vote, the *Daily News* remarked, "Bousfield, recently appointed to the board as an advocate of school reforms, did an agile flip-flop."[44]

While most black activists were indifferent toward reformers' efforts to depoliticize the public schools, they did want Bousfield to do something about the double-shift issue and to stand up against bias in education. Yet Bousfield's presence on the Board of Education had little apparent effect on South Side schools. Extreme overcrowding still plagued the ghetto, and underfunding and other forms of discrimination continued unabated. Ghetto leaders gradually became impatient. On the second anniversary of Bousfield's appointment, the *Defender* asserted that he "has had ample time to demonstrate that he is capable of serving the people who insisted that a Negro should be on the Board of Education." The paper concluded, "Dr. Bousfield should be able now to report some progress which benefits all of the people. . . . He must produce results or state that he is not able to get results and state why, as well as who is preventing him from getting results."[45]

Although blacks realized that one board member could not eradicate discrimination from the school system, they did expect Bousfield to show some display of activity. But the first Negro school trustee denied South Siders even this satisfaction. In 1941, after the Washington Park subdivision had become predominantly black, a delegation of mothers from A. O. Sexton Elementary visited Bousfield. They had learned of plans to put their school on a double-shift schedule and wanted Bousfield to help prevent the change. To their dismay, he refused, telling them that he would support the school administration. He claimed that Sexton children could have no guarantee of a full school day when many other black schools operated double shifts. An exasperated reporter declared, "Dr. Midian O. Bousfield . . . has once more indicated that he does not intend to make any clear-cut fight for patent rights of taxpayers and citizens who happen to be Negroes, if it involves a real fight." For his part, Bousfield would not forsake the approach that had won him his school board seat. Since open dissent was ungentlemanly and probably futile as well, he stated that if he believed it necessary to act, he would speak to fellow board members individually. If he succeeded, the result would reflect his efforts. But blacks discerned no improvement in their schools and wondered if Bousfield was doing anything on their behalf. The *Defender* decided, "He should fight . . . in the Board of Education, not member by member in a close huddle but on the basis of an issue."[46]

Black activists had won a major victory in 1939 when Mayor Kelly named Bousfield to the school board. But their triumph was hollow because of the very circumstances of Bousfield's appointment. Although his selection symbolized the ghetto's political importance and seemed to indicate that black demands would receive attention, Bousfield also won a place on the school board because whites knew that he would not upset the status quo. The black press and civic organizations wanted Bousfield to be a "race man" and felt disillusioned and betrayed when he refused to assume this role. Bousfield was a token, a man who owed his position on a citywide agency to influential whites who desired a black representative. Bousfield's record on the Board of Education suggests that he sensed that his real constituency was the white power structure, not the black ghetto. While Bousfield escaped the situation by resigning in 1942 to become an officer in the United States Army Medical Corps, his successors on the school board in the 1940s faced the same dilemma and responded similarly.[47]

Although ghetto civic groups did win black representation on the Chicago Board of Education, their campaigns to improve school accommodations during the 1930s had only mixed results. Although the majority of movements to get renovations, additions, or new buildings at individual schools succeeded, a vigorous drive against communitywide overcrowding failed to eliminate or even reduce the hated double shifts.

The most militant and most successful civic actions to improve school facilities for blacks in the Depression were efforts based in individual districts. The first of these, at Betsy Ross Elementary School in September, 1933, took place in a neighborhood whose residents were bitter about segregation as well as poor facilities. Located at Sixty-first Street and Wabash Avenue near the southern edge of the ghetto, Ross had been a junior high school for a number of years. Parents had asked officials several times for a new building to replace the structure erected in 1885, but the Board of Education failed to act. Early in 1933, citizens also complained that authorities sent black graduates of nearby elementary schools to Ross for ninth grade instead of directing them to Englewood High. Although these students did enter Englewood as sophomores, the arrangement reduced the high school's black enrollment and deprived the freshmen of some high school courses and facilities. For example, Ross did not offer Latin, a college preparatory course available to the average high school freshman. Moreover, blacks objected that the Ross building had an inadequate gymnasium, no swimming pool, and short-ages of certain equipment. Administrators ignored the grievances. Told that the three-story school had no fire escape, Ross's principal reportedly answered, "Well, the building is not very tall, anyway."[48]

When the school system's financial crisis caused the Board of Educa-tion to change Ross from a junior high to an elementary school in Sep-tember, 1933, discontent in the Ross district flared higher than ever before. As I explained in chapter 2, it was at this time that the board satis-fied white segregationists in the adjacent Washington Park subdivision by revising the Sexton-Ross boundary. The decision, which shifted black children from previously integrated Sexton to Betsy Ross, incensed black parents, for it switched their youngsters from a modern, well-equipped school to an antiquated, poorly maintained building on a double-shift schedule. On September 19, a thousand parents met at Brown Memorial Presbyterian Church and threatened "a wholesale strike." One woman vowed, "Those who must go to Betsy Ross will remain at home until the school is sufficiently repaired and equipped to care for them." The residents made good their threat, for on September 25, the first day of school, over four-fifths of Ross's students did not go to class. When a politician threatened parents with prosecution, they replied, "We'll pay fines, even go to jail, rather than submit to the injustice. We value the health of our children greater than we do their education."[49]

While black parents could not restore integration, the boycott did win better conditions at Ross. On the day of the protest, Superintendent of Schools William J. Bogan met with the boycott's leaders, visited Ross, and announced several improvements. He ordered establishment of a kindergarten, the delivery of more textbooks, removal of supplies from hallways, and increased supervision of toilet rooms. New books arrived quickly, but Ross parents had to send a second delegation to school headquarters before authorities fulfilled Bogan's three other promises. By mid-November, school officials had also closed a nearby alley to en-large play areas during recess and had permitted some black students to return to Sexton. Although Ross remained overcrowded and on double shifts, parents realized that they had made an impact on the school system. They organized the Fifth Ward Citizens Protective Association, which monitored school conditions and increased neighborhood cohesion by holding block meetings, a dance, and a tea. One member declared, "Through the militant and aggressive stand taken by the association, the board of education has shown signs of relenting from their former position." Three years later, Ross parents won their greatest victory when the school board announced plans for a building addition. At dedication ceremonies for the new facility in January, 1938, one of the speakers was G. McKay Miller, minister at Brown Memorial and a boycott leader four and one-half years before.[50]

Three years after the Ross boycott, a second black community used direct action to secure better school accommodations. Lilydale, which straddled State Street from Ninety-first to Ninety-seventh Streets, was a black island in the largely white Far South Side. Founded in 1912, the black enclave numbered 1,254 residents by 1930. Since Lilydale was far from other schools and at first had too few pupils to justify a permanent building, the area's children attended classes in portables. But even when enrollment rose above 200 in the late 1920s, officials made no plans to provide a regular school. In 1931 and 1933, local women's clubs objected to the portables and called for a new school. Some of their complaints concerned inadequate maintenance: dirty and broken windows, gaps in floors, dilapidated toilet facilities, and unsatisfactory landscaping. The women also protested conditions inherent to the temporary classrooms, such as uneven heating, low-quality construction, and lack of alternative exits in case of fire. The school board ordered its employees to wash windows and make other cosmetic improvements, but it ignored the plea for a new building. As had been the case at Ross, segregation accompanied inadequate facilities in Lilydale. Since 1924, the Board of Education had designated the portables as Branch One of Ryder Elementary, an all-white school twelve blocks away. Blacks pointed out that whereas area whites enrolled at Ryder, that school excluded Negro children. Lilydale residents, however, mostly ignored this situation; as one contemporary put it, people were "not too concerned with segregation." Attendance at Ryder would have required a three-mile round trip daily, and blacks feared mistreatment by hostile whites. Like the majority of Morgan Park blacks a decade earlier, Lilydale preferred new accommodations nearby to the inconvenience and harassment which integration would have entailed.[51]

In January and February, 1936, blacks renewed their demands for a permanent school. The PTA created a committee to lobby Board of Education administrators, and the *Defender* publicized Lilydale's grievances, calling the portables "a strange looking assortment of packing box structures which might easily be mistaken for one of those abortive hobo villages which occasionally spring up on city dumps!" Soon the most important civic organizations within the enclave created the Citizens Committee of Lilydale to lead the campaign for a new building. Beginning with six members, the committee soon included over twenty representatives of neighborhood groups, including all three churches, the Lilydale Community Club, the Women's Community Club, and the Monarch Social and Athletic Club. The protest leaders were persons already active in Lilydale civic affairs. The core of eight prominent individuals (five officers and three other organizers) included two Republican precinct captains, two clergymen, the founder of the local women's club, and two women who were, in the words of one resident, "active in mostly everything around."[52]

At first, the Citizens Committee followed a moderate course. It authorized a study by National Youth Administration workers to determine the number of school-age children in the neighborhood and to verify reports that some avoided the portables through truancy, while others falsified their addresses and enrolled in other school districts. The committee also compared Ryder Branch One facilities with other portables attended by white students. Having assembled evidence, the protest leaders mobilized community support. Some three hundred persons appeared at a mass meeting at St. James A.M.E. Church on March 30 to hear ten speakers, including representatives from the CUL, CCNO, YMCA, and *Defender*. Several hundred residents signed a petition describing the portables' shortcomings and asking the Board of Education for "the immediate replacement of the present obsolete school buildings with a new and modern school building."[53]

The Citizens Committee's conventional protest apparently succeeded four days later when school board president McCahey announced that construction of a new school would start in late June. During April and May, the board considered land purchases for the expanded school site, but by the end of the summer it had done nothing more. In August, Lilydale leaders blasted the failure to begin work on the permanent structure as "a break in faith" and complained that school authorities had ignored their inquiries. In early September, the committee learned that the board's failure to obtain a federal grant had resulted in postponement of Lilydale's new building. With another school year approaching and no replacement for the objectionable portables in sight, Lilydale activists grew increasingly impatient.[54]

From the beginning of the campaign, a frequent criticism of the makeshift schoolhouses had been their susceptibility to fire. Flimsy construction, individual heating units, and the single doorways could spell disaster for pupils and teachers. In February, Citizens Committee vice-chairman Juanita Grammar had warned, "The close proximity of the portables [makes them] firetraps. Panic-stricken children would become wedged between the buildings being exposed to fire or injury." Grammar's concerns won further credence on March 20, when flames caused $1,185 worth of damage to one of the Branch One structures. This blaze, combined with frequent use of the "firetrap" label in Citizens Committee propaganda, led some Lilydale youths to prod the school board more vigorously. In late August, when community spokesmen were voicing frustration at broken promises, a second fire inflicted minor damage on the portables. The Board of Education then received an unsigned letter promising more arson if authorities did not grant the demand for a new school. When officials failed to respond, the incendiaries struck again on September 10. They ignited three portable units, demolishing one and damaging two others. Repair costs were estimated at five thousand dollars.[55]

Police immediately charged seven Lilydale teenagers with arson. The youths readily admitted the crime, explaining that they had hoped to destroy all the portables and thus force school administrators to provide a new building. Although police attempted to link the fires to Communist agitators or to local adults, the youths had evidently acted on their own, inspired by flyers denouncing the "firetrap" portables. Most Lilydale residents regarded the arsonists with tolerance or approval. When one of the teens announced, "I'm doing you a favor," many of his neighbors seemed to agree. As Citizens Committee chairman Robert Campbell recalled, "People wasn't too down on them." None of the seven firebugs received harsh punishment. Four were placed in custody of juvenile authorities and apparently released after less than a week at the juvenile detention home. The three others, a Works Progress Administration laborer and two students, each received one year probation on reduced charges of malicious mischief.[56]

By the beginning of the fall semester, the Lilydale classrooms were in deplorable condition. An observer noted, "Fire and vandals have reduced the tinder box portables . . . to mere shells in which most of the windows are broken." Local blacks were more determined than ever to continue the pressure on school officials until victory was assured. At a rally at St. James Church on the rainy evening of September 11, more than one hundred persons heard speakers express outrage at the conduct of the Board of Education. A reporter stated, "It was pointed out that not one promise made by the board had been kept, and that in some instances positive discourtesy was shown the committee by school board officials." Concluding that only "a drastic program" would bring results, the crowd approved three proposals: picketing and boycotting the portables, disrupting board headquarters, and exploring the possibility of legal action.[57]

On September 14 and 15, a half-dozen women picketed the portables. Urging passers-by to support the protest, they carried signs reading, "No kennels wanted," "Empty these tin cans," and "No more T-B tolerated." The Citizens Committee declared a boycott of the school, and about half the pupils stayed home. Although the predominantly black teaching force remained in their classrooms, several instructors offered the committee advice and information about school administrators' attitudes. Authorities reacted patiently. School officials, according to Campbell, "didn't take a hard line" toward the protest, declining to charge parents for withholding their children from classes. Although police kept pickets across the street from the school, they did not attempt to disperse the women. For its part, the committee limited its effort to a two-day "show of concern," rather than increasing tensions by an extended boycott. Moreover, while Lilydale citizens had considered seeking an injunction to ban the use of the portables and had approved plans to send their children to school board headquarters for a full day "to get into the officials' hair," they did not implement either of these actions.[58]

Nevertheless, the prospect of litigation and further demonstrations, combined with the recent arson and boycott, apparently persuaded the Board of Education that Lilydale blacks were serious. Whereas school authorities had earlier pleaded lack of funds, they now moved to achieve a solution. Nine days after the boycott, the board's chief architect, John Christensen, informed President McCahey that $152,000 of a previously secured $2,000,000 federal public works grant remained unspent. The grant had financed fifteen new schools, but nearly all these projects were located in white districts. Christensen suggested that the leftover money could pay for a new building in Lilydale. After its September 28 meeting, the school board announced that Lilydale would have a $125,000 permanent school within a year. At first, blacks reacted suspiciously. Juanita Grammar warned, "We were fooled once . . . but we are going to keep on fighting from now until the school is built and the children safely housed in it." "The citizens committee of Lilydale is still to be convinced," added Secretary Arcola Philpott. "Our eyes are not to be closed for one moment." This time, however, the community was not betrayed. Construction began October 26, and the new school opened officially May 3, 1937. Lilydale had won a great victory.[59]

The movements for better school facilities in the Ross and Lilydale districts were the only educational protests by Chicago blacks in the interwar era to use direct action techniques. The success of each effort demonstrated the advantages of picketing and boycotts for school activists. Neighborhood groups could use direct action on their own, unrestrained by the limitations of the courts, politicians, or the established black civic organizations. Because direct action required neither money, behind-the-scenes influence, nor technical training, it was well suited for ordinary people. Furthermore, by disrupting the school routine, boycotts and pickets were more effective than verbal protests in forcing authorities to confront blacks' grievances. Even though the white daily press ignored both the Ross and Lilydale episodes, school officials acted in each case and did so quickly. Despite these attractions, however, direct action did not become a frequently used weapon in black activists' arsenal during the 1920s and 1930s. As far as most people were concerned, direct action was extreme and dangerous, for it meant working outside the law. Parents who kept children home violated compulsory education statutes; mass occupation of school offices was illegal; and courts had not yet protected peaceful picketing. Accordingly, only the most dramatic grievances were likely to provoke such daring tactics. Ross parents had suffered the deprivation of having their youngsters moved from a desirable, integrated school to a dilapidated, overcrowded one. And Lilydale was the only black area in Chicago that relied exclusively on portables for its school accommodations. Other neighborhoods did not have such distinctive complaints. Moreover, Lilydale and Ross also had far more social cohesion than most black districts in the city. Lilydale had high rates of population stability, home ownership, and participation in voluntary associations, while the Ross area had relatively high levels of income and education. Since most ghetto neighborhoods did not have these strengths, whatever civic action took place was more likely to rely on methods requiring less intense commitment and less risk. Finally, although CUL-sponsored groups like the CCNO and the Negro Labor Relations League marched, boycotted, and picketed during the Depression, much of the established black leadership still viewed such activities as radical and would not encourage nonviolent direct action. Thus, direct action in school controversies remained rare until both the outlook of blacks and the political climate in general changed by the 1960s.

About the time of the Ross and Lilydale protests, there were also vigorous but more conventional movements seeking better facilities for ghetto high school students. As stated earlier, Wendell Phillips High, the black belt's only secondary school, had become seriously overcrowded by the early part of the Depression. In 1933, 4,200 junior and senior high pupils used a building originally designed for 1,200. Reporters who visited the school found "crowded classrooms, crowded halls, [and] school children standing in rooms with their books in their hands because there were not enough seats to accommodate them." In the assembly hall, pupils had to write without desks, while in one over-crowded classroom, journalists saw a boy trying to draw without a table. "To do this he had to sit hunched over his chair—a position which would detract from the ability of stronger wills than that of a high school boy to concentrate." Sighed Phillips principal Chauncey Willard, "It's too bad, but we can't stretch brick!"[60]

During the mid-twenties, Willard and local PTA officers began call-ing for construction of a new high school to supplement Phillips. After several delays, the Board of Education broke ground early in 1931 at a site bounded by State Street and Wabash Avenue between Forty-ninth and Fiftieth Streets. But after contractors erected the structure's steel framework, the school system ran out of money, leaving the project and several others in the city uncompleted. Blacks were angry at the failure to finish the badly needed school, for the steel girders constantly reminded them that, as the *Defender*'s Dewey R. Jones put it, "Wen-dell Phillips is the stepchild of the board of education." The head of a South Side parents' club complained to Mayor Kelly that black children attended overcrowded classes, "while the steel skeleton of a new Phillips stood rusting in the rain, a monument to broken promises." The *Defender* called the project "mute evidence of the fact that the board of education is not keeping faith with taxpayers of Chicago" and demanded that authorities complete the school "before it rots and falls to pieces." After the local NAACP and South Side aldermen joined the *Defender* in lobbying local and federal officials, the Public Works Ad-ministration in December, 1933, lent the school board the money to finish Phillips.[61]

Just before New Phillips (which soon became Du Sable) was dedicated in February, 1935, a fire destroyed the gymnasium, assembly hall, and lunchroom at Old Phillips and seriously damaged other parts of the building. Despite promises to act, a year and a half later authorities still had not made the necessary repairs. Old Phillips was without library services or assemblies, and students had to walk to the Wabash Avenue YMCA three blocks away for physical education classes. Students formed "bucket brigades" to catch rain dripping into their classrooms, and during winter they had to wear coats for protec-tion against the cold. Even though a second high school now served the ghetto, Old Phillips was still overcrowded, accommodating high school pupils in the morning and children from four area elementary schools in the afternoon. The damaged building, according to the *Defender,* had "conditions far more deplorable than those that prevail in the backwoods of the darkest part of the South."[62]

In February, 1936, the Phillips PTA and State Representative Charles Jenkins persuaded school board president McCahey to pledge needed renovations. Seven months later, however, authorities had neither begun to repair the old building nor started to construct a new one promised for elementary students. In October, the PTA, Jenkins, and a newly established Phillips Alumni Association lobbied Mayor Kelly and gave Board of Education members petitions signed by nearly 3,000 local residents. A mass meeting also demonstrated community support. Along with these verbal protests, Phillips activists threatened more militant measures, perhaps inspired by the boycott and picketing in Lilydale. Jenkins gave school system attorneys the draft of a legal brief arguing that courts could compel school boards to repair buildings that jeopardized pupils' health or safety. In addition, after officials had once again agreed to begin construction but before it had actually started, Edward M. Joseph, chairman of the Alumni Association's civic committee, stated, according to a reporter, "that action must supplant words and that all action that is not violent would be attempted." When school administrators finally showed good faith, Joseph remarked that he would halt a planned boycott by Phillips students. The petitions and lobbying, combined with threats of direct action, made the campaign a success. Kelly and McCahey promised that the Board of Education would authorize the desired construction, contractors broke ground in December, and the remodeled school opened in September, 1937.[63]

Soon after administrators placed a refurbished Phillips in use, attention shifted back to Du Sable. Although planners had originally designed the new school to hold 3,300 students, when it opened in 1935, its capacity was only 2,400. Because of this unannounced change, which administration critics attributed to political corruption, Du Sable was overcrowded from its first day. Enrollment was 3,426 during the first semester, and after declining to a low of 3,100 in the fall of 1936, it rose to 4,056 by September, 1939. Features commonly found at other high schools, such as wastebaskets, bookcases, and exterior landscaping, were missing at Du Sable. While its curriculum included courses in drawing, woodworking, and mechanical trades, the only equipment was what teachers obtained on their own. Excessive enrollments required multiple shifts and forced classes to meet in ill-adapted rooms. By 1938, a protest movement had begun in the Du Sable district. The Du Sable Alumni Association, formed by graduates who had moved as students from Old to New Phillips, led the criticism of inadequate school conditions. The association was assisted by Frazier Lane and Joseph Jefferson of the CUL and by the CCNO and the Negro Labor Relations League. Activists complained to Mayor Kelly, school officials, and alderman, held mass meetings, and publicized their cause in the black press. In December, 1938, the Board of Education announced plans for a $750,000 addition to Du Sable. Though authorities soon acquired land and demolished buildings, by the summer of 1941, construction had not begun. Protest leaders and school administrators traded verbal salvos. McCahey called South Side dissidents "nincompoops and crackpots," while blacks charged that Du Sable construction funds had been diverted for private gain. Activists demanded that the school board "quit dilly-dallying and build the addition . . . which it has promised year after year," but no further progress occurred before World War II.[64]

By this time, concern over inadequate educational facilities in the ghetto had grown from demands for new construction in individual school districts to a ghetto-wide movement against overcrowding. To be sure, there were still campaigns at the end of the interwar period for better accommodations in specific areas. In the McCosh Elementary district at the southern edge of the black belt, 1,600 children occupied a building intended for 1,340. In 1938 and 1939, the PTA persuaded residents to petition the Board of Education for a building addition and got their alderman to introduce a resolution in the City Council. Officials authorized the addition in March, 1939, and it opened in September, 1941. While McCosh's activists were successful, a similar campaign among poorer blacks ended in failure. In the fall of 1941, tenants of the recently completed Ida B. Wells Homes, one of Chicago's early public housing projects, established the Wellstown Parents Civic Organization to protest classroom overcrowding. Complaining that double-shift schedules were hurting their children's educations, the WPCO collected 3,000 signatures on petitions calling either for transfers to schools with empty seats or for additions to existing buildings. The school board provided neither. For the most part, however, multipurpose civic organizations such as the CUL, CCNO, CCNNC, and the women's clubs led the fight against the double shift between 1939 and 1941. These activists both utilized existing opportunities and created new forums to voice their grievances. Beginning in 1939, blacks denounced overcrowding at the annual Board of Education budget hearings. For example, in 1940, thirteen speakers presented the special needs of ghetto schools; among them were three aldermen, the CUL's Foster, Gaines of the CCNO, the head of the Chicago and Northern District Association of Colored Women, and representatives of several South Side PTAs. Following Dickerson's election to the City Council in April, 1939, that body approved his resolution authorizing a study of ghetto education "with reference to an inadequacy of facilities and a consequent denial of equal educational facilities to children in that district." In June, the council's schools committee heard testimony from CUL and PTA representatives. The same year, the state legislature created an Illinois State Commission on the Condition of the Urban Colored Population, which held hearings in East St. Louis and Chicago on black life in these cities. Black critics of the school system testified not only about overcrowding in black Chicago's classrooms but also about segregation and racial bias in vocational education and teacher training programs. Although the commission issued recommendations against separate schools, it offered no conclusions about black Chicago's overcrowding problem.[65]

One distinctive feature of the lobbying efforts against double-shift classes in the ghetto between 1939 and 1941 was the presence of the largely white Citizens Schools Committee. Black activists had received very little white assistance since World War I, other than from the few whites who served as CUL officers. This situation would change at the end of the thirties, when the CSC, concerned about general mismanagement in the schools, finally discovered ghetto overcrowding. The CSC was an outgrowth of the Citizens Save Our Schools Committee, established in July, 1933, by several principals' and teachers' organizations to oppose the Board of Education's drastic cutbacks in school programs. Ten months after its formation, nearly 90 percent of the new group's members were public school instructors. The new organization, which would become the Citizens Schools Committee in 1935, began to expand its base when it persuaded the Illinois PTA president, Mrs. Holland Flagler, to become its first chairman. In addition to the PTA backing that Flagler mobilized, the CSC attracted support from such upper-status Protestant groups as the City Club of Chicago, the Woman's City Club, the Union League, and the League of Women Voters. The CSC thus gradually came to speak not only for teachers resisting educational retrenchment but also for the social and academic elite that ran Chicago's universities, charitable agencies, and professional associations. This group wanted government to be efficient, honest, and economical, and it viewed with distaste the politicians and ethnic groups who controlled the City Council. For this reason, the CSC bitterly fought the McCahey-Johnson regime, which the committee blamed for ruining the school system through political patronage, financial corruption, high administrative expenses, and disregard for merit. During its first six years, the CSC stressed restoration of educational programs and opposition to political influence in the schools and was oblivious to blacks' concerns. For example, it claimed that the real lesson of the Morgan Park High School branch conflict of 1934 was the evil of mayoral intervention in school affairs.[66]

In 1939, however, the CSC realized that it could use ghetto school overcrowding and the double-shift issue to dramatize the failures of the McCahey-Johnson administration. Over the next several years, the CSC was an energetic lobbyist on behalf of South Side schools. CSC chairman Arnold Baar testified at the 1940 Board of Education budget hearing about the need for more school accommodations in black districts, and Charles Gilkey, dean of the University of Chicago's Rockefeller Chapel, delivered a similar appeal as the CSC's representative the following year. In addition, the CSC assailed overcrowding by holding meetings, releasing statements to the press, and sponsoring tours of South Side schools that CUL staff members conducted. The CSC had been late in understanding the special problems of ghetto education, and circumstances suggest that the organization was using blacks' complaints for its own purposes. Nonetheless, black activists welcomed CSC assistance, for it gave their campaign against overcrowding greater publicity and communicated black concerns to the important segment of white society that constituted the CSC's following.[67]

Although black activists and their white supporters demanded that the school board act immediately to reduce or abolish double-shift schedules, they differed among themselves as to how this should be done. The majority of black civic leaders, and especially those with ties to the school system or the regular Democratic organization, simply called for more classrooms within the black belt. This solution, if adopted, would have eased overcrowding without disturbing whites in neighborhoods adjacent to the ghetto. Asked in 1938 to give her remedy for school congestion, Maudelle Bousfield, one of the system's two Negro principals, replied tersely, "More schools." Three years later, a black member persuaded the Chicago Teachers Union to call for "immediate use of building funds for the improvement and expansion of the schools in the South Side area of Chicago." Despite the unpopularity of portables, some blacks advocated their use to furnish needed seating as rapidly as possible. In 1940, Alderman Benjamin A. Grant, Democrat from the Third Ward, proclaimed, "Put up portables and relieve the situation." A year later, an instructor at Du Sable High declared, "Our big problem is to get the students off the streets. If we don't get an addition to the school, I hope the Board of Education will provide some portables." On the other hand, political independents of both races wanted to reduce segregation as well as overcrowding by loosening or abolishing the neighborhood school system. Alderman

Dickerson argued that since portables merely reinforced segregation, the school board should remap attendance areas to create "a democratic school system" in which black children could attend classes in nearby white neighborhoods. George McCray and H. M. Smith of the local National Negro Congress chapter agreed that authorities could alleviate much of the overcrowding by increasing school integration. As Smith told the Board of Education in January, 1940, "Let children attend school regardless of boundaries." Some white reformers concurred. Edwin H. Wilson, minister of Third Unitarian Church on the city's West Side, seconded Dickerson's opposition to portables. Criticizing the school board's inaction on overcrowding, the Chicago Woman's Club stated in 1939, "It seems both short-sighted and unethical to maintain district lines which separate uncrowded schools with extra rooms and white pupils from adjacent overpopulated districts where colored children have half-day sessions and double schools."[68]

School administrators, however, rejected suggestions to solve classroom overcrowding by modifying the neighborhood school structure. In 1941, Board of Education districting expert Don C. Rogers opposed a plan to transfer double-shift students to less crowded schools because, "I think that would create a social problem." Rogers also ruled out a revision of boundary lines to ease ghetto school congestion. "It always leads to trouble," he remarked, "so we just don't change boundaries." Although Rogers ignored the occasions in which the Board of Education had changed attendance areas to accommodate white separatists, he was undoubtedly correct to predict that transfers or redistricting to reduce black overcrowding would have touched off white protests. School officials, though, seemed uncertain about how to cope with double-shift schools in a time of financial exigency. Some administrators declared that ghetto overcrowding was temporary and would disappear (in an unexplained fashion), so there was no need to construct permanent school facilities. Since there was no evidence to substantiate this theory, by the late 1930s, authorities replied to criticism by listing new buildings and additions they had planned or completed. These announcements claimed huge appropriations for black school construction and argued that a disproportionately large amount of money for new classrooms went to black districts. "The Board of Education has not been fiddling while Rome burns," one employee said in 1939. "We know the conditions; we know the cause of them, and we are striving to overcome them." Although many new seats were added in the ghetto during the late 1930s, the additional classrooms were insufficient to meet rising enrollments.[69]

Between the world wars, black activists were deeply concerned about the schools their children attended. Though often discouraged by unpleasant realities, black community leaders tried to secure a full day's schooling for each child in a modern, well-equipped building. Representation on the Board of Education would further these aims and guarantee that a black voice would be heard in school affairs. In pursuit of these goals, black activists used a wide variety of methods, ranging from behind-the-scenes lobbying to verbal protest, from court litigation to direct action. Blacks chose their tactics reasonably and used them flexibly, shifting methods when necessary. Black activists not only played the game but sometimes won as well. By World War II, a Negro sat on the school board and movements for improved building accommodations had succeeded at Ross, Lilydale, Phillips High, and McCosh Elementary schools. Clearly, blacks had an impact on public school policies.

And yet overall, black activism had failed. Although blacks won some battles, none of their victories in school disputes reversed the basic trends of the era—rigid racial isolation, overcrowding, financial inequities, and prejudiced teachers. Black reaction to these trends varied considerably. Overcrowding, as I have shown, was the object of a full-fledged protest effort. But ghetto organizations were less vigorous about the other basic problems. Except for George McCray, who assembled a comparative study of school budgets in 1940, activists were unaware of the ghetto's increasingly inferior position in educational finances. Though black spokesman voiced occasional complaints about biased instructors, this issue never won concerted attention. While ghetto civic groups never repudiated the goal of integration and continued to defend it in the 1920s and 1930s, their devotion to mixed schools was rather mild. Black activists did not take the initiative or offensive to expand integration, and they never gave it as much time and energy as they poured into the school board and building facilities campaigns. In fact, neither the Shoop-Esmond boundary suit of 1927 nor the Dickerson-CCNNC position of curbing overcrowding by modifying the neighborhood school system had solid black support. Whether blacks' limited interest in integration was due to the attractions of separate schools or the futility of the integrationist cause is difficult to assess.

It is clear, however, that black activists had relatively little influence in school affairs. Despite the weaknesses of ghetto civic associations, it was whites—not blacks—who were responsible for classroom racism, unequal funding, and segregation. Overcrowding, on the other hand, had more complex origins. The double-shift classes that plagued the South Side in the late 1930s not only resulted from the confinement of blacks to the ghetto but also stemmed from the sharp increase in black enrollment and the drastic cutbacks in school construction resulting from the Depression. When black activists in the interwar years sought limited goals like a new building addition at a specific school, they were frequently successful. But white racism, the mass migration, and the Great Depression severely restricted black influence and imposed underfinanced schools and the double shift upon black Chicago.

NOTES

1. St. Clair Drake, *Churches and Voluntary Associations in the Chicago Negro Community* (Chicago, 1940), pp. 146-53, 209-11; St. Clair Drake and Horace R. Cayton, *Black Metropolis: A Study of Negro Life in a Northern City* (New York, 1945), ch. 19-23; Edward C. Banfield and James Q. Wilson, *City Politics* (Cambridge, 1963), pp. 293-302; James Q. Wilson, "The Strategy of Protest: Problems of Negro Civic Action," *Journal of Conflict Resolution,* 5 (Sept., 1961), 291-303; Arthur G. Falls, interview, Western Springs, Ill., July, 1980.

2. Arvarh E. Strickland, *History of the Chicago Urban League* (Urbana, Ill., 1966), pp. 29-34, 38, 41-50, 54, 56, 59, 67-76, 83-86, 89-94.

3. Drake and Cayton, *Black Metropolis,* pp. 734-37, 743-44; Chicago Urban League, *Annual Report,* 1937, Pt. 1, p. 2, Pt. 3, pp. 4, 7-8, Pt. 4, pp. 1-3; Strickland, *Chicago Urban League,* pp. 115-34; Drake, *Churches and Voluntary Associations,* pp. 252-53; August Meier and Elliott Rudwick, "The Origins of Nonviolent Direct Action in Afro-American Protest: A Note on Historical Discontinuities," in Meier and Rudwick, *Along the Color Line: Explorations in the Black Experience* (Urbana, Ill., 1976), pp. 327-28.

4. Chicago Urban League, *Twentieth Annual Report of the Chicago Urban League,* 1934-35, Pt. 1, p. 6; *Chicago Defender,* Apr. 30, 1932, p. 3, Jan. 21, 1933, p. 24, June 8, 1935, p. 6, Jan. 14, 1939, p. 1, June 10, 1939, p. 2, Feb. 22, 1941, p. 6, Oct. 4, 1941, p. 9, Sept. 21, 1940, p. 4, Oct. 5, 1940, pp. 1-2; "Notes on 1940 School Budget at Hearings of January 10, 1940," Mary Herrick Papers, Chicago Historical Society; *Chicago's Schools,* 7 (Feb.-Mar., 1941), 1, 4; Mary J. Herrick, interview, Chicago, Nov., 1969; *Chicago Daily News,* Oct. 1 and 3, 1940.

5. A. L. Foster, *The Urban League and the Negro Community: The Eighteenth Annual Report of the Chicago Urban League* (Chicago [1932]), pp. 21-25; Strickland, *Chicago Urban League,* pp. 106-7, 112, 114; Lovelyn Evans, interview, Chicago, July, 1980; Falls, interview; Chicago Urban League, *Twentieth Annual Report,* pp. 11-12.

6. Chicago Urban League, *Annual Report,* 1937, Pt. 1, pp. 4-5; Drake and Cayton, *Black Metropolis,* pp. 737-39; Raymond Wolters, *Negroes and the Great Depression: The Problem of Economic Recovery* (Westport, Conn., 1970), p. 358; Chicago Council of Negro Organizations, "To All Organized Groups Working in the Interest of Negroes in Chicago" [1935], NAACP Papers, Branch Files, Box G52, Library of Congress; *Defender,* Jan. 1, 1938, p. 4, Oct. 7, 1939, p. 13, Mar. 16, 1940, p. 22.

7. Drake and Cayton, *Black Metropolis,* pp. 738, 743-44; Strickland, *Chicago Urban League,* pp. 130-32; Drake, *Churches and Voluntary Associations,* p. 280; *Defender,* Oct. 7, 1939, p. 13, Mar. 16, 1940, p. 22, Sept. 21, 1940, p. 4, Jan. 11, 1941, p. 24, June 14, 1941, p. 3; Chicago Council of Negro Organizations, "To All Organized Groups Working in the Interest of Negroes in Chicago"; Chicago Council of Negro Organizations, flyer [Nov. 14, 1937], Welfare Council of Metropolitan Chicago Papers, Box 277, Chicago Historical Society; Falls, interview.

8. Allan H. Spear, *Black Chicago: The Making of a Negro Ghetto, 1890-1920* (Chicago, 1967), pp. 87-89; Charles Flint Kellogg, *NAACP: A History of the National Association for the Advancement of Colored People* (Baltimore, 1967), pp. 124-25; Chicago Commission on Race Relations, *The Negro in Chicago: A Study of Race Relations and a Race Riot* (Chicago, 1922), p. 148; B. Joyce Ross, *J. E. Spingarn and the Rise of the NAACP, 1911-1939* (New York, 1972), p. 23; Robert W. Bagnall to James Weldon Johnson [1918], NAACP Papers, Branch Files, Box G48.

9. Drake and Cayton, *Black Metropolis,* pp. 103, 106, 108, 184-87, 190, 530, 543, 554, 565; Falls, interview. From NAACP Branch Files: Harold L. Ickes to Robert W. Bagnall, Nov. 6, 1924, Box G48; Chicago Branch NAACP Memo [Feb., 1933], Box G51; A. C. MacNeal to Walter F. White, May 27, 1933, *ibid.;* E. Frederic Morrow to White, Nov. 14, 1938, Box G54; Morrow to National Office NAACP, Nov. 15, 1939, *ibid.;* Morris Lewis, Annual Report of the Executive Secretary, Chicago Branch NAACP, Feb. 1 to Dec. 31, 1923, Box G48; Archie L. Weaver to National Office NAACP, Jan. 28, 1930, Box G49; Chicago Branch NAACP, Press Releases, May 19, 1933, May 24, 1933, June 1, 1933, Box G51; Chicago Branch NAACP, "A Progressive Program for a Progressive Chicago," Sept., 1933, *ibid.;* Morrow to Executive Staff, Dec. 15, 1939, Box G54; "Report of the President of the Chicago Branch NAACP at the Annual Meeting—January 8, 1939," *ibid.*

10. Spear, *Black Chicago,* pp. 57-58, 85, 87-88, 186, 218; Falls, interview. From NAACP Branch Files: Robert W. Bagnall to Archie L. Weaver, Nov. 7, 1930, Box G49; Morris Lewis to Walter White, Feb. 3, 1922, Box G48; Lewis to Bagnall, Mar. 27, 1922, Mar. 30, 1923, *ibid.;* Bagnall to Carl G. Roberts, Mar. 31, 1925, *ibid.;* Harold L. Ickes to Bagnall, May 24, 1924, *ibid.;* Weaver to Bagnall, Nov. 20, 1930, Box G49; New York Office, Memorandum, July 23, 1933, Box G51; A. C. MacNeal to Frank Parker, Apr. 17, 1933, *ibid.;* R. E. Wood to MacNeal, June 20, 1933, *ibid.;* MacNeal to White, July 17, 1933, *ibid.;* MacNeal to Edwin Embree, July 5, 1933, *ibid.;* MacNeal to Roy Wilkins, Aug. 7, 1933, *ibid.;* Weaver to William Pickens, Oct. 26, 1934, Box G52.

11. Data on membership and budget are derived from Chicago Branch NAACP Annual Reports in NAACP Papers, Branch Files. Also from the Branch Files: Mary White Ovington to Jane Addams, Oct. 23, 1922, Box G48; Morris Lewis to Robert W. Bagnall, Feb. 8, 1924, *ibid.;* Kathryn M. Johnson to Walter White, Mar. 3, 1930, Box G49; A. C. MacNeal to White, May 27, 1933, Box G51; E. Frederic Morrow to Executive Staff, Dec. 15, 1939, Box G54.

12. *Defender,* Apr. 27, 1935, p. 4, July 27, 1935, p. 5, Oct. 26, 1935, p. 11. From NAACP Branch Files: Archie L. Weaver, Annual Report of the Secretary, Chicago Branch NAACP, Dec. 1, 1932 to Dec. 31, 1933, Jan. 14, 1934, Box G52; Chicago Branch NAACP, Press Release, July 18, 1935, *ibid.;* C.

180 Down from Equality

A. Hansberry to Roy Wilkins, Mar. 16, 1936, Box G53; Morris Lewis to Walter F. White, Oct. 3, 1923, Box G48; Chicago Branch NAACP, Press Release, June, 1937, Box G53; White to Edward J. Kelly, Oct. 9, 1934, Box G52; White to A. C. MacNeal, Oct. 9, 1934, *ibid.* The role of the Chicago Urban League in the Morgan Park controversy was reported in *Pittsburgh Courier,* Oct. 6, 1934, sec. 1, p. 6.

13. Drake and Cayton, *Black Metropolis,* p. 737; Ralph J. Bunche, "Extended Memorandum on the Programs, Ideologies, Tactics and Achievements of Negro Betterment and Interracial Organizations" (working memorandum for Gunnar Myrdal, *An American Dilemma),* pp. 342-43; Wolters, *Negroes and the Great Depression,* p. 359; Steven R. Tallackson, *"The Chicago Defender* and Its Reaction to the Communist Movement in the Depression Era" (M.A. thesis, University of Chicago, 1967), pp. 44, 59; Falls, interview.

14. Horace R. Cayton and George S. Mitchell, *Black Workers and the New Unions* (Chapel Hill, N.C., 1939), p. 419; Wolters, *Negroes and the Great Depression,* p. 461; Drake and Cayton, *Black Metropolis,* pp. 738, 744; *Defender,* Nov. 25, 1939, p. 1, Dec. 23, 1939, p. 8, Jan. 13, 1940, pp. 1-2; George F. McCray, "Jim Crow Goes to School," *The Record Weekly,* Dec. 9, 1939, Chicago Teachers Union Papers, Newsclipping Series, Box 10, Chicago Historical Society.

15. Wolters, *Negroes and the Great Depression,* pp. 353-82; Cayton and Mitchell, *Black Workers and the New Unions,* pp. 415-24.

16. Spear, *Black Chicago,* pp. 101-2; Drake and Cayton, *Black Metropolis,* pp. 531-37, 688-710; Evans, interview; Chicago Commission on Race Relations, *Negro in Chicago,* p. 142; "Stenographic Report of Public Hearing on the Proposed 1941 Budget of the Board of Education of the City of Chicago," Jan. 10, 1941, Mary Herrick Papers; *Defender,* Sept. 14, 1935, p. 3, Mar. 5, 1938, p. 2, Feb. 11, 1939, p. 16, Feb. 25, 1939, p. 8, Mar. 11, 1939, p. 17, Jan. 13, 1940, pp. 1-2, Sept. 11, 1943, p. 15; Chicago Council of Negro Organizations, "To All Organized Groups Working in the Interest of Negroes in Chicago"; Chicago and Northern District Association of Colored Women, *Annual Report,* 1937-38, pp. 6, 26, Irene McCoy Gaines Papers, Chicago Historical Society.

17. M. Morton Strassman, "The Activities of Parent-Teacher Associations in Elementary Schools in Chicago" (M.A. thesis, University of Chicago, 1936), pp. 1-4, 7, 17-39, 43-44, 61; Evans, interview; Alfreda Duster, interview, Chicago, July, 1980; *Defender,* June 6, 1936, p. 12, Aug. 14, 1937, p. 4, June 10, 1939, p. 2, Jan. 13, 1940, p. 1, Apr. 6, 1940, p. 12; "Notes on 1940 School Budget"; "Stenographic Report of Public Hearing on the Proposed 1941 Budget," pp. 104-5, 121, 130-31.

18. Regina Falls Merritt, interview, Western Springs, Ill., May, 1973; *Defender,* Dec. 1, 1928, sec. 1, p. 3, May 9, 1936, p. 16, May 13, 1939, p. 8, May 27, 1939, p. 9, Nov. 4 and Dec. 7, 1939, p. 26; Evans, interview; Howard S. Becker, "Role and Career Problems of the Chicago Public School Teacher" (Ph.D. diss., University of Chicago, 1951), p. 302.

19. Becker, "Role and Career Problems," pp. 97, 117, 303-4; Arthur N. Turnbull, interview, Chicago, Ill., Nov. and Dec., 1969; Edward E. Keener, interview, Chicago, Nov., 1969; Merritt, interview; Evans, interview; *Defender,* June 3, 1939, p. 6, Oct. 18, 1941, p. 2.

20. Duster, interview; *Defender,* Apr. 13, 1940, p. 1, Apr. 20, 1940, pp. 1-2, Oct. 18, 1941, p. 2, Oct. 28, 1933, p. 4.

21. Spear, *Black Chicago,* pp. 120, 187-88; Harold F. Gosnell, *Negro Politicians: The Rise of Negro Politics in Chicago* (Chicago, 1935), pp. 15-17; Drake and Cayton, *Black Metropolis,* pp. 342-43.

22. John M. Allswang, *A House for All Peoples: Ethnic Politics in Chicago, 1890-1936* (Lexington, Ky., 1971), pp. 52-53, 84, 148-49; Gosnell, *Negro Politicians,* pp. 41, 43-46, 67-68, 75, 153-95, 285-87; Spear, *Black Chicago,* pp. 122-23, 189-90; *Defender,* June 21, 1919, p. 16, Apr. 17, 1920, p. 12, Dec. 2, 1922, p. 3; *Chicago Whip,* Apr. 24, 1920, p. 7.

23. Rita Werner Gordon, "The Change in the Political Alignment of Chicago's Negroes during the New Deal," *Journal of American History,* 56 (Dec., 1969), 593-98, 602; Ralph J. Bunche, *The Political Status of the Negro in the Age of FDR* (Chicago, 1973), pp. 575-76; Perry R. Duis, "Arthur W. Mitchell: New Deal Negro in Congress" (M.A. thesis, University of Chicago, 1966), pp. 68, 72, 83-84, 96-97; Evans, interview; Drake and Cayton, *Black Metropolis,* p. 354; Gosnell, *Negro Politicians,* pp. x, 79; Earl B. Dickerson, interview, Chicago, Dec., 1969.

24. Gosnell, *Negro Politicians,* p. 376; *Defender,* Feb. 18, 1939, pp. 8-9, Apr. 1, 1939, p. 9, June 3, 1939, pp. 1-2; Dickerson, interview, Dec., 1969, July, 1980; Karen Gardner, "Earl B. Dickerson at 88," *Law School Record,* 26 (Spring, 1980), 24-25; Robert C. Puth, "Supreme Life: The History of a Negro Life Insurance Company, 1919-1962," *Business History Review,* 43 (Spring, 1969), 5-6, 15; Archie L. Weaver to Walter F. White, Robert W. Bagnall, and William Pickens, June 15, 1931, NAACP Papers, Branch Files, Box G50; Daisy E. Lampkin to Juanita Jackson, Nov. 11, 1936, Branch Files, Box G53; Strickland, *Chicago Urban League,* pp. 119, 123; Associated Negro Press, Press Release, Feb., 1933, Branch Files, Box G51; City of Chicago, *Journal of the Proceedings of the City Council,* May 24, 1939, p. 292; Falls, interview; Evans, interview.

25. *Defender,* Aug. 26, 1922, p. 15, Nov. 27, 1926, and Feb. 19, 1927, sec. 2, p. 2; Horace Mann Bond, *The Education of the Negro in the American Social Order* (New York, 1966), p. 385.

26. *Defender,* July 1, 1916, p. 8, Nov. 27, 1926, May 28, 1927, and Apr. 14, 1928, sec. 2, p. 2; Morris Lewis, Annual Report of the Executive Secretary, Chicago Branch NAACP, Feb. 1 to Dec. 31, 1923, p. 2, NAACP Papers, Branch Files, Box G48. See also *Defender,* Nov. 12, 1910, p. 1, Feb. 3, 1912, p. 4.

27. Ernest W. Burgess and Charles Newcomb, eds., *Census Data of the City of Chicago, 1930* (Chicago, 1933), p. 189; *Defender,* Apr. 19, 1924, p. 1, Jan. 15, 1927, p. 1; Herman H. Long and Charles S. Johnson, *People vs. Property: Race Restrictive Covenants in Housing* (Nashville, 1947), p. 50; Spear, *Black Chicago,* p. 210; Chicago Commission on Race Relations, *Negro in Chicago,* pp. 137-38; "Chicago Commission on Race Relations Housing," Part VIII, Outlying Neighborhoods, p. 3, Victor Lawson Papers, Incoming Letters: Chicago Commission on Race Relations, Newberry Library.

28. Chicago Board of Education, *Annual Directory,* 1924-25, p. 136, 1926-27, p. 193; *Defender,* Apr. 19, 1924, p. 1; Board of Education, *Proceedings,* July 28, 1926, p. 16, Aug. 25, 1926, pp. 166-67.

29. *Defender,* Nov. 13, 1926, p. 1.

30. Board of Education, *Proceedings,* Nov. 10, 1926, p. 448; *Defender,* Jan. 15, 1927, p. 1, Jan. 29, 1927, sec. 1, p. 5, July 2, 1927, sec. 1, p. 2.

31. *Defender,* Jan. 15 and May 21, 1927, p. 1, July 9, 1927, sec. 1, p. 3;

182   *Down from Equality*

Henry W. Hammond, interview, Chicago, Oct., 1969; Spear, *Black Chicago,* pp. 61, 87; Morris Lewis, Report of Chicago Branch NAACP, June 16, 1926-June 15, 1927, NAACP Papers, Branch Files, Box G49; People of the State of Illinois *ex rel.* Edith Richardson v. Board of Education of Chicago, B145922, Cook Co. Circuit Ct., 1927, Petition for Mandamus, May 17, 1927, Demurrer, May 25, 1927.

32. *Defender,* Sept. 22, 1928, p. 1.

33. *Messenger,* 7 (May, 1925), 196-97; G. Victor Cools, "New Tendencies in Negro Education," *School and Society,* 23 (Apr. 17, 1926), 485-86; *Defender,* Feb. 11, 1922, p. 16, Nov. 27, 1926, sec. 2, p. 2, Aug. 27, 1938, p. 18, July 6, 1940, p. 13. See also August Meier and Elliott M. Rudwick, "Negro Boycotts of Jim Crow Schools in the North, 1897-1925," *Integrated Education,* 5 (Aug.-Sept., 1967), 57-68.

34. George S. Counts, *School and Society in Chicago* (New York, 1928), pp. 48-51; Jean Everhard Fair, "The History of Public Education in the City of Chicago, 1894-1914" (M.A. thesis, University of Chicago, 1939), pp. 3-6.

35. *Defender,* Feb. 24, 1912, p. 5, Oct. 16, 1915, p. 4, Mar. 17, 1917, p. 1, Jan. 1 and Feb. 19, 1938, p. 4, Sept. 30, 1939, p. 1; *Opportunity,* 17 (Nov., 1939), 322; *Chicago Tribune,* Aug. 20, 1918, p. 8; George W. Ellis, "Reform and the Negro in Chicago," Irene McCoy Gaines Papers.

36. *Defender,* Dec. 13, 1913, p. 1, Sept. 23, 1933, pp. 1, 24; *Broad Ax* (Chicago), May 26, 1917, p. 1.

37. *New York Age,* May 30, 1907, p. 1; *Broad Ax,* Aug. 3, 1912, p. 1; *Defender,* Feb. 24, 1912, p. 5, Feb. 5, 1913, p. 2.

38. *Broad Ax,* May 26, 1917, p. 1, Mar. 16, 1918, p. 2, Aug. 24, 1918, p. 4, May 24, 1919, p. 5; *Defender,* Apr. 24, 1915, pp. 1, 4, Oct. 16, 1915, p. 4, Mar. 3, 1917, p. 10, May 24, 1919, p. 15, Oct. 21, 1939, p. 1; *Whip,* Jan. 3, 1920, p. 8; Dickerson, interview, Dec., 1969; Archibald J. Carey, Jr., interview, Chicago, May, 1973; Gosnell, *Negro Politicians,* pp. 49-51, 98, 201; Mary Josephine Herrick, "Negro Employees of the Chicago Board of Education" (M.A. thesis, University of Chicago, 1931), p. 69.

39. *Defender,* Mar. 28, 1931, p. 13, Apr. 11, 1931, pp. 1-2, Apr. 30, 1932, p. 3, Jan. 21, 1933, p. 24, Feb. 11, 1933, p. 7, Sept. 14, 1935, p. 3, Oct. 26, 1935, p. 11, May 9, 1936, p. 16, May 29, 1937, p. 1, Jan. 1, 1938, p. 4, Jan. 22 and Feb. 5, 1938, p. 1, Feb. 19, 1938, p. 4, Mar. 5, 1938, p. 19, May 28, 1938, p. 1, Oct. 7, 1939, p. 13, Oct. 21, 1939, p. 1, Mar. 16, 1940, p. 22; Duster, interview; Chicago Council of Negro Organizations, flyer [Nov. 14, 1937]; Chicago Branch NAACP, Press Release, July 18, 1935, NAACP Papers, Branch Files, Box G52; Chicago and Northern District Association of Colored Women, *Annual Report,* 1937-38, pp. 6, 26-27.

40. Mary J. Herrick, *The Chicago Schools: A Social and Political History* (Beverly Hills, Calif., 1971), p. 231; *Tribune,* Feb. 17, 1939, p. 3; *Chicago's Schools,* 5 (Apr., 1939), 3; *Defender,* Feb. 18, 1939, p. 8, Feb. 25, 1939, p. 1, Apr. 1, 1939, p. 9, Apr. 29, 1939, pp. 1-2.

41. *Defender,* June 24, 1939, p. 6, July 15, 1939, p. 3, July 22, 1939, p. 6, Aug. 12, 1939, p. 28, Sept. 23, 1939, p. 19, Sept. 30 and Oct. 7, 1939, p. 1; *Tribune,* May 27, 1939, p. 5, Oct. 19, 1939, p. 13; *Daily News,* Oct. 18, 1939, p. 10; Carey, interview; Duis, "Arthur W. Mitchell," p. 95.

42. *Daily News,* Oct. 18, 1939, p. 10; *Tribune,* Oct. 19, 1939, p. 13; *Defender,* Oct. 21, 1939, pp. 1-2, Oct. 28, 1939, p. 3; *Opportunity,* 3 (July,

1925), 222; Board of Education, *Proceedings,* Feb. 25, 1948, p. 1061; Sterling D. Spero and Abram L. Harris, *The Black Worker* (New York, 1931), p. 124.

43. Falls, interview, May 1973; Carey, interview; Dickerson, interview, July 1980.

44. *Defender,* Oct. 28, 1939, p. 3; *Opportunity,* 17 (Nov., 1939), 322-23; *Daily News,* Oct. 20, 1939, p. 24, Apr. 12, 1940, p. 18; Board of Education, *Proceedings,* Nov. 8, 1939, pp. 397, 401, Apr. 10, 1940, p. 1441, May 28, 1941, p. 1559, Mar. 11, 1942, p. 1432.

45. *Defender,* Oct. 11, 1941, p. 13.

46. *Ibid.,* Nov. 15, 1941, pp. 1, 11, 17.

47. James Q. Wilson, *Negro Politics: The Search for Leadership* (Glencoe, Ill., 1960), pp. 261-64; *Chicago Herald-American,* May 23, 1942, Chicago Teachers Union Papers, Newsclipping Series, Box 11; *Chicago Sun,* June 3, 1942, p. 4; *Defender,* Apr. 11, 1942, pp. 1-2.

48. *Defender,* Mar. 1, 1930, p. 2, May 17, 1930, p. 6, Feb. 4, 1933, pp. 1-2, Feb. 11, 1933, pp. 1, 23.

49. *Ibid.,* Sept. 23, 1933, pp. 1, 3, Sept. 30, 1933, pp. 1, 15.

50. *Ibid.,* Sept. 30, 1933, p. 1, Oct. 28, 1933, p. 4, Nov. 4, 1933, p. 3, Nov. 11 and 18, 1933, p. 16, Dec. 19, 1936, p. 5, Aug. 28, 1937, p. 6, Dec. 11, 1937, p. 5, Jan. 22, 1938, p. 6.

51. Ruth Evans Pardee, "A Study of the Functions of Associations in a Small Negro Community in Chicago" (M.A. thesis, University of Chicago, 1937), pp. 13-14; Burgess and Newcomb, *Census Data of the City of Chicago, 1930,* p. 139; Board of Education, *Annual Directory,* 1914-15 to 1929-30; *Defender,* Feb. 8, 1936, p. 3, Feb. 29, 1936, p. 9, Mar. 28, 1936, p. 2, Apr. 29, 1939, p. 7; Robert Campbell, interview, Chicago, May, 1973. For a description of Lilydale and a fuller account of the 1936 protest, see Michael W. Homel, "The Lilydale School Campaign of 1936: Direct Action in the Verbal Protest Era," *Journal of Negro History,* 59 (July, 1974), 228-41.

52. Pardee, "Functions of Associations," pp. 42, 44, 48; *Defender,* Jan. 18, 1936, p. 5, Feb. 8, 1936, pp. 1, 3, 11, Feb. 29 and Mar. 7, 1936, p. 9, Mar. 14, 1936, p. 6, Dec. 12, 1936, p. 9; Wesley Greenwood, interview, Chicago, May, 1973.

53. *Defender,* Feb. 8, 1936, p. 3, Mar. 21, 1936, p. 8, Mar. 28, 1936, p. 2, Apr. 4, 1936, pp. 1, 3.

54. *Ibid.,* Apr. 4, 1936, p. 1, Apr. 18, 1936, p. 7, Aug. 29, 1936, p. 4; Board of Education, *Proceedings,* Apr. 16, 1936, p. 1118, May 13, 1936, p. 1297, May 27, 1936, p. 1350.

55. *Defender,* Feb. 15, 1936, p. 7, Feb. 29, 1936, p. 8, Mar. 28, 1936, p. 4; Board of Education, *Proceedings,* June 26, 1936, p. 1476; Sept. 11, 1936: *Tribune,* p. 1; *Daily News,* p. 8; *Chicago Daily Times,* p. 20.

56. *Tribune,* Sept. 12, 1936, p. 15, Nov. 8, 1936, Pt. 1, p. 7; Campbell, interview; *Daily News,* Sept. 12, 1936, p. 4; *Daily Times,* Sept. 11, 1936, p. 9; Greenwood, interview; Mary Scott, interview, Chicago, May, 1973; Pardee, "Functions of Associations," pp. 25, 47-48; *Defender,* Sept. 19, 1936, p. 12; *People of the State of Illinois v. Richard Winesberry,* City of Chicago, Boys Court, Case 1448092, Sept. 12, 1936; *People of the State of Illinois v. George Brooks,* City of Chicago, Boys Court, Case 1448094, Sept. 12, 1936; *People of the State of Illinois v. Toussaint Johnson,* City of Chicago, Boys Court, Case 1448096, Sept. 12, 1936; City of Chicago, Boys Court, *Probation Record,* 1936.

57. *Defender,* Sept. 12, 1936, pp. 1, 6, Sept. 19, 1936, p. 7.

58. *Ibid.,* Sept. 19, 1936, p. 7, Oct. 3, 1936, p. 25; Campbell, interview.

59. Board of Education, *Proceedings,* Sept. 28, 1936, p. 210, Oct. 14, 1936, pp. 248, 263-64; *Tribune,* Oct. 4, 1936, Pt. 3, p. 5S; *Defender,* Oct. 3, 1936, p. 25, Oct. 10, 1936, p. 20, Oct. 17, 1936, p. 14.

60. *Tribune,* Mar. 29, 1931, sec. 7, p. 1S; *Defender,* Jan. 21 and Sept. 23, 1933, p. 3, Sept. 30, 1933, p. 24.

61. *Defender,* Apr. 10, 1926, sec. 1, p. 12, June 25, 1927, sec. 1, p. 2, Apr. 27, 1929, sec. 1, p. 7, Aug. 2, 1930, p. 12, Sept. 27, 1930, p. 1, Feb. 7, 1931, p. 22, Jan. 21, 1933, p. 3, July 22, 1933, p. 1, Sept. 23, 1933, p. 3, Sept. 30, 1933, p. 24, Nov. 4 and Dec. 9, 1933, p. 13, Dec. 16, 1933, p. 6, Dec. 30, 1933, p. 4; Herrick, interview.

62. *Defender,* Feb. 2, 1935, p. 5, Feb. 8, 1936, p. 6, Oct. 3, 1936, p. 25, Oct. 10, 1936, p. 26.

63. *Defender,* Feb. 8, 1936, p. 6, Feb. 15, 1936, p. 7, Apr. 4, 1936, p. 17, Apr. 18, 1936, p. 7, Aug. 29, 1936, p. 4, Oct. 3, 1936, p. 25, Oct. 10, 1936, pp. 9, 26, Oct. 17, 1936, p. 14, Oct. 31, 1936, p. 10, Dec. 12, 1936, pp. 6, 10, Dec. 26, 1936, p. 20, Aug. 28, 1937, p. 6, Nov. 8, 1941, p. 26.

64. *Chicago's Schools,* 7 (Feb.-Mar., 1941), 4; *Defender,* Oct. 19, 1929, p. 8, June 11, 1938, pp. 1-2, Oct. 22, Nov. 5, and Dec. 17, 1938, p. 1, June 10, 1939, p. 2, Oct. 28, 1939, p. 5, Sept. 7, 1940, pp. 1-2, Oct. 5, 1940, p. 2, Oct. 12, 1940, pp. 1-2, Oct. 19, 1940, p. 3, Oct. 26, 1940, p. 2, Nov. 9, 1940, p. 28, Aug. 2, 1941, p. 4.

65. *Chicago's Schools,* 6 (Oct., 1939), 3; *Journal of the Proceedings of the City Council,* Feb. 15, 1939, pp. 8043-44, May 24, 1939, p. 292; *Defender,* Jan. 14, 1939, p. 1, Jan. 28, 1939, p. 22, Apr. 1, May 27, and June 3, 1939, p. 1, June 10, 1939, p. 2, Jan. 13, 1940, p. 1, Jan. 11, 1941, pp. 1-2, Oct. 4, 1941, p. 3, Oct. 11, 1941, p. 2, Oct. 25, 1941, p. 18, Nov. 15, 1941, p. 4, Dec. 6, 1941, p. 26; "Notes on 1940 School Budget"; *Daily News,* Jan. 11, 1940, Chicago Teachers Union Papers, Newsclipping Series, Box 10; *Opportunity,* 17 (Oct., 1939), 311; Illinois State Commission on the Condition of the Urban Colored Population, hearings transcript, Jan. 3-4, 1941, Fair Employment Practices Commission, RG 228, National Archives; *Report of the Illinois State Commission on the Condition of the Urban Colored Population,* March, 1941, p. 12, Illinois State Library.

66. Martin Levit, "The Chicago Citizens Schools Committee: A Study of a Pressure Group" (M.A. thesis, University of Chicago, 1947), pp. 16-22, 90-98; Herrick, *The Chicago Schools,* pp. 209-13; *Chicago's Schools,* 1 (Nov., 1934), 4.

67. *Chicago's Schools,* 5 (Apr., 1939), 1; 6 (Oct., 1939), 1, 3; 7 (Feb.-Mar., 1941), 1, 4; Mabel P. Simpson, Annual Report of the Executive Secretary, Citizens Schools Committee, Jan. 5, 1940, Mary Herrick Papers; "Notes on 1940 School Budget"; "Stenographic Report of Public Hearing on the Proposed 1941 Budget," p. 157; *Daily News,* July 30, 1941, Chicago Teachers Union Papers, Newsclipping Series, Box 11; *Defender,* Aug. 2, 1941, p. 4; Levit, "Chicago Citizens Schools Committee," pp. 67-68, 71.

68. *Defender,* June 11, 1938, p. 19, Jan. 13, 1940, pp. 1-2, Feb. 22, 1941, p. 6, Mar. 22, 1941, p. 12; *Chicago's Schools,* 6 (Oct., 1939), 1, 3; 6 (Feb., 1940), 4; Dickerson, interview, Dec., 1969; "Notes on 1940 School Budget"; *The Record Weekly,* Dec. 9, 1939, Chicago Teachers Union Papers, Newsclipping

Series, Box 10; Board of Managers, Chicago Woman's Club, "Even a Portable May Be Better Than Half-Day Divisions, Double Schools, and Staggered Shifts," Apr. 4, 1939, Mary Herrick Papers.

69. Commission on the Condition of the Urban Colored Population, hearings transcript, Jan. 3-4, 1941, pp. 201-6, 220-21, 226, 234; *Defender,* Aug. 28, 1937, p. 6, Jan. 21, 1939, p. 4, June 3, 1939, p. 2, Jan. 11, 1941, p. 24; *Chicago's Schools,* 10 (Nov.-Dec., 1943), 3; Herrick, interview.

ALTHOUGH THE STORY of black Chicagoans and the public schools between the world wars is a fascinating mixture of hostility and hope, of tragedy and achievement, it would be incomplete unless we addressed two subjects hitherto neglected. First, we must look forward in time, however briefly, at black public schooling in Chicago during the four decades following World War II. Does what we find support this study's argument that the interwar years saw the establishment of persistent patterns in black education and educational activism in the Windy City? Second, since we have thus far considered Chicago in isolation, with little regard for developments elsewhere, we need to take a wider view and place the Chicago story in the context of its times. In so doing, we may learn how Chicago compared with other urban centers in the North during the 1920s and 1930s. We can, at the same time, find out how other recent scholars have approached black schooling and raise questions that deserve further study.

For Chicago, the last forty years have seen some dramatic changes in the status of blacks in the public education system. The most obvious shift has been demographic, with the schools reflecting the sharp increase in the city's black population. Black student enrollment has risen from about 46,000 in 1940 to 291,000 in 1980, and the number of black teachers has jumped from perhaps 500 during World War II to nearly 11,000. As a result of the white exodus from city to suburbs, today 61 percent of the public school pupils and 44 percent of their faculty members are black. These changes have reached the top levels of the system, where blacks now enjoy a prominence quite unlike their status prior to World War II. At the beginning of the 1980s, five blacks served on the eleven-member Board of Education, and in 1981 the board hired its first black superintendent of schools, Ruth B. Love. Significant changes in ghetto school facilities also occurred, as massive construction programs in the 1950s and 1960s modernized educational accommodations in black districts. At the same time, black activism was transformed as well. Black protest groups mobilized larger numbers of ghetto residents and used more aggressive tactics in school controversies, as the marches and boycotts of the 1960s illustrate. Meanwhile, the federal government has assumed a greater role in local education. Whereas federal involvement was negligible during the 1920s and 1930s, in recent years Washington has been a source of both educational funds and (at least until 1980) pressure for desegregation. All these factors have given black education more public attention than it had before World War II. Thus, in many respects, black education in Chicago differs considerably today from the interwar years.[1]

Despite these changes, however, many of the patterns that took shape in the 1920s and 1930s remain intact. The most important of these is racial segregation. Chicago classrooms, in fact, have become even more segregated than they were forty years ago. In 1965, 89 percent of Chicago's black pupils were enrolled at schools with 90-100 percent black enrollments, a figure slightly above the level of the 1930s. Over nine-tenths of the black teachers in 1965 worked in schools with black pupil majorities. In more recent years, segregation has remained intense. In 1976, the Board of Education admitted that only 5 percent of the city schools complied with state integration guidelines; two years later, the Chicago Urban League declared that two-thirds of the elementary schools were 90-100 percent black or white. In 1979, University of Illinois political scientist Gary Orfield calculated that the system's segregation index was 90.3 in the high schools and 93.0 in the elementary schools. Orfield concluded, "Chicago's schools are the most segregated of any major city." During the 1960s and 1970s, black activists and the federal government tried to force local authorities to relieve racial isolation in the classroom by several means, including the busing of children to schools outside their home districts. Such attempts provoked vehement opposition from those who argued that deviations from neighborhood schools shattered long-standing precedent. As chapter 2 has shown, however, officials had long used pupil transfers, boundary alterations, and portable buildings to intensify segregation above levels resulting from housing patterns alone.[2]

Unfortunately, segregation was not the only feature of black education in the interwar era to persist in succeeding decades. Black children long continued to suffer disproportionately from school overcrowding. In 1958, the local NAACP charged that over four-fifths of black Chicago's grade school pupils attended double-shift classes, while only one in fifty white institutions operated on a multiple-shift schedule. The average black elementary school housed nearly twice the number of children as the typical white school, extending the trend which had begun in the thirties. In 1961-62, nearly all double-shift schools were in black areas, and a study of selected elementary schools showed black ones averaging 39 pupils per class, as compared to 31 in white schools. Despite extensive school-building efforts, complaints about inadequate facilities continued during the 1960s and 1970s. At the start of the 1980s, federal officials accused local authorities of operating over-crowded classrooms for black children while underutilizing white schools. Other conditions emerging during the interwar decades also displayed strong staying power. For many years, black schools contin-ued to have a smaller share of regularly assigned teachers and a higher portion of substitutes and uncertified instructors. This meant that the ghetto still had the lowest teacher salaries and least experienced facul-ties, as was the case during the Depression. Urban League researchers found in the early 1960s that officials appropriated 50 percent more money per capita for operating expenses and 18 percent more for teachers' salaries in white schools than in black ones, a gap differing only marginally from that of 1940. Finally, although black activism has changed over the last several decades, it has still been unable to alter patterns of segregation and inequality in the local school system. In sum, black public education in Richard J. Daley's and Jesse Jackson's Chicago was essentially the product of the 1920s and 1930s.[3]

In *An American Dilemma* (1944), Gunnar Myrdal told his readers that in the North, "Negroes have practically the entire educational sys-tem flung open to them without much discrimination." Myrdal did ac-knowledge the existence of segregation and racial inequities in facilities and curriculum in northern public schools but seemed to regard most of these conditions as temporary. He advised, "It is unnecessary to take up the Negro school in the North since it hardly exists as a separate enti-ty." For more than two decades, scholars apparently heeded Myrdal's guidance. In recent years, however, this neglect has diminished with the convergence of two paths of historical inquiry. While books such as Gil-bert Osofsky's *Harlem* (1966), Allan Spear's *Black Chicago* (1967), and Kenneth Kusmer's *A Ghetto Takes Shape* (1976) have explained the evolution of urban ghettoes, Michael Katz, David Tyack, Joel Spring, Colin Greer, and others have redefined the history of American public education. The juncture of these two fields has produced a body of work that calls attention to the development of northern black educa-tion in the twentieth century. In addition to this study of Chicago, re-cent books include Vincent P. Franklin's monograph on Philadelphia; Ronald D. Cohen and Raymond A. Mohl's analysis of the Gary, In-diana, schools; and Judy Jolley Mohraz's comparison of Chicago, Philadelphia, and Indianapolis. As these and other studies have enhanced our knowledge, they also have reminded us how much of the story of black schooling in the North still remains untold.[4]

By proving that northern classrooms were highly segregated between the world wars, recent scholarship decisively rejects Myrdal's conclusion that separate black schools hardly existed. Current studies, however, document such a wide variety of local practices that one cannot assume that Chicago was typical during in the 1920s and 1930s. To be sure, in several other systems, housing patterns, reinforced by unofficial or informal manipulation of school boundaries and pupil transfers, produced racial isolation, just as they did in Chicago. Kusmer indicates that although the Cleveland schools formerly had been integrated, by the late 1920s, black population growth and the rise of the ghetto led to classroom segregation. During the Depression, authorities there permitted white children to transfer out of black districts for the first time. A similar pattern also apparently emerged in New York City during the 1920s and 1930s, although the treatment of the twentieth century in Carleton Mabee's *Black Education in New York State* (1979) is disappointingly sparse. In the Chicago suburb of Evanston, while junior high and high school education were racially mixed, pupil transfers fostered separation at the elementary level.[5]

On the other hand, most recent work on black schooling in the North deals with cities in which local officials formally authorized segregation. In their studies of black boycott movements, August Meier and Elliott Rudwick identify school systems in New Jersey, Pennsylvania, Ohio, and California which openly provided separate facilities for black children between the world wars. In Springfield, Ohio, for example, the Board of Education established an all-black elementary school in 1922, while Dayton administrators restricted black pupils to separate classes within regular schools. Richard Kluger's *Simple Justice* (1975) points out that Topeka, Kansas, source of *Brown* v. *Board of Education,* operated separate junior high schools until 1941 and segregated elementary schools into the 1950s. In Indianapolis, according to Mohraz, all-black elementary schools had long existed, but not all minority children attended them. In the late 1920s, however, racial isolation became complete when authorities removed the few black students from largely white grade schools and opened a separate all-black high school. Cohen and Mohl state that from the start, Gary officials isolated black elementary pupils either in separate schools or in separate classes within a predominantly white immigrant school. Though the latter arrangement ceased in 1917, most black youngsters attended officially separate schools through the 1940s. Franklin's volume on Philadelphia shows segregation and integration existing within the same system. High schools and junior highs were racially mixed, but the Board of Education maintained both integrated and all-black elementary schools. While the latter evidently never enrolled more than a third of the eligible students, officials increased their number from eight in 1908 to fourteen in the mid-1920s. Philadelphia was not unique in this regard, for Cincinnati likewise operated both separate and racially mixed grade schools and integrated high schools.[6]

Even though recent work has documented patterns of school segregation in a number of northern cities, our knowledge of the subject is not far advanced from the 1920s and 1930s, when Horace Mann Bond, Louise V. Kennedy, and others described current policies. These observers distinguished between the "lower North" (New Jersey westward to southern Illinois) and the "upper North" (New England to northern Illinois). In the former region, school boards openly and formally segregated black students, while in the latter area, separate schools stemmed from housing barriers and from unofficial decisions of authorities. This geographic distinction seems accurate in general, but we still do not have enough information to be sure. The history of black education in such eastern and midwestern cities as Boston, New York, Newark, Pittsburgh, and Detroit remains largely ignored for the decisive years from World War I through World War II. The same is true for nonsouthern cities west of the Mississippi River, where only Wichita, Omaha, and Los Angeles had sizable black populations in 1940. Moreover, little work has been done on smaller cities in the North. Robert Austin Warner's study of one such community, *New Haven Negroes* (1940), found that even though black children were overconcentrated at one grade school, there was no segregation, and they participated in extracurricular activities in both elementary and secondary schools. How common this situation was we do not know. Only when more local studies of the extent and causes of school segregation in the North during the formative interwar period have been published will we be able to go beyond case studies and impressionistic judgments. At that point, we will at least be able to correlate separate schools with such variables as geographic region, city size and population, number and percentage of black population and black school enrollment, rate of black population and enrollment increase, and extent of housing segregation. But results may not be easy to obtain if racial enrollment data is as elusive for other cities as it is for Chicago.[7]

While observers used to cite Chicago for liberally hiring black teachers, comparison with other cities weakens its reputation. It is true that Chicago, with some 300 Negro faculty members in 1930, and New

York City, with about 800, were the leading employers of black educators among northern cities with ostensibly integrated systems. But formally segregated districts used relatively more black instructors. In 1930, in five cities with formal school segregation, there were on the average 323 black teachers for every 100,000 black inhabitants, more than triple the ratio in nine systems with supposedly integrated schools (97 per 100,000). Gary and Dayton, with 17,000-18,000 blacks, employed about as many Negro instructors (75-84) as did Cleveland (71,900 blacks) or Detroit (120,000). Among officially integrated systems, Pittsburgh had only three Negro faculty members in 1930, Newark eleven, and Buffalo twelve (1927). As these figures suggest, administrators usually hired black faculty to teach black children, and the recent studies of Philadelphia, Gary, and Indianapolis confirm this. With few exceptions, however, distribution of Negro instructors in formally integrated systems is poorly documented. We have seen the transition from faculty integration to segregation in Chicago in the 1920s. By contrast, Kusmer finds that at the same time Cleveland's 84 Negro teachers were located at 41 different schools, most of them predominantly white. During the thirties, though, authorities there began to place black new hires in ghetto districts. In Depression-era New Haven, two Negro instructors were in overwhelmingly white buildings and two in mixed districts with sizable black enrollments. Practices in Detroit, Los Angeles, and New York City, among others, remain unmapped. Mabee states that New York scattered Negro teachers throughout the system, but he offers no substantiating data. He also says nothing about the distribution of black personnel in the Buffalo schools.[8]

Besides our need for more information about the extent of integration of Negro instructors, other questions about black educators in the public schools demand answers. How does one account for wide variations in hiring practices among cities with allegedly integrated schools? New York, for example, hired proportionately twice the number of black teachers as Chicago, Cleveland, or Los Angeles which, in turn, far outpaced Detroit. What were the barriers to black advancement to high school and administrative positions? Who were the Negro teachers and what were their social backgrounds and career patterns? We know rather little about the educational role black instructors fulfilled and the similarities and differences between them and white teachers in the classroom. Black community reaction to black faculty members is also largely uncharted. On the one hand, Mohraz and Cohen and Mohl suggest that black teachers were a source of racial pride and solidarity and functioned as role models for black youth. On the other hand, some

Negro instructors were unsympathetic to children from lower-class backgrounds, and black parents in integrated systems occasionally regarded black teachers as unwelcome symbols of segregation.

While much remains to be learned about numbers and distribution of northern black students and teachers in the 1920s and 1930s, our understanding of the school facilities issue is even weaker. The comparative analysis of buildings, budgets, and overcrowding in Chicago found in this book has not been done for other northern cities. Franklin reports that double shifts and deteriorated buildings existed in black Philadelphia in the twenties. While he says that outmoded accommodations served whites as well as blacks, he does not explore the topic further. Cohen and Mohl offer a similar verdict about Gary but do even less with the question than Franklin. Mabee and Mohraz ignore the matter almost entirely, the latter instead emphasizing curricular problems and segregation. Those hoping to learn about public school accommodations for blacks must turn to contemporary sources. Even here, though, the evidence is frequently unsatisfactory. Mayor Fiorello La Guardia's New York City riot study commission of 1935 found Harlem schools old, overcrowded, and dilapidated. But the group based its conclusions on impressionistic rather than statistical evidence and failed to compare black institutions to schools in white neighborhoods. Even though one can assume that data on funding and facilities by race would be available for both formally segregated and allegedly integrated systems, neither type has been thoroughly analyzed. Thus, the question of how often separate meant unequal in the interwar North remains unanswered.[9]

While educational historians have largely neglected the school accommodations issue, they have engaged in lively debate over educational policies relating to social mobility. Despite demonstrating the prevalence of segregation, recent scholars have tended to view black schooling in the context of progressive education in general, rather than as a distinct entity. With a thesis that belies its title, Mohraz's *The Separate Problem* argues that school personnel used industrial education, intelligence testing, ability grouping, and vocational counseling to reinforce the subordinate position of blacks and poor whites alike. Advisers discouraged these children from enrolling in academic courses and urged them to adjust career plans to more "realistic" levels. Science and statistics became tools in building an efficient, specialized social order in which blacks joined immigrants in the lower ranks of manual laborers. Although Mohraz has little room for complexity or ambiguity and is somewhat stronger at outlining her theory than at showing how educators applied these principles in specific settings, others reach similar conclusions. In Philadelphia, according to Franklin, authorities channeled blacks and immigrants into manual training courses that officials justified by citing high rates of retardation in academic classes. Intelligence-test scores helped bolster racial and ethnic bias and provided a rationale for a separate curriculum for blacks. In Cleveland, as black enrollment in certain schools rose, foreign languages, clerical training, and elective courses dwindled and industrial education expanded. Labor unions excluded blacks from technical high schools offering skilled trades instruction, just as they did in Chicago, New York City, and Buffalo. In Buffalo, where the ban against blacks covered Polish children as well, officials established a curiously named Opportunity School, which taught rug and broom making to those barred from skilled trades apprenticeships. The Gary schools did much the same thing, but Cohen and Mohl warn against simplistic verdicts. They argue that progressive education encompassed democratic radicalism as well as the efficiency, social control, and class bias that Mohraz, Katz, Spring, and others emphasize. While Cohen and Mohl view the policies of administrators in much the same way as revisionist authors, they refuse to see the school as a triumphant juggernaut, crushing the independent aspirations of children and parents. Cohen and Mohl remind us that the public school was merely one of many educational agencies for immigrants and blacks (a point also made by Franklin and Mabee, who deal with non-public schools and community education in Philadelphia and New York). Furthermore, Cohen and Mohl argue that lower-class residents were not helpless victims but discerning "educational consumers" who rejected some aspects of public schooling and molded others to fit their own needs. In amending both traditional and revisionist approaches, Cohen and Mohl raise issues that future students of black schooling must address. Other problems on the agendas of educational historians include determining how well black pupils actually did in school and exploring the relationships between home culture and academic success, between school performance and occupational achievement, and between black and immigrant education.[10]

Turning to black civic action on school issues, we find Chicago differing from other northern cities that have been examined in recent years. Although a few Chicago blacks favored separate schools, at no time was there a significant body of black opinion openly endorsing segregation. As we have seen, local activists defended integration, even after the school facilities issue assumed top priority during the Depression. Elsewhere, however, blacks appear to have been bitterly divided over the separate schools issue, while the question of inadequate accommodations seems to have aroused little protest. In Philadelphia, anti-segregation movements spearheaded by the *Tribune* and the NAACP failed to unite blacks in the 1910s and 1920s. Negro teachers supported separate schools as their only opportunity for employment, and black politicians were unwilling to antagonize the dominant Republican organization. Not until the 1930s with the creation of the Educational Equality League and the rise of the Democratic party did blacks succeed in eliminating separate eligibility lists for Negro instructors. Gary blacks were even more badly split: Cohen and Mohl describe them as "torn between advocating integration in principle and accepting segregation in practice." Some, including the NAACP and school principal H. Theodore Tatum, protested segregation, while others, led by a rival principal, Garveyite F. C. McFarlane, defended separate schools as a catalyst for group solidarity and community pride, as well as a source of jobs for educated blacks. This lack of consensus prevented effective challenge to the policies of Superintendent William Wirt. Philadelphia and Gary show that when authorities formally segregated the public schools, a substantial number of blacks supported separation. But, as the boycott studies of Meier and Rudwick demonstrate, the integration-segregation division varied from place to place, differing according to local circumstance. In Springfield, Ohio, blacks' attachment to the Republican organization nourished tolerance for segregation, while political independents were ardent integrationists. Recent arrivals in Dayton were the most committed integrationists there (unlike in Chicago), while in the East Orange, New Jersey, boycott of 1905-6, social class was a significant variable. Here the elite supported integration, and lower-class blacks were indifferent or opposed to the protest. Despite such studies, we still lack a clear picture of school protest movements in ostensibly integrated systems other than Chicago, and more work on black activism and the public schools needs to be done. For example, was black support for segregation in the North as strong as Franklin, Mohraz, and Cohen and Mohl demonstrate? Can black opinion on this issue be understood primarily in terms of local conditions, as Meier and Rudwick indicate, or can we identify more general factors? Mohraz, for example, suggests that the relatively greater opportunities for black professionals and business people in Chicago made the prospect of separate schools less attractive for the city's Negro elite. This hypothesis needs testing. Other questions about school protest remain. What conditions were necessary for viable protest movements? What influenced the tactics blacks used in school controversies? How can their successes and failures be explained?[11]

   Although the study of the history of black public education in the twentieth-century North has moved ahead in recent years, the field is still in its formative stage. As mentioned, much more work must be done on specific locales to permit students of the subject to generalize about segregation, facilities, educational policies, and black activism from a broader base of evidence. Some research will be undertaken by those primarily interested in the history of education. But students of ghetto development and urban race relations should give schooling more prominence than they have done to date. With contributions from both kinds of historians, we will be able to fashion the synthesis that we lack at present.

NOTES

1. Robert J. Havighurst, *The Public Schools of Chicago* (Chicago, 1964), p. 54; Mary-Jane Grunsfeld, *Negroes in Chicago* (Chicago, 1944); *New York Times,* Sept. 25, 1980, p. 20, Mar. 6, 1979, p. 14, Feb. 18, 1977, p. 16, May 28, 1977, p. 8; U.S. Commission on Civil Rights, *Desegregation of the Nation's Public Schools: A Status Report* (Washington, 1979), p. 35.

2. U.S. Commission on Civil Rights, *Racial Isolation in the Public Schools* (Washington, 1967), I, 4, 7; "Anything but Busing," *Time,* Dec. 11, 1978, p. 71; *New York Times,* Jan. 25, 1976, p. 39, Mar. 6, 1979, p. 14. The segregation index is the proportion of black students who would have to attend a different school in order for the system to achieve desegregation.

3. Will Maslow, "De Facto Public School Segregation," in Hubert H. Humphrey, ed., *School Desegregation: Documents and Commentaries* (New York, 1964), p. 168; U.S. Commission on Civil Rights, *Civil Rights U.S.A.: Public Schools: Cities in the North and West* (Washington, 1962), pp. 216-26, 241-48; Havighurst, *Public Schools of Chicago,* p. 170; *New York Times,* Apr. 11, 1979, p. 15, Sept. 26, 1980, p. 12.

4. Gunnar Myrdal, *An American Dilemma* (New York, 1944), pp. 879, 945; Gilbert Osofsky, *Harlem: The Making of a Ghetto* (New York, 1966); Allan H. Spear, *Black Chicago: The Making of a Negro Ghetto, 1890-1920* (Chicago, 1967); Kenneth L. Kusmer, *A Ghetto Takes Shape: Black Cleveland, 1870-1930* (Urbana, Ill., 1976); Michael B. Katz, *The Irony of Early School Reform* (Cambridge, 1968) and *Class, Bureaucracy, and Schools* (New York, 1971); David B. Tyack, *The One Best System: A History of American Urban Education* (Cambridge, 1974); Joel H. Spring, *Education and the Rise of the Corporate State* (Boston, 1972); Colin Greer, *The Great School Legend* (New York, 1972); Vincent P. Franklin, *The Education of Black Philadelphia* (Philadelphia, 1979); Ronald D. Cohen and Raymond A. Mohl, *The Paradox of Progressive Education: The Gary Plan and Urban Schooling* (Port Washington, N.Y., 1979); Judy Jolley Mohraz, *The Separate Problem: Case Studies of Black Education in the North, 1900-1930* (Westport, Conn., 1979).

5. Kusmer, *A Ghetto Takes Shape,* pp. 182-83; Carleton Mabee, *Black Education in New York State* (Syracuse, 1979), pp. 247-49; Dominic J. Capeci, Jr., *The Harlem Riot of 1943* (Philadelphia, 1977), p. 40; Bettye Sledge, "Black Education in Evanston Public Schools: A Look at the Twenties and Thirties," *Integrated Education,* 12 (Sept.-Oct., 1974), 26-29.

6. August Meier and Elliott Rudwick, "The Origins of Nonviolent Direct Action in Afro-American Protest: A Note on Historical Discontinuities," in Meier and Rudwick, *Along the Color Line: Explorations in the Black Experience* (Urbana, Ill., 1976), pp. 312-14; Meier and Rudwick, "Negro Boycotts of Jim Crow Schools in the North, 1897-1925," *Integrated Education*, 5 (Aug.-Sept., 1967), 61-65; Richard Kluger, *Simple Justice* (New York, 1976), pp. 375, 379, 382; Mohraz, *Separate Problem*, pp. 93-97, 123-30; Cohen and Mohl, *Paradox of Progressive Education*, pp. 110-16, 120, 138-39; Franklin, *Education of Black Philadelphia*, pp. 35-85; Thomas J. Woofter, ed., *Negro Problems in Cities* (New York, 1928), pp. 177-78; Horace Mann Bond, *The Education of the Negro in the American Social Order* (New York, 1966), p. 380.

7. Bond, *Education of the Negro*, pp. 373-74, 378-82; Louise Venable Kennedy, *The Negro Peasant Turns Cityward* (New York, 1930), pp. 194-95; Woofter, *Negro Problems*, pp. 177-83; Robert Austin Warner, *New Haven Negroes: A Social History* (New Haven, 1940), pp. 277-78.

8. The five segregated systems were Cincinnati, Columbus, Dayton, Gary, and Philadelphia, while the nine "integrated" cities were Chicago, Cleveland, Detroit, Buffalo, Los Angeles, New Haven, Newark, New York City, and Pittsburgh. Tyack, *One Best System*, pp. 225-28; William B. Thomas, "Urban Schooling for Black Migrant Youth: A Historical Perspective, 1915-25," *Urban Education*, 14 (Oct., 1979), 278; Warner, *New Haven Negroes*, pp. 279-80; Cohen and Mohl, *Paradox of Progressive Education*, pp. 117-18, 138-40; Mohraz, *Separate Problem*, pp. 94-97, 127; Franklin, *Education of Black Philadelphia*, pp. 40-41, 48-49, 71-77, 135-50; Kusmer, *A Ghetto Takes Shape*, pp. 183-84; Mabee, *Black Education in New York State*, p. 268.

9. Franklin, *Education of Black Philadelphia*, pp. 48-51; Cohen and Mohl, *Paradox of Progressive Education*, p. 115; *The Complete Report of Mayor La Guardia's Commission on the Harlem Riot of March 19, 1935* (New York, 1969), pp. 78-81.

10. Mohraz, *Separate Problem*, pp. 50-81; Tyack, *One Best System*, pp. 198-225; Franklin, *Education of Black Philadelphia*, pp. 44-47, 53-59; Kusmer, *A Ghetto Takes Shape*, pp. 184, 197-98; Thomas, "Urban Schooling for Black Migrant Youth," pp. 275-82; *Complete Report of Mayor La Guardia's Commission*, pp. 85-87, 90; Cohen and Mohl, *Paradox of Progressive Education*.

11. Franklin, *Education of Black Philadelphia*, pp. 71-85, 121-50; Mohraz, *Separate Problem*, pp. 25, 87-93, 109-23; Cohen and Mohl, *Paradox of Progressive Education*, pp. 119-21, 139-40, 154-56; Meier and Rudwick, "Negro Boycotts," pp. 57-68.

BIBLIOGRAPHICAL ESSAY

Chicago Board of Education

Unpublished records of the Chicago public schools for the interwar decades apparently have been discarded, thereby limiting our knowledge of the history of education in that city. The three main Board of Education sources for this study were the *Proceedings,* the *Annual Report,* and the *Directory of the Public Schools of the City of Chicago (Annual Directory).* The *Proceedings,* available continuously from 1871, are the official record of school board business. They include school budgets, textbook lists, and district boundaries; though they note double-shift schools, they rarely report policy discussions and sometimes omit other important information. Moreover, as already noted, an examination of the *Proceedings* would lead one to conclude that Chicago had no black students or predominantly black schools during the 1920s and 1930s. Before 1920, the annual reports carried extensive statistical data and descriptions of educational programs. From 1920 to 1936, however, the reports were no longer annual, and those that did appear were less informative than their predecessors. The reports resumed in 1936 but were in large part advertisements for the McCahey-Johnson administration. The annual directories underwent a similar trend. In the 1920s, they listed each teacher's name, address and school assignment, and described every school's facilities and curricular programs, but most of this information disappeared in the 1930s. Even so, the directories still gave pupil-teacher totals for individual schools, information essential for determining distribution of resources within the system.

Newspapers and Periodicals

As the notes reveal, the *Chicago Defender,* founded by Robert S. Abbott in 1905, was the single most important source for this study. The *Defender,* available on microfilm from 1909, was one of the nation's most successful black newspapers between the world wars, and it was indispensable for learning about black Chicago. Two other local black weeklies were of lesser value. Julius Taylor's *Broad Ax* (1895-1927) covered school issues to some degree before 1920, and microfilm copies of the *Chicago Whip* between 1919 and 1922 contained little on public education. I also consulted several black newspapers published outside of Chicago. The *Pittsburgh Courier* occasionally supplemented the *Defender* for the interwar period, while the *New York Age* was helpful for the early twentieth century, especially because of the dispatches of Fannie Barrier Williams.

The white daily press in Chicago generally ignored blacks during the 1920s and 1930s. For example, the papers reported whites' boycotts against black children but omitted black protests against segregation and inadequate accommodations. The *Chicago Tribune* and *Chicago Daily News* were the most likely to cover school affairs, while the *Chicago Daily Journal, Chicago Times,* and *Chicago Herald and Examiner* carried some information. Neighborhood newspapers are an often-overlooked source for urban historians. During the Depression, the *Woodlawn Booster* covered housing and school rivalries between the races in Washington Park and Woodlawn from a white segregationist point of view. For the early twentieth century, the *Chicago Record-Herald, Chicago Herald, Chicago Evening Post,* and the *Inter-Ocean* supplemented the *Daily News* and *Tribune.* For the 1860s, I also used the *Chicago Times,* the *Daily Democratic Press,* and the *Chicago Evening Journal.*

Three nationally circulated black journals helped shed light on developments in Chicago. The NAACP's monthly *Crisis* and the National Urban League's *Opportunity* carried Chicago news as well as more general articles with local relevance. The *Messenger* (1917-28), edited by A. Philip Randolph and Chandler Owen, covered the debate among blacks over school segregation. Locally, the predominantly white Citizens Schools Committee issued *Chicago's Schools* beginning in 1933; after 1939, the publication stressed school overcrowding in the ghetto. For the history of the CSC, see Martin Levit, "The Chicago Citizens Schools Committee: A Study of a Pressure Group" (M.A. thesis, University of Chicago, 1947). The *Chicago Schools Journal* (1918-65) occasionally carried articles about black education, while the most useful educational journals of national scope are the *Journal of Negro Education, School and Society,* and *Integrated Education.*

Interviews

A number of former teachers, principals, and civic activists of both races helped enrich my understanding of events in Chicago by offering windows to the past that printed sources cannot provide. I appreciate the contributions of Irene K. Berger, Sylvia Bonheim, Maudelle B. Bousfield, Sydney P. Brown, Robert Campbell, Judge Archibald J. Carey, Jr., Earl B. Dickerson, Alfreda M. Duster, Lovelyn Evans, Dr. Arthur G. Falls, Wesley Greenwood, Henry W. Hammond, Mary J. Herrick, Ethel M. Hilliard, Ruth S. Jewell, Edward E. Keener, Harry L. Manley, Regina Falls Merritt, Annabelle Carey Prescott, John T. Rose, Mary Scott, Madeline R. Stratton, Samuel B. Stratton, and Arthur N. Turnbull.

Census Data

I used federal census information for tracing aggregate population and enrollment trends and for identifying predominantly black school districts, drawing data from two compilations edited by Ernest W. Burgess and Charles Newcomb and published by the University of Chicago Press: *Census Data of the City of Chicago, 1920* (published in 1931) and *Census Data of the City of Chicago, 1930* (1933), as well as from U.S. Department of Commerce, Bureau of the Census, *Fifteenth Census of the United States, 1930: Population,* I (1933); *Sixteenth Census of the United States, 1940: Population,* IV, Pt. 2 (1943); and *Sixteenth Census of the United States: 1940, Population and Housing, Statistics for Census Tracts and Community Areas, Chicago, Illinois* (1943), which were published in Washington by the Government Printing Office. Two valuable works based on census returns are Louis Wirth and Margaret Furez, eds., *Local Community Fact Book 1938* (Chicago: Chicago Recreation Commission, 1938), which helped me organize the comparison of school resources in chapter 3, and Otis Dudley Duncan and Beverly Duncan, *The Negro Population of Chicago: A Study in Residential Succession* (Chicago: University of Chicago Press, 1957), a statistical analysis of black migration to the city and residential segregation within it.

Manuscript Collections

Manuscript collections contain little material on black public education in Chicago. As mentioned earlier, Board of Education files apparently cannot be retrieved, and the papers of most black civic leaders and organizations have not been preserved. The best sources of this kind remain the Chicago Branch Files in the NAACP Papers at the Library of Congress and the Mary Herrick Papers and Irene McCoy Gaines Papers at the Chicago Historical Society. Of less value for this study were "The Negro in Illinois," the Works Progress Administration's Illinois Writers Project (George Cleveland Hall Branch, Chicago Public Library), Chicago Teachers Union Papers and Welfare Council of Metropolitan Chicago Papers (both at Chicago Historical Society), Julius Rosenwald Papers (University of Chicago Library), and the Victor Lawson Papers (Newberry Library).

Textbooks

The Chicago Board of Education *Proceedings,* Aug. 9, 1933, pp. 69-107, offered a comprehensive list of textbooks used in local classrooms; partial lists are scattered elsewhere in the *Proceedings.* The Center for Research Libraries in Chicago has a large collection of schoolbooks that includes the great majority of those used in the city. My discussion of textbook racism in chapter 4 is based upon the following sources: Eugene C. Barker, William E. Dodd, and Walter P. Webb, *The Story of Our Nation* (Evanston: Row, Peterson and Co., 1929), *Our Nation Begins* (1932) and *Our Nation Grows Up* (1932); Charles A. Beard and William C. Bagley, *The History of the American People* (New York: Macmillan Co., 1924); Charles A. Beard and Mary R. Beard, *History of the United States* (Macmillan Co., 1925); Marion G. Clark and Wilbur Fisk Gordy, *The First Three Hundred Years in America* (New York: Charles Scribner's Sons, 1931); Henry William Elson, *History of the United States of America* (Macmillan Co., 1923); Wilbur Fisk Gordy, *Leaders in Making America* (Charles Scribner's Sons, n.d.); Reuben Post Halleck, *History of Our Country* (New York: American Book Co., 1923); Reuben Post Halleck and Juliette Frantz, *Our Nation's Heritage: What the Old World Contributed to the New* (American Book Co. 1925), *Founders of Our Nation* (1929), and *Makers of Our Nation* (1930); Mary G. Kelty, *The Growth of the American People and Nation* (Boston: Ginn and Co., 1931) and *The Beginnings of the American People and Nation* (1937); Thomas M. Marshall, *American History* (Macmillan Co., 1930); Edna

McGuire and Claude Anderson Phillips, *Adventuring in Young America* and *Building Our Country* (Macmillan Co., 1931); David Saville Muzzey, *History of the American People* (Ginn and Co., 1929); Harold Rugg, *An Introduction to American Civilization* (Ginn and Co., 1929) and *A History of American Civilization* (1930); Henry Noble Sherwood, *Our Country's Beginnings* (Indianapolis: Bobbs-Merrill Co., 1924); Rolla M. Tryon and Charles R. Lingley, *The American People and Nation* (Ginn and Co., 1927): Grace Vollintine, *The American People and Their Old World Ancestors* (Ginn and Co., 1930); Ruth West and Willis Mason West, *The Story of Our Country* (Boston: Allyn and Bacon, 1935); James A. Woodburn and Howard C. Hill, *Historic Background of Our United States* (New York: Longmans, Green and Co., 1938); and James Albert Woodburn, Thomas Francis Moran, and Howard Copeland Hill, *Our United States* (Longmans, Green and Co., 1935). For contemporary discussions of the problem of classroom bigotry, see Carter G. Woodson, "The Miseducation of the Negro," *Crisis,* 38 (Aug., 1931), 266-67, and Alice Dunbar-Nelson, "Text Books in Public Schools: A Job for the Negro Woman," *Messenger,* 9 (May, 1927), 149, 169. Harold R. Isaacs, *The New World of Negro Americans* (New York: Viking Press, 1964), mentions how schoolbooks portrayed Africa, while Frances FitzGerald, *America Revised* (Boston: Little, Brown and Co., 1979), is a stimulating history of American history texts.

Books, Articles, and Dissertations

An excellent introduction to the problems of public schools in large cities is David B. Tyack, *The One Best System: A History of American Urban Education* (Cambridge: Harvard University Press, 1974). See also Tyack's "Growing Up Black: Perspectives on the History of Education in Northern Ghettos," *History of Education Quarterly,* 9 (Fall, 1969), 287-97. Other works on urban education include Raymond E. Callahan, *Education and the Cult of Efficiency* (Chicago: University of Chicago Press, 1962); Lawrence A. Cremin, *The Transformation of the School: Progressivism in American Education, 1876-1957* (New York: Alfred A. Knopf, 1961); Colin Greer, *The Great School Legend* (New York: Basic Books, 1972) and "Immigrants, Negroes, and the Public Schools," *Urban Review,* 3 (Jan., 1969), 9-12; Michael B. Katz, *Class, Bureaucracy, and Schools* (New York: Praeger, 1971); and Clarence J. Karier, Paul Violas, and Joel Spring, *Roots of Crisis: American Education in the Twentieth Century* (Chicago: Rand McNally College Publishing Co., 1973).

Studies focusing specifically on black education are Horace Mann Bond, *The Education of the Negro in the American Social Order* (1934; reprinted, New York: Octagon Books, 1966); Judy Jolley Mohraz, *The Separate Problem: Case Studies of Black Education in the North, 1900-1930* (Westport, Conn.: Greenwood Press, 1979); and Meyer Weinberg, *Race and Place: A Legal History of the Neighborhood School* (Washington: Government Printing Office, 1967). August Meier, *Negro Thought in America, 1880-1915* (Ann Arbor: University of Michigan Press, 1963), describes the industrial education movement among blacks; see also Sol Cohen, "The Industrial Education Movement, 1906-17," *American Quarterly,* 20 (Spring, 1968), 95-110. Contemporary accounts dealing with black education in the North from the 1920s to the 1940s are G. Victor Cools, "New Tendencies in Negro Education," *School and Society,* 23 (Apr. 17, 1926), 484-87; Reid E. Jackson, "The Development and Character of Permissive and Partly Segregated Schools," *Journal of Negro Education,* 16 (Summer, 1947), 301-10; William R. Ming, Jr., "The Elimination of Segregation in the Public Schools of the North and West," *Journal of Negro Education,* 21 (Summer, 1952), 265-75; E. George Payne, "Negroes in the Public Elementary Schools of the North," *Annals of the American Academy of Political and Social Science,* 140 (Nov., 1928), 224-33; L. A. Pechstein, "The Problem of Negro Education in Northern and Border Cities," *Elementary School Journal,* 30 (Nov., 1929), 192-99; Charles Predmore, "The Administration of Negro Education in the Northern Elementary School," *School and Society,* 39 (June 9, 1934), 751-53; Charles H. Thompson, "The Negro Separate School," *Crisis,* 42 (Aug., 1935), 230-31, 242, 247, 252; and Doxey A. Wilkerson, "The Negro in American Education," unpublished working memorandum for Gunnar Myrdal, *An American Dilemma.*

Two useful contemporary works on black life in the North are Louise Venable Kennedy, *The Negro Peasant Turns Cityward* (New York: Columbia University Press, 1930), and Thomas J. Woofter, ed., *Negro Problems in Cities* (Garden City, N. Y.: Doubleday, Doran & Co., 1928). Kenneth L. Kusmer, *A Ghetto Takes Shape: Black Cleveland, 1870-1930* (Urbana: University of Illinois Press, 1976), has a strong comparative dimension. For an introduction to the history of Chicago, see Bessie Louise Pierce, *A History of Chicago* (3 vols., New York: Alfred A. Knopf, 1937-57), and Harold M. Mayer and Richard C. Wade, *Chicago: Growth of a Metropolis* (Chicago: University of Chicago Press, 1969).

The only general history of public education in Chicago, Mary J. Herrick, *The Chicago Schools: A Social and Political History* (Beverly

Hills, Calif., Sage Publications, 1971), emphasizes the conflicts between teachers and reformers on one side and administrators and politicians on the other; Herrick, a former teacher and civic activist, sides squarely with the teachers and reformers. George S. Counts, *School and Society in Chicago* (New York: Harcourt, Brace and Co., 1928), remains a convincing account of school politics of the twenties. George D. Strayer, *Report of the Survey of the Schools of Chicago, Illinois* (New York: Teachers College, Columbia University, 1932), has valuable data on building quality and classroom overcrowding, while Robert J. Havighurst, *The Public Schools of Chicago* (Chicago: Board of Education of the City of Chicago, 1964), updates Strayer. Two school history studies are Henry Evert Dewey, "The Development of Public School Administration in Chicago" (Ph.D. dissertation, 1937) and Jean Everhard Fair, "The History of Public Education in the City of Chicago, 1894-1914" (M.A. thesis, 1939). Both of these were written for the University of Chicago, where graduate students in education, sociology, and political science in the 1920s and 1930s conducted extensive research on Chicago's people and institutions. All of the other theses and dissertations mentioned in the following pages were also products of the University of Chicago.

Literature on blacks in Chicago is abundant. For the 1860s, V. Jacque Voegeli, *Free but Not Equal: The Midwest and the Negro during the Civil War* (University of Chicago Press, 1967), provides context, while a report from Chicago in U.S. Commissioner of Education, *History of Schools for the Colored Population* (New York, Arno Press, 1969), states that school integration resumed in 1865, not 1874, as others have claimed. For the early twentieth century, Allan H. Spear, *Black Chicago: The Making of a Negro Ghetto, 1890-1920* (University of Chicago Press, 1967), has been a model for other scholars. William M. Tuttle, Jr., *Race Riot: Chicago in the Red Summer of 1919* (New York: Atheneum, 1970) is broader than its title suggests; see also Tuttle, "Labor Conflict and Racial Violence: The Black Worker in Chicago, 1894-1919," *Labor History,* 10 (Summer, 1969), 408-32; and Arthur I. Waskow, *From Race Riot to Sit-In, 1919 and the 1960s* (Garden City, N.Y.: Doubleday Anchor Books, 1967). Primary sources include Alfreda M. Duster, ed., *Crusade for Justice: The Autobiography of Ida B. Wells* (University of Chicago Press, 1970); Louise De Koven Bowen, *The Colored People of Chicago* (Chicago: Juvenile Protective Association, 1913); Fannie Barrier Williams, "Social Bonds in the 'Black Belt' of Chicago," *Charities,* 15 (Oct. 7, 1905), 40-44; and Richard R. Wright, Jr., "The Industrial Condition of Negroes in Chicago" (B.D. thesis, 1901). Two directories that help identify black teachers are D. A.

204   *Down from Equality*

Bethea, *Colored People's Blue Book and Business Directory of Chicago, Illinois* (Chicago: Celerity Printing Co., 1905), and Ford S. Black, *Black's Blue Book* (Chicago: Ford S. Black, 1917 and 1918). For the information about black Chicagoans between the world wars, St. Clair Drake and Horace R. Cayton, *Black Metropolis: A Study of Negro Life in a Northern City* (New York: Harcourt, Brace and Co., 1945), is a monument in a class of its own. Two other books that were essential for my work are Chicago Commission on Race Relations, *The Negro in Chicago: A Study of Race Relations and a Race Riot* (University of Chicago Press, 1922), and Harold F. Gosnell, *Negro Politicians: The Rise of Negro Politics in Chicago* (University of Chicago Press, 1935). The commission's volume, compiled after the 1919 riot, is both massive and comprehensive; its account of blacks in the schools was unduplicated anywhere else during the next several decades. Gosnell is not only basic for black politics but also includes a valuable chapter on Negro teachers. Other general sources are Drake, *Churches and Voluntary Associations in the Chicago Negro Community* (Chicago: Works Projects Administration, 1940); Commission on Intercommunity Relationships of the Hyde Park-Kenwood Council of Churches and Synagogues, "The Negro Problems of the Community to the West" (1940); Mary Elaine Ogden, *The Chicago Negro Community: A Statistical Description* (Chicago: Works Progress Administration, 1939); Frederick H. Robb, ed., *1927 Intercollegian Wonder Book, or The Negro in Chicago, 1779-1927* (Chicago: Washington Intercollegiate Club, 1927) and *The Book of Achievement Featuring the Negro in Chicago, 1779-1929* (1929); and W. Lloyd Warner, Buford H. Junker, and Walter A. Adams, *Color and Human Nature* (Washington: American Council on Education, 1941).

Among treatments of residential segregation, Thomas Lee Philpott's *The Slum and the Ghetto: Neighborhood Deterioration and Middle-Class Reform, Chicago, 1880-1930* (New York: Oxford University Press, 1978) stands out as especially valuable. Robert C. Weaver, *The Negro Ghetto* (New York: Harcourt, Brace and Co., 1948), is an older work with material on Chicago. Rose Helper, "The Racial Practices of Real Estate Institutions in Selected Areas of Chicago" (Ph.D. dissertation, 1958), and Herman H. Long and Charles S. Johnson, *People vs. Property: Race Restrictive Covenants in Housing* (Nashville: Fisk University Press, 1947), deal with selected aspects of racial segregation in housing. For the Washington Park subdivision and the restrictive covenants fight there, see Cayton, "Negroes Live in Chicago," *Opportunity*, 15 (Dec., 1937), 366-69; Frederick Burgess Lindstrom, "The Negro Invasion of the Washington Park Subdivision" (M.A. thesis, 1941);

Robert E. Martin, "Racial Invasion," *Opportunity,* 19 (Nov., 1941), 324-28; I. F. Stone, "The Rat and Res Judicata," *Nation,* 151 (Nov. 23, 1940), 495-96; and Clement E. Vose, *Caucasians Only: The Supreme Court, the NAACP, and the Restrictive Covenant Cases* (Berkeley: University of California Press, 1959).

Evidence on social conditions within the ghetto also can be found in E. Franklin Frazier, *The Negro Family in Chicago* (University of Chicago Press, 1932); Earl R. Moses, "Community Factors in Negro Delinquency," *Journal of Negro Education,* 5 (Apr., 1936), 220-27; Clifford R. Shaw, *Delinquency Areas* (University of Chicago Press, 1929); and Frederic M. Thrasher, *The Gang: A Study of 1,313 Gangs in Chicago* (University of Chicago Press, 1927).

For introductions to black activism and black politics, see—in addition to Gosnell—Edward C. Banfield and James Q. Wilson, *City Politics* (Cambridge: Harvard University Press, 1963); Wilson, *Negro Politics: The Search for Leadership* (Glencoe: The Free Press, 1960); and Wilson, "The Strategy of Protest: Problems of Negro Civic Action," *Journal of Conflict Resolution,* 5 (Sept., 1961), 291-303. August Meier and Elliott Rudwick have analyzed black protests against separate schools in "Negro Boycotts of Jim Crow Schools in the North, 1897-1925," *Integrated Education,* 5 (Aug.-Sept., 1967), 57-68; for a broader treatment of one type of black protest, see "The Origins of Nonviolent Direct Action in Afro-American Protest: A Note on Historical Discontinuities," in their book, *Along the Color Line: Explorations in the Black Experience* (Urbana: University of Illinois Press, 1976), pp. 307-404. For one such movement in Chicago described in chapter 5, refer to Michael W. Homel, "The Lilydale School Campaign of 1936: Direct Action in the Verbal Protest Era," *Journal of Negro History,* 59 (July, 1974), 228-41. Ruth Evans Pardee, "A Study of the Functions of Associations in a Small Negro Community in Chicago" (M.A. thesis, 1937) analyzes civic life in Lilydale.

Although Arvarh E. Strickland's *History of the Chicago Urban League* (University of Illinois Press, 1966) capably covers the CUL, nothing similar exists for other black civic groups between the world wars. Information on the National Negro Congress and its local affiliate comes from Ralph J. Bunche, "Extended Memorandum on the Programs, Ideologies, Tactics and Achievements of Negro Betterment and Interracial Organizations" (unpublished working memorandum for Myrdal, *An American Dilemma*); Horace R. Cayton and George S. Mitchell, *Black Workers and the New Unions* (Chapel Hill: University of North Carolina Press, 1939); Steven R. Tallackson, "*The Chicago Defender* and its Reaction to the Communist Movement in the Depression" (M.A. thesis, 1967); and Raymond Wolters, *Negroes and the Great Depression: The Problem of Economic Recovery* (Westport, Conn.: Greenwood Press, 1970).

Black politics in Chicago is better documented than any other form of civic activity. Besides the titles already mentioned, consult John M. Allswang, "The Chicago Negro Voter and the Democratic Consensus: A Case Study, 1918-1936," *Journal of the Illinois State Historical Society,* 60 (Summer, 1967), 145-75, and *A House for All Peoples: Ethnic Politics in Chicago, 1890-1936* (Lexington: University of Kentucky Press, 1971); Ralph J. Bunche, *The Political Status of the Negro in the Age of FDR* (University of Chicago Press, 1973); Perry R. Duis, "Arthur W. Mitchell: New Deal Negro in Congress" (M.A. thesis, 1966); Rita Werner Gordon, "The Change in the Political Alignment of Chicago's Negroes during the New Deal," *Journal of American History,* 56 (Dec., 1969), 584-603; and Gosnell, "How Negroes Vote in Chicago," *National Municipal Review,* 22 (May, 1933), 238-43.

Besides *The Negro in Chicago,* which described race relations in the schools, assessed black pupils' progress, and provided estimates of black enrollment at specific schools, another essential source for this book was Mary Josephine Herrick, "Negro Employees of the Chicago Board of Education" (M.A. thesis, 1931). Herrick not only detailed the status of black teachers in the city schools but also offered the most thorough racial enrollment figures available for the interwar era. Secondary works on black education in Chicago are the Mohraz book previously cited and Harold Baron, "History of Chicago School Segregation to 1953," *Integrated Education,* 1 (Jan., 1963), 17-19, 30. Contemporary articles dealing with blacks in the local schools include "John Farren School, Chicago," *Journal of Education,* 73 (Feb. 2, 1911), 119; Susan L. Gorman, "Character Education under Difficulties," *Chicago Schools Journal,* 20 (Jan.-Feb., 1939), 117-22; Anna E. Harmon, "Orienting First-Graders," *ibid.,* 22 (Sept.-Oct., 1940), 10-13; and Marion Sykes, "Training for Courtesy," *ibid.,* 13 (June, 1931), 471-72.

On curricular issues, one can trace the IQ debate in Herman G. Canady, "The Methodology and Interpretation of Negro-White Mental Testing," *School and Society,* 55 (May 23, 1942), 569-75; E. L. Thorndike, "Intelligence Scores of Colored Pupils in High Schools," *School and Society,* 18 (Nov. 10, 1923), 569-70; Morris S. Viteles, "The Mental Status of the Negro," *Annals of the American Academy of Political and Social Science,* 140 (Nov., 1928), 166-77; Horace Mann Bond, "Intelligence Tests and Propaganda," *Crisis,* 28 (June, 1924), 61-64, and "Some Exceptional Negro Children," *ibid.,* 34 (Oct., 1927), 257-59, 278, 280; and Albert Sidney Beckham, "Race and Intelligence," *Op-*

portunity, 10 (Aug., 1932), 240-42. E. E. Keener, *Mental Ability of High School Freshmen in Relation to Problems of Adjustment* (Chicago: Board of Education, Bureau of Standards and Statistics, 1924), illustrates how authorities used IQ scores to limit children's educational options.

The occupational aspirations of black pupils are the concern of Letitia Fyffe Merrill, "Children's Choice of Occupations," *Chicago Schools Journal,* 5 (Dec., 1922), 154-60, and Theophilus Lewis, "Where Do They Go from School?" *Commonweal,* 29 (Oct. 28, 1938), 6-7. For the Chicago Board of Education's vocational training programs, see Marjorie Lord Dunnegan, "Vocational Education at Dunbar," *Integrated Education,* 1 (June, 1963), 29-35, and John A. Lapp, *The Washburne Trade School* (Chicago, 1941). Grade retardation and pupil failure are examined by Alicia Treanor Doran, "Retardation among Negro Pupils in the Junior High School" (M.A. thesis, 1934), and Don C. Rogers, "Retardation from the Mental Standpoint," *Chicago Schools Journal,* 9 (Apr., 1927), 302-3, and "A Study of Pupil Failures in Chicago," *Elementary School Journal,* 26 (Dec., 1925), 273-77. Graduate students examining the educational achievement of black children included Maudelle Brown Bousfield, "A Study of the Intelligence and School Achievement of Negro Children" (M.A. thesis, 1931); William Henry Burton, "The Nature and Amount of Civic Information Possessed by Chicago Children of Sixth Grade Level" (Ph.D. dissertation, 1924); Julia Hermine Lorenz, "The Reading Achievements and Deficiencies of Ninth Grade Negro Pupils" (M.A. thesis, 1937); Charles Henry Thompson, "A Study of the Reading Accomplishment of Colored and White Children" (M.A. thesis, 1920); and Gertrude Whipple, "An Analytical Study of the Reading Achievement of Three Different Types of Pupils" (M.A. thesis, 1927).

Ghetto teachers reveal their opinions in Howard S. Becker, "Role and Career Problems of the Chicago Public School Teacher" (Ph.D. dissertation, 1951). Other studies treating local faculty members are Reuben Freedman, "The Problem of the Unassigned Teacher," *Chicago Schools Journal,* 6 (Jan., 1924), 170-72; Miriam Wagenschein, " 'Reality Shock': A Study of Beginning Elementary School Teachers" (M.A. thesis, 1950); and John A. Winget, "Teacher Inter-School Mobility Aspirations: Elementary Teachers, Chicago Public School System, 1947-48" (Ph.D. dissertation, 1952). Parent-teacher relations are the subject of Ruth Rosner Kornhauser, "Parents and the School: A Study of Clients' Expectations and Demands" (M.A. thesis, 1957), and PTAs are described by M. Morton Strassman, "The Activities of Parent-Teacher Associations in Elementary Schools in Chicago" (M.A. thesis, 1936).

INDEX

Abbott, Robert S.: on racial conflict in schools, 8; on education and success, 88; on prejudice of black teachers, 111; on vocational education, 119; defends school integration, 151, 155. See also *Chicago Defender*
Addams, Jane, 10, 139
Africa: in textbooks, 112, 116
Albany Park, 60
Alcohol: use of, 96; opposition to, 96, 145
Altgeld Elementary School: protest against black teacher at, 31
Anderson, Louis B., 20, 148
Archer Heights, 33, 60
Armour Square, 39, 60
Arson: in Lilydale, 168
Arthur, George, 154
Avalon Park, 60

Baar, Arnold, 175
Bagnall, Robert W. 139, 141
Barnett, Ferdinand L., 9, 10
Beckham, Albert, 117
Beecher, Roxanna, 3
Bentley, Charles E.: organizes Equal Opportunity League, 9; opposes separate schools, 11; and Chicago NAACP, 140
Betsy Ross Elementary School. *See* Ross Elementary School
"Better Schools for Negro Children" (committee), 143
Beverly, 60
Binet, Alfred, 116
"The Birth of a Nation," 139
Black activism: appraisal of, 134-35, 177-78; changes in, 1960s, 186-87; in

North, 1920s and 1930s, 193-94. *See also individual groups*
Black Laws, 2, 4
Black schools: compared with categories of white schools, 59-60, 61-74, 124. *See also individual schools*
Board of Education: and Colored School, 3-4; and transfer issue, 10; and Loeb-Thompson issue, 19; and boundary changes, 39; and Morgan Park High School branch, 43-44; segregates Sexton Elementary School, 47-52, 165; financial crisis and retrenchment program of, 50, 165, 174; and unequal school budgets, 65, 69-70, 71, 73; and overcrowding, 73, 75-81; and textbook racism, 115-16; and vocational education, 120-22; budget hearings of, 120, 136-37, 143, 144, 145, 173, 175; and Shoop-Esmond issue, 154-56; composition of, 158, 159; Bousfield on, 163-64; and Lilydale school campaign, 166-69 *passim;* Citizens Schools Committee opposition to, 174-75; black membership of, 1980s, 186. *See also* School administrators *and individual officials*
Board of Education campaign: and Chicago Urban League, 136, 160; and Chicago Council of Negro Organizations, 138, 139, 158, 160, 161; and Chicago NAACP, 142; and National Negro Congress (Chicago Council), 143; and women's clubs, 144, 160; and black politicians, 150, 159-60; 161; arguments of, 158-59; before 1931, 159-60; 1931-39, 160-62
Bogan, William J.: cancels transfer

Plant operation and maintenance budgets: compared by school category, 66, 69-70; and school size, 71, 74
Platoon system, 76, 77-78
Politicians: in 1930s, 43, 148-50; and school issues, 137, 148, 149-50, 171, 175-76; in 1920s, 147-48; power of, 147. *See also individual names*
Population, black, 5, 29
Portable schools: described, 41-42; and segregation, 48, 152, 154, 166; protest against in Lilydale, 59, 104 *(illus.)*, 166-69, 170; number of, 75; advantages and disadvantages of, 75-76; in Morgan Park, 152, 154; as overcrowding remedy, 175; mentioned, 76, 77
Poverty: and black education, 89
Principals, school: and segregation of black teachers, 32-33; encourage white pupil transfers, 40; and pupil segregation, 42; racism of, 42, 109; praised by blacks, 108; and parents, 146-47
Progressive Negro League, 16
Property owners' associations, 30, 39
Public Works Adminstration, 50, 80, 171
Pullman, 33, 60
Pupil performance: assessment of, 122-23, 126-27; on subject-matter tests, 123; and failure rate, 123-24; and retardation, 124-26
Pupils, black: excluded, 1; integrated, 1; distribution of (1861), 1-2, (1905-16) 6, (1916-40), 27; school attendance of (1900-20), 6, (1920-30) 78, (1930-40) 80; number of, 29-30; increased school enrollment of, 80
Pupil-teacher ratio: compared by school category, 63-64, 70; and per pupil spending, 69; and school enrollment size, by school category, 71-72
Pupil transfers: by whites avoiding blacks, 9-10, 40; by blacks, 13, 41, 176; black opposition to, 40, 142, 144; officials' opposition to, 41, 176; public support for, 41; in Morgan Park, 154, 155, 156
Race riot (1919), 5; and segregation proposals, 20; and NAACP legal defense, 139, 141
Racial conflict: increases after 1900, 1, 5,

7-14 *passim;* in Civil War, 2; relative lack of before 1920, 4-5, 7; and racial violence, 5, 9, 13, 14, 30; at Phillips, 14-18; in Morgan Park, 42-44; varies among white areas, 45-46; at Fenger, 46-47; in Washington Park subdivision, 47-52; education as weapon in, 88
Racism: varies in different areas, 28-29, 45-46; of white teachers, 42, 109-10, 152, 177; and school budgets, 65, 69-70, 71, 73; of textbooks, 111-16; and intelligence tests, 116-17; and pupil performance, 122, 127
Randolph, A. Philip, 142, 144
Raymond Elementary School: and racial harmony, 7
Reading, 90
Reconstruction: as treated in textbooks, 113
Relay system, 77
Rented classrooms, 73, 75, 76
Republican party: wins 1864-65 elections, 4; and Loeb segregation inquiry, 19-20; blacks' role in, 147-48; and Board of Education campaign, 161
Restrictive covenants: definition and scope of, 30; in Washington Park subdivision, 48, 52; opposition to, 138, 140
Retardation: definition of, 123, 124; frequency and degree of, 124-25; causes of, 125, 126; problems for pupils of, 125-26
Rock Island Railroad, 36, 154, 155
Rogers, Don C., 33, 176
Rogers Park, 60
Rosenwald, Julius: and Chicago Urban League, 135, 137; and Chicago NAACP, 139; influence on race relations of, 162
Rosenwald Fund, 141, 162
Ross Elementary School: converted from junior high school, 50-51; protest against conditions at, 51, 59, 164-66, 169-70; Fifth Ward Citizens Protective Association at, 52, 147; impact of double shift at, 81-82
Rotary school, 76
Ryder Elementary School: and segregation in Lilydale, 166

A NOTE ON THE AUTHOR

MICHAEL W. HOMEL, a native of Chicago, is a pro-
fessor of history at Eastern Michigan University, Ypsi-
lanti, Michigan. He received his bachelor's degree from
Grinnell College (1965) and his M.A. and Ph.D. from
the University of Chicago (1966 and 1972, respectively).
He has published articles in *Integrated Education,* the
Journal of Negro History, and the *Journal of Negro
Education,* and contributed to the *Biographical Dic-
tionary of American Mayors, 1820-1980,* edited by
Melvin G. Holli and Peter D'A. Jones.